The Victorian Sages

An Anthology of Prose

edited by Alan W. Bellringer
and C. B. Jones,
Department of English,
University College of North Wales,
Bangor

Dent, London
Rowman and Littlefield, Totowa, N.J.

© Introduction, selection and commentary
J. M. Dent & Sons Ltd, 1975

All rights reserved
Made in Great Britain
at the
Aldine Press · Letchworth · Herts
for
J. M. DENT & SONS LTD
Aldine House · Albemarle Street · London
First published 1974

First published in the United States 1975
by ROWMAN AND LITTLEFIELD, Totowa, New Jersey

This book is set in 10 on 11 Baskerville 169

Dent edition
Hardback ISBN: 0 460 10730 5
Paperback ISBN: 0 460 11730 0

Rowman and Littlefield edition
Library of Congress Cataloging in Publication Data

Bellringer, Alan W.   comp.
   The Victorian sages: an anthology of prose.

   (Rowman and Littlefield university library)
   Includes bibliographical references.
   1.   Great Britain—Intellectual life—19th century—
Addresses, essays, lectures. I. Jones, C. B., joint comp.
II.   Title.
DA533.B46 1974   914.2'03'8108   74-6364
ISBN 0-87471-553-9
ISBN 0-87471-554-8 (pbk.)

Contents

Introduction   vii
Select Bibliography   xvii

THE PROPHETIC VOICE   1
    J. Sterling; extract from 'The State of Society in England'.   2
    T. Carlyle; extracts from 'Signs of the Times', 'Sartor
    Resartus', II, Chs. 7 and 9, and *Past and Present*, Part II,   7
    Chs. 6, 7, 8 and 10.

THE WHIG VIEW OF HISTORY   35
    T. B. Macaulay; extracts from 'Southey's Colloquies' and
    History of England, Ch. 3.   35

SOCIAL PROBLEMS IN FICTION   49
    B. Disraeli; extracts from *Coningsby*, IV, Ch. 13, and VII,
    Ch. 2.   49
    C. Kingsley, extract from 'Yeast', Ch. 14.   52

THE RISE OF SOCIOLOGY   56
    J. S. Mill; extract from *Autobiography*, 'The Spirit of the
    Age', *Principles of Political Economy*, IV, Ch. 6, and
    The Subjection of Women, Ch. 2.   57
    G. H. Lewes; extract from *Comte's Philosophy of the Sciences*,
    Part II, Section 12.   95
    F. Harrison; extract from 'A Few Words about the Nineteenth
    Century'.   97

THE RELIGIOUS DILEMMA   102
    T. Arnold; extract from *Principles of Church Reform*.   103
    J. H. Newman; extracts from *Apologia Pro Vita Sua*,
    Part VII, and *An Essay in Aid of a Grammar of Assent*,
    Ch. 4, Sections 2 and 3.   108
    L. Stephen; extract from *An Agnostic's Apology*, 2,
    'The Scepticism of Believers'.   129

MATTHEW ARNOLD   136
    M. Arnold; *Culture and Anarchy*, Chs. 1 and 3.   136

EVOLUTION AND SOCIETY   188
    H. Spencer; extract from *Social Statics*, Part III, Ch. 25,
    'Poor-Laws'.   189
    C. Darwin; extracts from *The Origin of Species*, Chs. 4 and 14. 191
    S. Butler; extracts from *Erewhon*, Chs. 21, 22 and 23.   196
    T. H. Huxley; extract from 'The Struggle for Existence:
    A Programme'.   202

ART AND SOCIETY   207
    J. Ruskin; extracts from *The Stones of Venice*, II, Ch. 6, 'Unto
    this Last', Essay IV, and *Sesame and Lilies*, Lecture III.   208
    W. H. Pater; extracts from 'Poems by William Morris',
    'Notes on Leonardo Da Vinci', and 'The School of
    Giorgione'.   226
    W. Morris; 'How I became a Socialist'.   236

Introduction

The purpose of this anthology is to provide a selection of texts which represent the wide range of Victorian thought. In general we have aimed to reproduce the first printed versions of the passages so as to acquaint the reader with them in the form in which they made their original impact. We have tried to avoid both the tedium of long passages of undistinguished or repetitive prose and the frustration arising from inadequate representation of complex arguments. The extracts are chosen and arranged more as illustrations of the ideas by which the Victorians interpreted their society than as a study of prose-style.

Victorian prose offers a rich variety of styles, but to concentrate on its idiosyncrasies tends to obscure the widely shared problems which provoked an ideological as well as stylistic commitment. Indeed the importance of style actually focuses one of the major problems of the day: the dependence on rhetorical style rather than on rational argument reflects the feeling that the methods of reason were either inadequate or even harmful when applied to the most important subjects. The first extended examination of this aspect of the period was John Holloway's *The Victorian Sage* (1953). Reason and science, through geology, biology and the 'higher criticism', were shaking literal belief in the Biblical narratives; the new 'dismal science' of political economy with its statistics, its 'factual' educational programme, and its harsh Malthusian attitude towards the poor, seemed to deny the humanitarianism which was its professed motive; equality and freedom, which had been the watchwords of reason in the days of Godwin and Hazlitt, had become the banner of unscrupulous *laissez-faire* capitalism and of the advancing armies of Democracy. Progress itself seemed to mean a race

in which the weakest went to the wall. Unless he clung to a
faith in reason and science, like Huxley, Stephen or J. S. Mill,
the Victorian thinker was drawn towards a style which sought
to express a deeper truth than that accessible to normal consciousness. Carlyle was the most imitated writer, and his style
exhibits startling innovations in rhetorical technique.

The feeling of intimacy with the reader, which Carlyle at
times almost parodies, was a keynote of the Victorian Sage.
One might almost feel an air of religious self-examination or of
the confessional in the accounts given by public figures of their
private struggles and commitments: Carlyle's record of his
triumph over despair, Newman's expression of his deep
personal need for a firm faith, Mill's account of his dejection
at the inadequacy of utilitarian doctrines, even Darwin,
lamenting that his mind had become a machine for grinding
out general laws. In this mode of communication one continually suspects some posturing, some surrender of the reason
to emotional appeals. The calls to personal regeneration almost
become reminiscent of revivalist techniques. In the best
writing of the time, however, this personal commitment is the
spur to reasoned argument and an attempt to extend its
significance in general social terms. There is no doubt that in
their stress on personal feelings and the need for commitment,
purpose and duty, the Victorian writers were responding to a
mood of deep uncertainty, and offering a faith which addressed
itself to the emotions of the individual in a society increasingly
composed of organised masses. But the Victorians were not
merely prolific exponents of emotional rhetoric. The creeds
which they offered were ideas, ideas charged with emotion and
tried against the realities of life. Carlyle, as George Eliot
commented in 1855, 'does not, perhaps, convince you, but he
strikes you, undeceives you, animates you'. Many writers bear
witness to Carlyle's animating power but few could remain
content with rhetorical exhortation. 'Carlyle led us out into the
desert and he has left us there,' Arnold had said in 1848,
Arnold's phrase for good art—'the powerful application of
ideas to life'—catches the concern of Victorian thinkers to
engage wholeheartedly with the problems of the day. One can
see the force of this engagement in many instances, some ex-

travagant to modern eyes: Mill arrested for distributing advice on birth control, Thomas Arnold civilising the brutality of the public school, Matthew Arnold serving as inspector of schools in the East End, Ruskin founding the utopian Guild of St George, Morris deserting society drawing-rooms to address meetings of workers. The urgent engagement with reality contributes to the 'impurity' of much Victorian prose: Carlyle's lapses into strident bullying, Morris's threadbare Marxist jargon, Newman's occasional descents to the debating-floor, the ugly emphases that intrude into the elegant prose of Matthew Arnold, and the unevenness of the social novel, teetering on the boundary of art and journalism. It is true that the Victorians tended to write too much. Working from day to day with incredible energy, they produced their unwieldy *œuvres*, monuments to their almost obsessive sense of mission, in part ineffectual through sheer unevenness and repetitiveness. The anthologiser's duty to make cuts comes lightly here.

The ideas with which the Victorians confronted their problems owed a lot to the Romantics who had perceived the dangers of contemporary developments. They had seen the catastrophic failure of Reason in the progress of the French Revolution, and had founded their trust in the feelings such as family affections, local attachments, patriotism and love of nature, and in the institutions which provided the focus and symbol of these feelings. They championed the traditional sense of community found in the village and the parish, the 'feudal' idea of property regarded as a trust, and religion as an active force for social good and a symbol of a higher unity. In terms of sensibility Wordsworth exercised a domina-ting influence over the nineteenth century, as 'Nature' became a refuge from the doubts, distractions and fears of contemporary debate.

But it was Coleridge who provided much of the intellectual stimulus. His arguments transformed emotional convictions of the existence of God, the force of conscience and the grip of sin into practical ideas which gave order and direction to the active life, such as the establishment of a state-paid 'clerisy'. In discountenancing literal interpretations of the Bible Coleridge managed to place religious truths beyond the assaults of 'scientific' and sceptical scholars. For him the evidences of religion were to be found only in the constitution of the human mind. This aspect of Coleridge's thought heavily influenced the nineteenth-century religious debate. F. D. Maurice, John Sterling and Newman all echoed his assertion that religious truths were the objects of intuition rather than of mere reasoning. Newman, although he claimed never to have read Coleridge before he took up his major positions, reflects his ideas especially in his definition of liberalism as 'false liberty of thought, or the exercise of thought upon matters, in which, from the constitution of the human mind, thought cannot be brought to any successful issue, and therefore is out of place', and in his distinction between 'notional', or passive, assent to a mechanically derived truth, and 'real' practical assent to the inner truths on which all our actions are based. The diffusion of Coleridge's ideas, however, was not dependent upon direct influence. As the sage of Highgate he had his 'Thursday evenings', attended by a numerous reverential company as well as by the more sceptical Carlyle; and, especially through Julius Hare, his ideas passed into general currency among the University generation. His ideas were discussed among the Cambridge 'Apostles', founded by F. D. Maurice, whose membership included Hallam and Tennyson. It was through Maurice and Sterling that J. S. Mill came under the influence of Coleridge's ideas and acknowledged him as one of the seminal minds of the century. Mill attempted to combine Benthamite utilitarianism with Coleridgean ideas by recognising that man had certain spiritual and moral 'self-directed' aims, as well as the desire for material comfort and happiness. 'Self-culture' or 'cultivation of the feelings' was only a part of one's life to Mill; it was not the sense of self-hood that controlled all one's actions and thoughts as it was to Coleridge, Carlyle and Newman.

In *On the Constitution of the Church and State** Coleridge had proposed a National Church as a unifying spiritual and

* Available as an Everyman University Paperback, edited by John Barrell.

educational force. This National Church was to be a non-sectarian institution outside politics, which would ensure the primacy of its inner truths by directing the machinery of education and welfare and taking a leading role in the affairs of the community. As this picture suggests, Coleridge played a major role in the Romantic rehabilitation of the Middle Ages. This use of the past to evoke a more satisfactory sense of community is evident throughout the nineteenth century, from Carlyle's *Past and Present* to Ruskin's observations on Gothic art and the social relationships which it reflects. The need for strong national institutions was the starting-point of many Victorian thinkers. Thomas Arnold at Rugby produced a miniature of the Christian State: a chain of authority from the headmaster through the prefectorial system instilling a sense of social duty, reinforced by religion and centred on the concept of 'The School', an institution which was also an emotional and ethical Idea. In his *Proposals for Church Reform* he sought to create a truly national Church, incorporating all denominations and including laymen in the government. For Thomas Arnold conduct was central; religion was not a matter of theological doctrines but of moral and religious affections which were the basis of good citizenship. He attacked as socially irrelevant the preoccupation of Newman and his followers with hierarchy, sanctity and ceremony. Newman shared the position that only our inner feelings could place before us the idea of a holy life, and this idea should be represented by an institution, but to him the 'sovereign authority' of a Protestant Church was an impossibility. Protestantism encouraged the clash of personal opinions, wranglings over Biblical interpretation, and was part of the movement of rationalism and individualism which had been sapping true religion since the Reformation. In a world riven with conflict, sin and corruption, an infallible centre of spiritual authority was necessary. In the end there seemed to be no middle path between the Atheism towards which the 'intellect' seemed to be moving and the Catholic Church which affirmed the truth of inner feeling.

Most of those who, like Matthew Arnold, were unable to accept Catholic dogma, were certainly attracted by the appeal to romantic fervour and the inner life which Newman exerted, but could not abandon the use of their rational faculties. Arnold was well aware of the anarchy of opinion in religious life, the 'Protestantism of the Protestant Religion', just as he was aware of the chaos of political views, but he believed with his father that religion and moral conduct rested on a community of feeling, and had its authority from the facts of human inner experience which could not be controverted by empirical arguments. He was aware of the new 'higher criticism' of the Bible in the work of German writers such as Strauss and Feuerbach. In these works the attacks on the historical accuracy of the Bible, which were rocking English minds at the time, had been sustained and transcended by placing the Bible on the level of myth. This view sees all religions as deifications of human values, and puts them on the same plane as literature as an appeal to the 'buried life' of common inner ideas. Arnold said that the strongest part of religion was its unconscious poetry, and while he urged his readers to consider religion not as fact or science but literature, he also approached literature with an almost religious demand for high moral and spiritual standards. The establishment of standards in literature (he pointed to the example of the French Academy), is reflected by his desire for worthy national institutions in other areas of life. Such a discriminating centre of authority concentrates that impulse towards human perfection which Arnold calls 'culture', and in a divided society he located this impulse in individuals who are critical of their own class. The idea of the State is not only of an administrative centre, planning and supervising national works, welfare and education. It is also a symbol, a focus for moral and social aspirations. But it is important that such an institution should live up to the grandeur and beauty of these aspirations. In 'The Function of Criticism at the Present Time' he warns his readers not to be content with the practical achievements in praise of which practical men are so eloquent. Criticism's task is to make constructive contrasts and fine distinctions, to compare the grandeur of the ideal with the often shoddy achievement, to set the achievements of other national cultures against our own, and to teach us not to be

content with 'the grand name without the grand thing'.
In *Culture and Anarchy* this type of criticism is pervasive. Mrs
Gooch's Golden Rule stands beside 'Be Ye Perfect'; Right
Reason is faced with the *British Banner* and the Licensed
Victuallers. It is by this indirect, ironic method that criticism
strives 'to keep man from a self-satisfaction which is retarding
and vulgarising, to lead him towards perfection'. It is only in
the pursuit of culture that men are truly equal, when they are
searching for the same goal of perfection in individual and
social life, and it is to this basis of common aspirations that
Arnold appeals.

J. S. Mill was another who felt that Coleridge was right in
stressing the importance of State institutions, but his conception lacks the inward moral and spiritual dimension of
Coleridge or Arnold. Mill believed in the effectiveness of
private opinion, which could grow unassisted by powerful
institutions. For him the State would have a purely administrative function. Government was a matter of calculation and
expertise and, as only a limited number of people could be
expected to attain this expertise, an elitist framework seemed
inevitable. Men must be told, argued with or even constrained
to follow the course of action which produces happiness. Men
(and also women) are considered in their separateness, not
as unified by a common bond of moral feeling, and indeed
there is profit in the interplay of individuality: wealth comes
from free competition, truth from free discussion. Yet against
this is set a kind of State Socialism which interferes with this
freedom in the name of social justice. Mill wrestled with this
problem in *On Liberty* (1859) and *Utilitarianism* (1863) and
decided that social justice or the love of humanity should be
taught as a religion. These moral feelings are not considered as
natural, as a common humane spirit which is its own evidence,
but are to be instilled as a means to personal happiness.

In his exploitation of religion for social ends, as in his attempt
to combine inductive and deductive thinking, Mill was influenced by Auguste Comte (1798–1851), the founder of
Sociology. It was Comte's aim to bring to social phenomena the
scientific methods which had proved so successful in the
physical sciences and thus bring them into line with the march

of human progress. The worship of God or Nature would give way to the worship of man, a creed which would have the advantage of unifying Science and Religion in one purpose, the enrichment of human life. Comte's crusading spirit caught many English minds filled with the wonders of material progress, such as G. H. Lewes and Charles Kingsley. Kingsley entered the Great Exhibition of 1851 as if into a cathedral, and shared the Whig notion that increasing trade and industrialisation would actually bring peace and plenty to nations. Herbert Spencer, H. T. Buckle and W. E. H. Lecky all wrote enthusiastically in praise of progress, that assumption to which theories of evolution came as a triumphant proof. Several thinkers, however, though sharing the conviction that science was the means by which society could be ameliorated, were neither convinced of the unmixed blessings of progress, nor viewed with entire satisfaction Comte's plan of future social organisation. J. S. Mill was disturbed by the rigidity of Comte's system. T. H. Huxley foresaw that progress would intensify the struggle for existence, and insisted that those most fitted to survive were not the highest ethical types, but 'the strongest, the most self-assertive'.

To most Victorians the struggle for existence was only too painfully obvious as the industrial revolution gathered pace, and Manchester became the city that symbolised the problems of the age. Through novels such as those of Disraeli and Mrs Gaskell, and social criticism like that of Engels, the evils which competition and industrial development involved were brought home to the conscience of the nation. Struggle and competition were, however, regarded as painful necessities by most Victorians. Kingsley combined a deep sympathy with the oppressed poor with a deeper conviction that life is a battle in which the strongest must impose and perpetuate their superior ideology in the name of progress. The Carlylean vision of history as a record of great men in whom we see that right and might are inseparable permeates the age and competes with the view of history as a succession of historical eras progressing according to their own laws. Marx, although his ideas are dominated by a theory of historical movements rather than of great men, also emphasised the element of struggle. The idea of class-conflict, however, took a long time to penetrate the traditional moral ideas of community. Only in the 1880s and 90s did Marx's thought really become important. In William Morris we see the Romantic side of Socialism, the view that sees the present situation as an aberration from a 'natural' state of life rather than seeing it as a step towards new scientific State Socialism. This 'natural' way of life was described in the work of Ruskin, in which we see the common Romantic return to the Middle Ages as a model of community. For both Ruskin and Morris the Gothic style meant an unforced individual expression of the practical and spiritual realities of life. It became associated in Morris's mind with folk-art, the art of the English people in fashioning common practical implements, and in lavishing a personal attention on details, before industrial organisation made workers fractions of men and divided life into the utilitarian and the artistic. Under the influence of Marxist thought Morris increasingly tended to see the class-struggle as the main question of the day and to separate popular art and high art, being willing to see the obliteration of all 'artificial' culture if society could recapture the 'natural' basis which is the condition of all true popular art in contact with the life of the people.

Walter Pater represents a reaction against the moral strenuousness of the period. For him art was not the reflection of the economic relationships of society nor an urgent message to contemporaries, but the record of a subtle artistic craftsman working at the focus of the most vital aspects of the life of his day and capturing a unique, fugitive, imaginative vision. He can echo Arnold, as in the ideal of a 'general culture' animated by fresh and free ideas, but his theory postpones the establishment of central standards of judgement. He concentrates on the facts of the critic's appreciation and the exploration of the sources of his pleasure, the complex discriminations which are the result of a cultivated aesthetic sense. To many this seems a comfortable scholar's creed, yet one cannot miss the note of desperation in the Conclusion of *The Renaissance*, the vision of life as a meaningless flux in which the bubble of human consciousness aimlessly floats, admiring the iridescence of its walls. It is this note of deep scepticism about the rational order of the world and human life that marks the transition to the apocalyptic pessimism of the later period, the *fin de siècle*, and the questioning of human ideals in the work of Conrad, Hardy and Yeats.

We should like to acknowledge assistance in compiling this anthology from Judith Chernaik, Brian Maidment and Professor Alun R. Jones.

Alan W. Bellringer

C. B. Jones

University College of North Wales, Bangor, 1974

Select Bibliography

J. M. Robertson, *Modern Humanists Reconsidered* (London, 1927); D. C. Somervell, *English Thought in the Nineteenth Century* (London, 1929); G. M. Young, *Victorian England* (London, 1936); G. Hough, *The Last Romantics* (London, 1949); B. Willey, *Nineteenth Century Studies* (London, 1949); B. Willey, *More Nineteenth Century Studies* (London, 1956); F. R. Leavis, *Mill on Bentham and Coleridge* (London, 1950); J. Buckley, *The Victorian Temper* (London, 1952); J. Holloway, *The Victorian Sage* (London, 1953); A Briggs, *Victorian People* (London, 1954); W. Houghton, *The Victorian Frame of Mind* (Yale, 1957); R. Williams, *Culture and Society 1780–1950* (London, 1958); R. Peters, *Victorians on Literature and Art* (New York, 1961); W. M. Simon, *European Positivism in the Nineteenth Century* (New York, 1963); A. O. J. Cockshut, *The Unbelievers* (London, 1964); B. M. S. Reardon, *Religious Thought in the Nineteenth Century* (London, 1966); G. Himmelfarb, *Victorian Minds* (New York, 1968); R. Chapman, *The Victorian Debate* (London, 1968); G. Levine and W. Madden, *The Art of Victorian Prose* (London, 1968); D. J. Delaura, *Hebrew and Hellene in Victorian England* (London, 1969); J. Gross, *The Rise and Fall of the Man of Letters* (London, 1969); P. M. Ball, *The Central Self* (London, 1971).

Select Bibliography

The Prophetic Voice

[Thomas Carlyle (1795–1881), the son of a Scottish stonemason, worked as a schoolmaster, translator of German literature and review-essayist, before moving from Scotland in 1834. Fame came to him with his *French Revolution* (1837); and as the 'Sage of Chelsea' he added to his reputation with an expansive output of lectures, pamphlets and biographical writings. His denunciations of material- istic Utilitarianism were founded on his personal religious feeling for the 'Unnameable' and Duty. In 'Signs of the Times' Carlyle applies a Romantic distinction between mechanism and life to the con- temporary situation, attacking most notably the tyranny of the machine in the economic sphere, of bureaucracy in the political sphere, and of money and popularity in the moral sphere. His sense of a nightmarish world without moral bearings is expressed with a stylistically disordered urgency in *Sartor Resartus*, where he adopts the mask of a bewildered and dejected German professor who undergoes a conversion to pantheism and the gospel of work. Carlyle's later political writings are anti-democratic, as is illustrated by the sequence from *Past and Present* on the 'emergence' of Samson as abbot. This study is one of a number of Victorian works which stress what could still be learned from mediaeval social practice.

In 1835 Carlyle met John Sterling (1806–1844), whose *Life* he was to publish in 1851. Sterling's writings on society and literature are much influenced by Coleridge, whom he knew personally and whose *Confessions of an Inquiring Spirit* he transcribed. In 1828 Sterling was, with F. D. Maurice, part-owner of *The Athenaeum*, where the essay with which we begin the anthology appeared. It contains an attack on Mammon and Utility in familiar Romantic terms and calls for a prophet or moral teacher to arise to carry on the work of Wordsworth and Coleridge. Sterling's appeal was to be loudly answered.]

JOHN STERLING

From *The State of Society in England*

[Sterling's 'The State of Society in England' is No. III of 'Fragments from the Travels of Theodore Elbert, a young Swede', in *The Athenaeum*, I, 487–8, No. 31 (28 May, 1828).]

... 'Wealth! wealth! wealth! Praise be to the god of the nineteenth century! The golden idol—the mighty Mammon!' Such are the accents of the time, such the cry of the nation. There never was an age when money could accomplish so much as now in England. There never was a time when it was so necessary for comfort. There may here and there be an individual who does not spend his heart in labouring for riches; but there is nothing approaching to a class of persons actuated by any other desire. To rest contented with poverty, demands more courage in any man than would furnish forth a score of martyrs, or a hundred heroes. He who would attempt to make the improvement of his own nature, and of his age, the business of his life, and therefore to remain satisfied with a spare and unostentatious subsistence, is railed at, as one knowing nothing of the true objects of existence, a useless and contemptible being, to be treated with haughtiness by every gambler in the funds, by every man whose soul is put out at compound interest, whose very being is garnered in a money-chest, by every owner of hereditary acres, and oracle of hereditary wisdom. To succeed in life is to make a large fortune, without doing any thing which would send a man to prison. To be unsuccessful is not the being ignorant, or luxurious, or envious, or sensual; but simply the being poor,— the one unpardonable sin—not against the Spirit of God, but against the spirit of the world. In England, the poor man walks surrounded with an atmosphere of shame. He lives upon bitter crumbs of insolence which fall from the rich man's table; and the common air of social humanity reaches him only in pinching blasts.

Wherefore is this? It is a dark ingrained spot in the national mind. It is a propensity which every good man must oppose;

and which, if the country were in a healthy state, could never have grown upon it. But, like everything else, it must have its cause, or its causes, for they probably are many; and those causes, it would be well worth while to discover. The chief of them seems to be the nature of the Government, which is founded, half on privilege, and half on wealth. But the wealth can buy the privilege; and with it, therefore, is ultimately lodged the whole political power of England. The Government is a Chrysocracy. Not that form of polity, in which power is adapted to property, and the greatest mass of property has the chief dominion in the commonwealth; but that in which a small number of the richest individuals retain, in their own hands, the whole energies of the state. The law of succession in England, which gives the whole landed property to the eldest son, has set the fashion with regard to other property; and it is the ambition of every man who can obtain a large fortune, to transmit it undiminished to some one of his family. Those great inheritances become the standards by which opinion measures wealth; and, as society is not parcelled out by any impassable barriers, there is a perpetual struggle upward, from step to step, in the scale of riches and of consequent estimation, which concentrates the whole mind, and every feeling of the country, into the voracity for gain. Power, rank, political influence, all the most splendid objects of human eagerness are, to an Englishman, comprised in wealth: and what is there of wonder, that the talents, and industry, and enterprise of the country, all that should be instruments of good, are devoted to this one pursuit?

Hence arises that indifference to everything in literature which does not minister either to amusement or profit. Hence it is, that novels, and works on political economy, are the only books that now find favour, except, indeed, those party histories which are intended as engines of attack or defence for profitable monopolies: and hence, our popular literature is completely stripped of that majestic character imprinted upon it of old, by minds which were directed to far other aims than the mere work-day business of vulgar interests. Hence it is, that nothing is an end in itself; nothing precious to man except as leading him to riches: and truth and benevolence are good only because they minister to the increase of the means of enjoyment.

The Englishman of the nineteenth century does not, indeed, like those who laud the wisdom of our ancestors for the things in which alone they were foolish, discover, in the errors of the past, the links that connect it with present; but he sees, in the merits of the present, a barrier that separates it from the past. In his view, we may analyse the mind by chemical solvents, and melt the heart in a blow-pipe; we may arrive at the innermost secrets of the universe by algebraic process; and, by extraction of the square root, lay bare the deepest fibres of the tree of knowledge. A pair of compasses and a quadrant are means, not only of intellectual progress, but of moral re-generation. He thinks to discover God amid the skies, by taking an observation; and physical science is not merely the wand of Moses to call forth water from the rock, and to govern natural causes, but the fiery presence and living glory of the Deity. To him the most spiritual of poetry is dreaming, religion is mysticism, and enthusiasm madness. His vocabulary is confined to the one word 'utility', and the beautiful, the true, the good, are its subservient offspring,—not princes and gods themselves, but slaves to the peddling merchant, ex-pediency. He weighs the happiness of mankind as a usurer his ingots, and numbers it as a farmer his sheaves: for to him it consists only in sheaves and ingots, and those faculties of our nature, which cannot employ themselves in reading bills of exchange, and reckoning oxen,—are a sound,—a fancy,—nothing. His philosophy is only another name for the general principles of profit and loss, and his mind is a blank signed with the style and title of MAN, but to be filled up as may be determined by the 'science of circumstances'. In defiance of all the records of poor men, whose good feelings have made them happy, he sees, in political economy, not merely the science of the laws which regulate wealth, but the science which alone must govern the welfare of our species; and he would be willing to sacrifice, not only sight, hearing, and speech, so that he might be wealthy, but earnestness, gentleness, courage, and love of truth,—faith, hope, and charity.

Such is the philosopher of the day, and so different his

wisdom from that which would have in it anything of a reforming or purifying power. But the most melancholy peculiarity of the age is, the effect on the great mass of the instructed classes of this inordinate and all-devouring eagerness for riches. There is nothing round us of that meditative calm in which the mind of a nation might deliberately address itself to high aims, and serenely take upon it the noble and laborious task of self-regeneration. The whole energies of the land and time, are given up to 'spending and getting';[1] and the exhausting anxiety for money leaves behind it a lassitude from which no stimulants can rouse, except those which embody the fiercest turbulence of evil passions. The nation is thus diseased to the very core. Its physicians offer it poisons for remedies, and the malady which preys upon it prevents it from discovering that it is not in the vigorous flush of health. Why does not a prophet arise among this great people, to lament over them, as did the Seers of Judah over their degraded country? To tell them of their lapses and their wanderings, and to exhibit, in mighty and terrible visions, the judgements which wait upon the ill-doings of nations? Yet, would the voice of an Isaiah be listened to on the Stock Exchange? or the pampered heart of aristocracy tremble at the accents of Ezekiel?

No: there are men in England who could accomplish this work, if it were to be done on a sudden. But this may not be. A change of institutions is necessary; and this change cannot take place without an alteration in the mind of the country. To this reform of thought and feeling, it is not likely that England will arrive, until she has been taught by much sorrow, been disciplined into wisdom by suffering, and learnt to listen to voices of teachers, of such men as Wordsworth and Coleridge, and, in another way, Chalmers,[2] who for years have been speaking to those that will not hear, and uttering truth to those that will not understand. What immediate change can be hoped for, when, even in the appointed places of education, the same profuse expenditure is observed as that which is seen through all the rest of England and which makes it necessary for every one, in the upper and middling classes, to think of scarce any thing but the means of gain. From these institutions men come into the world with habits of luxury, which are the curse of their future years, and which often make their lives but one long struggle of expense and anxiety, display and misery.

The evil does not reside in the want or in the superfluity of wealth, but in the inequality of its distribution. It is easy to refer this, as is so commonly and so vaguely done, to the influence of civilisation, and to look no further. But if, as is no doubt the case the division of labour and the progress of the arts tend to produce this result, wherefore should artificial institutions tend to increase the evil? Wherefore should the laws of inheritance be such as to perpetuate a moral mischief of the most lamentable kind,—such as to make the few rich, and the many poor, and thereby establish laws of opinion, which lead the many to drudge away their lives in seeking to gain the same level as the few? And, though it may be said that this can act but upon a small part of the community, and must leave the vast majority in the condition which they are found to exhibit elsewhere; yet, be it remembered, that the persons on whom it does act, are the very class among whom exist, in all countries, the seeds and promise of national improvement; that those whom these laws debase, and consign to lives of greediness and ostentation, are the strength and heart of the country; that it is from the aristocracy, and the largest instructed classes immediately below them, and especially acted upon by aristocratical ambition,—that it is from them we ought to be entitled to expect every thing for the education of the body of the people. When you degrade the gentry into machines of accumulation and votaries of luxury, and make them alternately misers and spendthrifts, you do almost all that is possible for destroying the best hopes of England; you do all that man can do to prevent the existence of man, who, with that freedom from manual labour which is necessary for the highest cultivation of the faculties, would also have those moderate and self-denying habits which are indispensable to the growth of virtue; all that is possible to deprive the people of moral teachers, and to quench for ever the light of wisdom. It illuminated the humble study of Milton, and brightened the page of Harrington.[3] Shall it now gleam only amid the mountains of Westmoreland, and scarce be known to anyone but some unregarded FRIEND?[4]

THOMAS CARLYLE

From 'Signs of the Times'

[Carlyle's 'Signs of the Times' was published anonymously as a review-article in *The Edinburgh Review*, XLIX, No. 98 (June, 1829).]

... Were we required to characterise this age of ours by any single epithet, we should be tempted to call it, not an Heroical, Devotional, Philosophical, or Moral Age, but above all others, the Mechanical Age. It is the Age of Machinery, in every outward and inward sense of that word; the age which, with its whole undivided might, forwards, teaches and practises the great art of adapting means to ends. Nothing is now done directly, or by hand; all is by rule and calculated contrivance. For the simplest operation, some helps and accompaniments, some cunning, abbreviating process is in readiness. Our old modes of exertion are all discredited, and thrown aside. On every hand, the living artisan is driven from his workshop, to make room for a speedier, inanimate one. The shuttle drops from the fingers of the weaver, and falls into iron fingers that ply it faster. The sailor furls his sail, and lays down his oar; and bids a strong, unwearied servant, on vaporous wings, bear him though the waters. Men have crossed oceans by steam; the Birmingham Fire-King has visited the fabulous East; and the genius of the Cape, were there any Camoens now to sing it, has again been alarmed, and with far stranger thunder than Gama's. There is no end to machinery. Even the horse is stripped of his harness, and finds a fleet fire-horse yoked in his stead. Nay, we have an artist that hatches chickens by steam,—the very brood-hen is to be superseded! For all earthly, and for some unearthly purposes, we have machines and mechanic furtherances; for mincing our cabbages; for casting us into magnetic sleep. We remove mountains, and make seas our smooth highway; nothing can resist us. We war with rude nature; and, by our resistless engines, come off always victorious, and loaded with spoils.

What wonderful accessions have thus been made, and are still making, to the physical power of mankind; how much better fed, clothed, lodged and, in all outward respects, accommodated men now are, or might be, by a given quantity of labour, is a grateful reflection which forces itself on every one. What changes, too, this addition of power is introducing into the social system; how wealth has more and more increased and at the same time gathered itself more and more into masses, strangely altering the old relations, and increasing the distance between the rich and the poor, will be a question for Political Economists and a much more complex and important one than any they have yet engaged with.

... Nowhere, for example, is the deep, almost exclusive faith, we have in Mechanism, more visible than in the Politics of this time. Civil government does, by its nature, include much that is mechanical, and must be treated accordingly. We term it, indeed, in ordinary language, the Machine of Society, and talk of it as the grand working wheel from which all private machines must derive, or to which they must adapt, their movements. Considered merely as a metaphor, all this is well enough; but here, as in so many other cases, the 'foam hardens itself into a shell', and the shadow we have wantonly evoked stands terrible before us and will not depart at our bidding. Government includes much also that is not mechanical, and cannot be treated mechanically; of which latter truth, as appears to us, the political speculations and exertions of our time are taking less and less cognisance.

Nay, in the very outset, we might note the mighty interest taken in *mere political arrangements*, as itself the sign of a mechanical age. The whole discontent of Europe takes this direction. The deep, strong cry of all civilised nations—a cry which, every one now sees, must and will be answered, is, Give us a reform of Government! A good structure of legislation, a proper check upon the executive, a wise arrangement of the judiciary, is *all* that is wanting for human happiness. The Philosopher of this age is not a Socrates, a Plato, a Hooker, or Taylor, who inculcates on men the necessity and infinite worth of moral goodness, the great truth that our happiness depends on the mind which is within us, and not on the circumstances which are without us; but a Smith, a De Lolme,[5] a Bentham, who chiefly inculcates the reverse of this—

that our happiness depends entirely on external circumstances; nay that the strength and dignity of the mind within us is itself the creature and consequence of these. Were the laws, the government, in good order, all were well with us; the rest would care for itself! Dissentients from this opinion, expressed or implied, are now rarely to be met with; widely and angrily as men differ in its application, the principle is admitted by all.

Equally mechanical, and of equal simplicity, are the methods proposed by both parties for completing or securing this all-sufficient perfection of arrangement. It is no longer the moral, religious, spiritual condition of the people that is our concern, but their physical, practical, economical condition, as regulated by public laws. Thus is the Body-politic more than ever worshipped and tended. But the Soul-politic less than ever. Love of country, in any high or generous sense, in any other than an almost animal sense, or mere habit, has little importance attached to it in such reforms, or in the opposition shown them. Men are to be guided only by their self-interests. Good government is a good balancing of these; and, except a keen eye and appetite for self-interest, requires no virtue in any quarter. To both parties it is emphatically a machine: to the discontented, a 'taxing-machine'; to the contented, a 'machine for securing property'. Its duties and its faults are not those of a father, but of an active parish-constable.

Thus it is by the mere condition of the machine; by preserving it untouched, or else by re-constructing it and oiling it anew, that man's salvation as a social being is to be insured and indefinitely promoted. Contrive the fabric of law aright, and without farther effort on your part, that divine spirit of freedom, which all hearts venerate and long for, will of herself come to inhabit it; and under her healing wings every noxious influence will wither, every good and salutary one more and more expand. Nay, so devoted are we to this principle, and at the same time so curiously mechanical, that a new trade, specially grounded on it, has arisen among us, under the name of 'Codification', or code-making in the abstract; whereby any people, for a reasonable consideration, may be accommodated with a patent code;—more easily than curious

individuals with patent breeches, for the people does *not* need
to be measured first.

. . . Again, with respect to our Moral condition: here also,
he who runs may read that the same physical, mechanical
influences are everywhere busy. For the 'superior morality',
of which we hear so much, we too would desire to be thankful:
at the same time, it were but blindness to deny that this
'superior morality', is properly rather an 'inferior criminality',
produced not by greater love of Virtue, but by greater perfection of Police; and of that far subtler and stronger Police,
called Public Opinion. This last watches over us with its
Argus eyes more keenly than ever; but the 'inward eye'
seems heavy with sleep. Of any belief in invisible, divine things,
we find as few traces in our Morality as elsewhere. It is by
tangible, material considerations that we are guided, not by
inward and spiritual. Self-denial, the parent of all virtue, in
any true sense of that word, has perhaps seldom been rarer:
so rare is it, that the most, even in their abstract speculations,
regard its existence as a chimera. Virtue is pleasure, is Profit;
no celestial, but an earthly thing. Virtuous men, Philanthropists, Martyrs, are happy accidents; their 'taste' lies the right
way! In all senses, we worship and follow after Power; which
may be called a physical pursuit. No man now loves Truth, as
Truth must be loved, with an infinite love; but only with a
finite love, and as it were *par amours*. Nay, properly speaking,
he does not *believe* and know it, but only '*thinks*' it, and that
'there is every probability'! He preaches it aloud and rushes
courageously forth with it,—if there is a multitude huzzaing
at his back! yet ever keeps looking over his shoulder, and the
instant the huzzaing languishes, he too stops short. In fact,
what morality we have takes the shape of Ambition, of
Honour; beyond money and money's worth, our only
rational blessedness is Popularity. It were but a fool's trick to
die for conscience. Only for 'character', by duel, or, in case of
extremity, by suicide, is the wise man bound to die. By
arguing on the 'force of circumstances', we have argued away
all force from ourselves; and stand leashed together, uniform
in dress and movement, like the rowers of some boundless
galley. This and that may be right and true; *but* we must not

do it. Wonderful 'Force of Public Opinion'! We must act and walk in all points as it prescribes; follow the traffic it bids us, realise the sum of money, the degree of 'influence' it expects of us, *or* shall be lightly esteemed; certain mouthfuls of articulate wind will be blown at us, and this what mortal courage can front? Thus, while civil Liberty is more and more secured to us, our moral Liberty is all but lost. Practically considered, our creed is Fatalism; and, free in hand and foot, we are shackled in heart and soul, with far straiter than feudal chains. Truly may we say, with the Philosopher, 'the deep meaning of the Laws of Mechanism lies heavy on us'; and in the closet, in the marketplace, in the temple, by the social hearth, encumbers the whole movements of our mind, and over our noblest faculties is spreading a nightmare sleep.

From 'Sartor Resartus'

['Sartor Resartus' ran in *Fraser's Magazine* from November, 1833 to August, 1834. The following extracts, from Book II, Chs. 7 and 9, appeared in March and April, 1834; Vol. IX, Nos. 51 and 52.]

... Thus must the bewildered Wanderer stand, as so many have done, shouting question after question into the Sibyl-cave of Destiny, and receive no Answer but an Echo. It is all a grim Desert, this once-fair world of his; wherein is heard only the howling of wild beasts, or the shrieks of despairing, hate-filled men and no Pillar of Cloud by day, and no Pillar of Fire by night, any longer guides the Pilgrim. To such length has the spirit of Inquiry carried him. "But what recks it (*was thut's*)?" cries he: "it is but the common lot in this era. Not having come to spiritual majority prior to the *Siècle de Louis Quinze*, and not being born purely a Loghead (*Dummkopf*), thou hast no other outlook. The world is, like thee, sold to Unbelief; their old Temples of the Godhead, which for long have not been rainproof, crumble down; and men ask now: Where is the Godhead? our eyes never saw him!".

Pitiful enough were it, for all these wild utterances, to call our Diogenes wicked.[6] Unprofitable Servants as we all are,

perhaps at no era of his life was he more decisively the
Servant of Goodness, the Servant of God, than even now when
doubting God's existence. "One circumstance I note," says he:
"after all the nameless woe that Inquiry, which for me, what
it is not always, was genuine Love of Truth, had wrought me,
I nevertheless still loved Truth, and would bate no jot of my
allegiance to her. 'Truth!' I cried, 'though the Heavens crush
me for following her: no Falsehood! though a whole celestial
Lubberland were the price of Apostacy'. In conduct it was the
same. Had a divine Messenger from the clouds, or miraculous
Handwriting on the wall, convincingly proclaimed to me
This thou shalt do, with what passionate readiness, as I often
thought, would I have done it, had it been leaping into the
infernal Fire. Thus, in spite of all Motive-grinders, and
Mechanical Profit-and-Loss Philosophies, with the sick
ophthalmia and hallucination they had brought on, was the
Infinite nature of Duty still dimly present to me: living without
God in the world, of God's light I was not utterly bereft; if my
as yet sealed eyes, with their unspeakable longing, could nowhere see Him, nevertheless in my heart He was present, and
His Heaven-written Law still stood legible and sacred there."

Meanwhile, under all these tribulations, and temporal and
spiritual destitutions, what must the Wanderer, in his silent
soul, have endured! "The painfullest feeling", writes he, "is
that of your own Feebleness (*Unkraft*); ever, as the English
Milton says, to be weak is the true misery.[7] And yet of your
Strength there is and can be no clear feeling, save by what you
have prospered in, by what you have done. Between vague
wavering Capability and fixed indubitable Performance, what
a difference! A certain inarticulate Self-consciousness dwells
dimly in us; which only our Works can render articulate and
decisively discernible. Our Works are the mirror wherein the
spirit first sees its natural lineaments. Hence too, the folly of
that impossible Precept, *know thyself*; till it be translated into
this partially possible one, *know what thou canst work at*.

"But for me, so strangely unprosperous had I been, the net
result of my Workings amounted as yet simply to—Nothing.
How then could I believe in my Strength, when there was as
yet no mirror to see it in? Ever did this agitating, yet as I now

perceive, quite frivolous question, remain to me insoluble: Hast thou a certain Faculty, a certain Worth, such even as the most have not; or art thou the completest Dullard of these modern times? Alas! the fearful Unbelief is unbelief in yourself; and how could I believe? Had not my first, last Faith in myself, when even to me the Heavens seemed laid open, and I dared to love, been all-too cruelly belied? The speculative Mystery of Life grew ever more mysterious to me: neither in the practical Mystery had I made the slightest progress, but been everywhere buffeted, foiled, and contemptuously cast-out. A feeble unit in the middle of a threatening Infinitude, I seemed to have nothing given me but eyes, whereby to discern my own wretchedness. Invisible yet impenetrable walls, as of Enchantment, divided me from all living: was there, in the wide world any true bosom I could press trustfully to mine? O Heaven, No, there was none! I kept a lock upon my lips: why should I speak much with that shifting variety of so-called Friends, in whose withered, vain and too-hungry souls, Friendship was but an incredible tradition? In such cases, your resource is to talk little, and that little mostly from the Newspapers. Now when I look back, it was a strange isolation I then lived in. The men and women round me, even speaking with me, were but Figures: I had, practically, forgotten that they were alive, that they were not merely automatic. In midst of their crowded streets, and assemblages, I walked solitary; and (except as it was my own heart, not another's, that I kept devouring) savage also, as the tiger in his jungle. Some comfort it would have been could I, like a Faust, have fancied myself tempted and tormented of the Devil; for a Hell, as I imagine, without Life, though only diabolic Life, were more frightful: but in our age of Downpulling and Disbelief, the very Devil has been pulled down, you cannot so much as believe in a Devil. To me the Universe was all void of Life, of Purpose, of Volition, even of Hostility: it was one huge, dead, immeasurable Steam-engine, rolling on, in its dead indifference, to grind me limb from limb. O, the vast, gloomy, solitary Golgotha, and Mill of Death! Why was the Living banished thither companionless, conscious? Why, if there is no Devil; nay, unless the Devil is your God?"

A prey incessantly to such corrosions, might not, moreover, as the worst aggravation to them, the iron constitution even of a Teufelsdröckh threaten to fail? We conjecture that he has known sickness; and, in spite of his locomotive habits, perhaps sickness of the chronic sort. Hear this, for example: "How beautiful to die of broken-heart, on Paper! Quite another thing in Practice; every window of your Feeling, even of your Intellect, as it were, begrimed and mud-spattered, so that no pure ray can enter; a whole Drugshop in your inwards; the fordone soul drowning slowly in quagmires of Disgust!"

Putting all which external and internal miseries together, may we not find in the following sentences, quite in our Professor's still vein, significance enough? "From Suicide a certain aftershine (*Nachschein*) of Christianity withheld me: perhaps also a certain indolence of character; for, was not that a remedy I had at any time within reach? Often, however, was there a question present to me: Should some one now, at the turning of that corner, blow thee suddenly out of Space, into the other World, or other No World, by pistol-shot,—how were it? On which ground, too, I have often, in sea-storms and sieged cities and other death-scenes, exhibited an imperturbability, which passed, falsely enough, for courage."

"So had it lasted," concludes the Wanderer, "so had it lasted, as in bitter protracted Death-agony, through long years. The heart within me, unvisited by any heavenly dew-drop, was smouldering in sulphurous, slow-consuming fire. Almost since earliest memory I had shed no tear; or once only when I, murmuring half-audibly, recited Faust's Deathsong, that wild *Selig der den er im Siegesglanze findet* (Happy whom He finds in Battle's splendour), and thought that of this last Friend even I was not forsaken, that Destiny itself could not doom me not to die. Having no Hope, neither had I any definite Fear, were it of Man or of Devil: nay, I often felt as if it might be solacing, could the Arch-Devil himself, though in Tartarean terrors, but rise to me, that I might tell him a little of my mind. And yet, strangely enough, I lived in a continual, indefinite, pining Fear; tremulous, pusillanimous, apprehensive of I knew not what: it seemed as if all things in the Heavens above and the Earth beneath would hurt me; as if the Heavens and the Earth were but boundless Jaws of a devouring Monster, wherein I, palpitating, waited to be devoured.

"Full of such humour, and perhaps the miserablest man in the whole French Capital or Suburbs, was I, one sultry Dogday, after much perambulation, toiling along the dirty little Rue Saint-Thomas de l'Enfer, among civic rubbish enough, in a close atmosphere, and over pavements hot as Nebuchadnezzar's Furnace, whereby doubtless my spirits were little cheered; when, all at once, there rose a Thought in me, and I asked myself: 'What *art* thou afraid of? Wherefore, like a coward, dost thou forever pip and whimper, and go cowering and trembling? Despicable biped! what is the sum-total of the worst that lies before thee? Death? Well, Death; and say the pangs of Tophet[8] too, and all that the Devil and Man may, will or can do against thee! Hast thou not a heart; canst thou not suffer whatso it be; and, as a Child of Freedom, though outcast, trample Tophet itself under thy feet, while it consumes thee? Let it come, then; I will meet it and defy it!' And as I so thought, there rushed like a stream of fire over my whole soul; and I shook base Fear away from me for ever. I was strong, of unknown strength; a spirit, almost a god. Ever from that time, the temper of my misery was changed: not Fear or whining Sorrow was it, but Indignation and grim fire-eyed Defiance.

"Thus had the EVERLASTING NO (*das Ewige Nein*) pealed authoritatively through all the recesses of my Being, of my ME; and then was it that my whole ME stood up, in native God-created majesty, and with emphasis recorded its Protest. Such a Protest, the most important transaction in Life, may that same Indignation and Defiance, in a psychologi-cal point of view, be fitly called. The Everlasting NO had said: 'Behold, thou art fatherless, outcast, and the Universe is mine (the Devil's)'; to which my whole Me now made answer: '*I* am not thine, but Free, and forever hate thee!'

"It is from this hour that I incline to date my Spiritual New-birth, or Baphometic,[9] Fire-baptism; perhaps I directly thereupon began to be a Man."

... So that for Teufelsdröckh also there has been a "glorious revolution": these mad shadow-hunting and

shadow-hunted Pilgrimings of his, were but some purifying
"Temptation in the Wilderness", before his apostolic work
(such as it was) could begin; which Temptation is now
happily over, and the Devil once more worsted! Was "that
high moment in the *Rue de l'Enfer*," then, properly the turning-
point of the battle; when the Fiend said, *Worship me or be torn
in shreds*, and was answered valiantly with *Apage Satanas*?[10]
Singular Teufelsdröckh, would thou hadst told thy singular
story in plain words! But it is fruitless to look there, in those
Paper-bags, for such. Nothing but innuendoes, figurative
crotchets: a typical Shadow, fitfully wavering, prophetico-
satiric; no clear logical Picture. "How paint to the sensual
eye," asks he once, "what passes in the Holy-of-Holies of
Man's Soul; in what words known to these profane times,
speak even afar off of the Unspeakable?" We ask in turn:
Why perplex these times, profane as they are, with needless
obscurity, by omission and by commission? Not mystical only
is our Professor, but whimsical; and involves himself, now more
than ever, in eye-bewildering *chiaroscuro*. Successive glimpses,
here faithfully imparted, our more gifted readers must endeavour to combine for their own behoof.

He says: "The hot Harmattan-wind had raged itself out;
its howl went silent within me; and the long-deafened soul
could now hear, I paused in my wild wanderings; and sat me
down to wait, and consider; for it was as if the hour of change
drew nigh. I seemed to surrender, to renounce utterly, and
say: Fly, then false shadows of Hope; I will chase you no more,
I will believe you no more. And ye too, haggard spectres of
Fear, I care not for you; ye too are all shadows and a lie. Let
me rest here: for I am way-weary and life-weary; I will rest
here, were it but to die: to die or to live is alike to me: alike
insignificant."—And again: "Here, then as I lay in that
CENTRE OF INDIFFERENCE; cast, doubtless by benignant upper Influence, into a healing sleep, the heavy dreams
rolled gradually away, and I awoke to a new Heaven and a
new Earth. The first preliminary moral Act, Annihilation of
Self (*Selbsttödtung*), had been happily accomplished; and my
mind's eyes were now unsealed, and its hands ungyved."

Might we not also conjecture that the following passage

refers to his Locality, during this same "healing sleep"; that his Pilgrim-staff lies cast aside here, on "the high table-land"; and indeed that the repose is already taking wholesome effect on him? Were it not that the tone, in some parts, has more of riancy, even of levity than we could have expected. However, in Teufelsdröckh, there is always the strangest Dualism, light dancing, with guitar-music, will be going on in the forecourt, while by fits from within comes the faint whimpering of woe and wail. We transcribe the piece entire:

"Beautiful it was to sit there, as in my skyey Tent, musing and meditating; on the high table-land, in front of the Mountains; over me, as roof, the azure Dome; and around me, for walls, four azure flowing curtains,—namely, of the Four azure Winds, on whose bottom-fringes also I have seen gilding. And then to fancy the fair Castles that stood sheltered in these Mountains' hollows: with their green flower-lawns, and white dames and damosels, lovely enough: or better still, the straw-roofed Cottages, wherein stood many a Mother baking bread, with her children round her:—all hidden and protect-ingly folded up in the Valley-folds; yet there and alive, as sure as if I beheld them. Or to see, as well as fancy, the nine Towns and Villages, that lay around my mountain-seat, which in still weather, were wont to speak to me (by their steeple-bells) with metal tongue; and, in almost all weather, proclaimed their vitality by repeated smoke-clouds; whereon, as on a culinary horolage, I might read the hour of the day. For it was the smoke of cookery, as kind housewives at morning, midday, eventide, were boiling their husbands' kettles; and ever a blue pillar rose up into the air, successively or simultaneously, from each of the nine, saying, as plainly as smoke could say: Such and such a meal is getting ready here. Not uninteresting! For you have the whole Borough, with all its love-makings and scandal-mongeries, contentions and contentments, as in miniature, and could cover it all with your hat.—If, in my wide Wayfarings, I had learned to look into the business of the World in its details, here perhaps was the place for combining it into general propositions, and deducing inferences therefrom.

"Often also could I see the black Tempest marching in

anger through the Distance: round some Schreckhorn, as yet grim-blue, would the eddying vapour gather, and there tumultuously eddy, and flow down like a mad witch's hair; till, after a space, it vanished, and, in the clear sunbeam, yon Schreckhorn stood smiling grim-white, for the vapour had held snow. How thou fermentest and elaboratest, in thy great fermenting-vat and laboratory of an Atmosphere, of a World, O Nature!.—Or what if Nature? Ha! why do I not name thee GOD? Art thou not the 'Living Garment of God?' O Heavens, is it, in very deed, HE then, that ever speaks through thee; that lives and loves in thee, that lives and loves in me?

"Fore-shadows, call them rather fore-splendours, of that Truth, and Beginning of Truths, fell mysteriously over my soul. Sweeter than Dayspring to the Shipwrecked in Nova Zembla; ah! like the mother's voice to her little child that strays bewildered, weeping, in unknown tumults; like soft streamings of celestial music to my too-exasperated-heart; came that Evangile. The Universe is not dead and demoniacal, a charnel-house with spectres; but godlike, and my Father's!

"With other eyes, too, could I now look upon my fellow man; with an infinite Love, an infinite Pity. Poor, wandering, wayward man! Art thou not tired, and beaten with stripes, even as I am? Ever, whether thou bear the Royal mantle or the Beggar's gabardine, art thou not so weary, so heavy-laden; and thy Bed of Rest is but a Grave. O my Brother, my Brother! why cannot I shelter thee in my bosom, and wipe away all the tears from thy eyes.—Truly, the din of many-voiced Life, which, in this solitude, with the mind's organ, I could hear, was no longer a maddening discord, but a melting one: like inarticulate cries, and sobbings of a dumb creature, which in the ear of Heaven are prayers. The poor Earth, with her poor joys, was now my needy Mother, not my cruel Stepdame; Man, with his so mad Wants and so mean Endeavours, had become the dearer to me; and even for his sufferings and his sins, I now first named him Brother. Thus was I standing in the porch of the '*Sanctuary of Sorrow*'; by strange, steep ways, had I too been guided thither; and ere long its sacred gates would open, and the '*Divine Depth of Sorrow*' lie disclosed to me."

The Professor says, he here first got eye on the Knot that had been strangling him, and straightway could unfasten it, and was free. "A vain interminable controversy," writes he, "touching what is at present called Origin of Evil, or some such thing, arises in every soul, since the beginning of the world; and in every soul, that would pass from idle Suffering into actual Endeavouring, must first be put an end to. The most in our time, have to go content with a simple, incomplete enough Suppression of this controversy; to a few some Solution of it is indispensable. In every new era too, such Solution comes out in different terms; and ever the Solution of the last era has become obsolete; and is found unserviceable. For it is man's nature to change his Dialect from century to century; he cannot help it though he would. The authentic *Church-Catechism* of our present century has not yet fallen into my hands: meanwhile, for my own private behoof, I attempt to elucidate the matter so. Man's Unhappiness, as I construe, comes of his Greatness; it is because there is an Infinite in him, which with all his cunning he cannot quite bury under the Finite. Will the whole Finance Ministers and Upholsterers and Confectioners of modern Europe undertake, in joint-stock company, to make one Shoeblack HAPPY? They cannot accomplish it, above an hour or two; for the Shoeblack also has a Soul quite other than his stomach, and would require, if you consider it, for his permanent satisfaction and saturation, simply this allotment, no more, and no less: *God's infinite Universe altogether to himself*, therein to enjoy infinitely, and fill every wish as fast as it rose. Oceans of Hochheimer, A Throat like that of Ophiuchus![11] speak not of them, to the infinite Shoeblack they are as nothing. No sooner is your ocean filled, than he grumbles that it might have been of better vintage. Try him with half of a Universe, of an Omnipotence, he sets to quarrelling with the proprietor of the other half, and declares himself the most maltreated of men.—Always there is a black spot in our sunshine: it is even, as I said, the *Shadow of Ourselves*.

"But the whim we have of Happiness is somewhat thus. By certain valuations, and averages of our own striking, we come upon some sort of average terrestial lot; this we fancy belongs to us by nature, and of indefeasible right. It is simple payment of our wages, of our deserts; requires neither thanks nor complaint: only such *overplus* as there may be do we account Happiness; any *deficit* again is Misery. Now consider that we have the valuation of our own deserts ourselves, and what a fund of Self-conceit there is in each of us,—do you wonder that the balance should so often dip the wrong way, and many a Blockhead cry: See there, what a payment; was ever worthy gentleman so used!—I tell thee, Blockhead, it all comes of thy vanity; of what thou *fanciest* those same deserts of thine to be. Fancy that thou deservest to be hanged (as is most likely), thou wilt feel it happiness to be only shot; fancy that thou deservest to be hanged in a hair-halter, it will be a luxury to die in hemp.

"So true is it, what I then said, that *the Fraction of Life can be increased in value not so much by increasing your Numerator, as by lessening your Denominator.* Nay, unless my Algebra deceive me, *Unity* itself divided by *Zero* will give *Infinity*. Make thy claim of wages a zero, then; thou hast the world under thy feet. Well did the Wisest of our time write: 'It is only with Renunciation (*Entsagen*) that Life, properly speaking, can be said to begin'.[12]

"I asked myself: What is this that, ever since earliest years, thou hast been fretting and fuming, and lamenting and self-tormenting, on account of? Say it in a word; is it not because thou art not HAPPY? Because the THOU (sweet gentleman) is not sufficiently honoured, nourished, soft-bedded, and lovingly cared for? Foolish soul! What Act of Legislature was there that *thou* shouldst be Happy? A little while ago thou hadst no right to *be* at all. What if thou were born and predestined not to be Happy, but to be Unhappy! Art thou nothing other than a Vulture, then, that fliest through the Universe seeking after somewhat to *eat*; and shrieking dolefully because carrion enough is not given thee? Close thy *Byron*; open thy Goethe."

"*Es leuchtet mir ein*, I see a glimpse of it!" cries he elsewhere: "there is in man a HIGHER than Love of Happiness: he can do without Happiness, and instead thereof find Blessedness! Was it not to preach-forth this same HIGHER that sages and martyrs, the Poet, and the Priest, in all times, have spoken and suffered; bearing testimony, through life and through death, of the Godlike that is in Man, and how in the Godlike only has he Strength and Freedom? Which God-inspired Doctrine art thou too honoured to be taught; O Heavens! and broken with manifold merciful Afflictions, even till thou become contrite, and learn it! O thank thy Destiny for these; thankfully bear what yet remain: thou hadst need of them; the Self in thee needed to be annihilated. By benignant fever-paroxysms is Life rooting out the deep-seated chronic Diseases, and triumphs over Death. On the roaring billows of Time, thou art not engulphed, but borne aloft into the azure of Eternity. Love not Pleasure; love God. This is the EVER-LASTING YEA, wherein all contradiction is solved: wherein whoso walks and works, it is well with him."

... "But indeed Conviction, were it never so excellent is worthless till it convert itself into Conduct. Nay properly Conviction is not possible till then: inasmuch as all Speculation is by nature endless, formless, a vortex amid vortices: only, by a felt indubitable certainty of Experience, does it find any centre to revolve round, and so fashion itself into a system. Most true is it, as a wise man teaches us, that 'Doubt of any sort cannot be removed except by Action'. On which ground too let him who gropes painfully in darkness or uncertain light, and prays vehemently that the dawn may ripen into day, lay this other precept well to heart, which to me was of invaluable service: '*Do the Duty which lies nearest thee*', which thou knowest to be a Duty! Thy second Duty will already have become clearer.

"May we not say, however, that the hour of Spiritual Enfranchisement is even this: When your Ideal World, wherein the whole man has been dimly struggling and inexpressibly languishing to work, becomes revealed, and thrown open; and you discover, with amazement enough, like the Lothario in *Wilhelm Meister*[13] that your 'America is here or nowhere'? The Situation that has not its Duty, its Ideal, was not yet occupied by man. Yes here, in this poor, miserable, hampered, despicable Actual, wherein thou even now standest, here or nowhere is thy Ideal: work it out therefrom; and, working, believe, live, be free. Fool! the Ideal is in thyself, the Impediment too is in thyself; thy Condition is but the stuff thou art to shape that same Ideal out of: what matters whether such stuff be of this sort or of that, so the Form thou give it be heroic, be poetic? O thou that pinest in the imprisonment of the Actual, and criest bitterly to the gods for a kingdom wherein to rule and create, know this is of a truth: the thing thou seekest is already with thee, 'here or nowhere', couldst thou only see!

"But it is with man's Soul as it was with Nature: the beginning of Creation is—Light. Till the eye have vision, the whole members are in bonds. Divine moment, when over the tempest-tost Soul, as once over the wild-weltering Chaos, it is spoken: Let there be Light! Ever to the greatest that has felt such moment is it not miraculous and God-announcing; even, as under simpler figures, to the simplest and least. The mad primeval Discord is hushed; the rudely-jumbled conflicting elements bind themselves into separate Firmaments: deep silent rock-foundations are built beneath; and the skyey vault with its everlasting Luminaries above: instead of a dark wasteful Chaos, we have a blooming,—fertile, Heaven-encompassed World.

"I too could now say to myself: Be no longer a Chaos, but a World, or even Worldkin. Produce! Produce! Were it but the pitifullest infinitesimal fraction of a Product, produce it in God's name! 'Tis the utmost thou hast in thee: out with it then. Up, Up! Whatsover thy hand findeth to do, do it with thy whole might. Work while it is called To-day, for the Night cometh wherein no man can work."

From *Past and Present*

[*Past and Present* was first published in 1843. The following extracts are from Part II, Chs. 6, 7, 8, and 10. The 'past' is that of a twelfth-century monastery re-created through the chronicle of a Jocelin of Brakelond.]

Within doors, down at the hill-foot, in our Convent here, we are a peculiar people,—hardly conceivable in the Arkwright Corn-Laws ages, of mere Spinning-Mills and Joe-Mantons.[14] There is yet no Methodism among us, and we speak much

Secularities: no Methodism; our Religion is not yet a horrible restless Doubt, still less a far horribler composed Cant; but a great heaven-high Unquestionability, encompassing, inter-penetrating the whole of Life. Imperfect as we may be, we are here, with our litanies, shaven crowns, vows of poverty, to testify incessantly and indisputably to every heart, That this Earthly Life, and *its* riches and possessions, and good and evil hap, are not intrinsically a reality at all, but *are* a shadow of realities eternal, infinite; that this Time-world, as an air-image, fearfully *emblematic*, plays and flickers in the grand still mirror of Eternity; and man's little Life has Duties that are great, that are alone great, and go up to Heaven and down to Hell. This, with our poor litanies, we testify and struggle to testify.

Which, testified or not, remembered by all men or forgotten by all men, does verily remain the fact, even in Arkwright Joe-Manton ages! But it is incalculable, when litanies have grown obsolete; when *fodercorns*,[15] *avragiums*,[16] and all human dues and reciprocities have been fully changed into one great due of *cash payment*; and man's duty to man reduces itself to handing him certain metal coins, or covenanted money-wages, and then shoving him out of doors; and man's duty to God becomes a cant, a doubt, a dim inanity, a 'pleasure of virtue' or suchlike; and the thing a man does infinitely fear (the real *Hell* of a man) is, 'that he do not make money and advance himself,'—I say, it is incalculable what a change has introduced itself everywhere into human affairs! How human affairs shall now circulate everywhere not healthy life-blood in them, but, as it were, a detestable copperas banker's ink; and all is grown acrid, divisive, threatening dissolution; and the huge tumultuous Life of Society is galvanic, devil-ridden, too trule possessed by a devil! For in short, Mammon *is* not a god at all; but a devil, and even a very despicable devil. Follow the Devil faithfully, you are sure enough to *go* to the Devil: whither else *can* you go? In such situations, men look back with a kind of mournful recognition even on poor limited Monk-figures, with their poor litanies; and reflect, with Ben Jonson,[17] that soul is indispensable, some degree of soul, even to save you the expense of salt!—

For the rest, it must be owned, we Monks of St. Edmundsbury are but a limited class of creatures, and seem to have a
somewhat dull life of it. Much given to idle gossip; having
indeed no other work, when our chanting is over. Listless gossip,
for most part, and a mitigated slander; the fruit of idleness, not
of spleen. We are dull, insipid men, many of us; easy-minded;
whom prayer and digestion of food will avail for a life. We
have to receive all strangers in our Convent, and lodge them
gratis; such and such sorts go by rule to the Lord Abbot, and
his special revenues; such and such to us and our poor
Cellarer, however straitened. Jews themselves send their
wives and little ones hither in war-time, into our *Pitanceria*;[18]
where they abide safe, with due *pittances,*—for a consideration.
We have the fairest chances for collecting news. Some of us
have a turn for reading Books; for meditation, silence; at
times we even write Books. Some of us can preach, in English-
Saxon, in Norman-French, and even in Monk-Latin; others
cannot in any language or jargon, being stupid.

Failing all else, what gossip about one another! This is a
perennial resource. How one hooded head applies itself to the
ear of another, and whispers *tacenda*. Willelmus Sacrista, for
instance, what does he nightly, over in that Sacristy of his?
Frequent bibations, *'frequentes bibationes et quaedam tacenda,'*—
eheu! We have *'tempora minutionis,'* stated seasons of blood-
letting, when we are all let blood together; and then there is
a general free-conference, a sanhedrin of clatter. For all our
vow of poverty, we can by rule amass to the extent of 'two
shillings'; but it is to be given to our necessitous kindred or in
charity. Poor Monks! Thus too a certain Canterbury Monk
was in the habit of 'slipping, *clanculo*,[19] from his sleeve',
five shillings into the hand of his mother, when she came to
see him, at the divine offices, every two months. Once, slipping
the money clandestinely, just in the act of taking leave, he
slipt it not into her hand but on the floor, and another had it;
whereupon the poor Monk, coming to know it, looked mere
despair for some days; till Lanfranc the noble Archbishop,
questioning his secret from him, nobly made the sum *seven*
shillings, and said, Never mind!

One Monk of a taciturn nature distinguishes himself among

these babbling ones: the name of him Samson; he that answered Jocelin, '*Fili mi*, a burnt child shuns the fire.' They call him 'Norfolk *Barrator*,' or litigious person; for indeed, being of grave taciturn ways, he is not universally a favourite; he has been in trouble more than once. The reader is desired to mark this Monk. A personable man of seven-and-forty; stout-made, stands erect as a pillar; with bushy eyebrows, the eyes of him beaming into you in a really strange way; the face massive, grave, with 'a very eminent nose', his head almost bald, its auburn remnants of hair, and the copious ruddy beard, getting slightly streaked with gray. This is Brother Samson; a man worth looking at.

He is from Norfolk, as the nickname indicates; from Tottington in Norfolk, as we guess; the son of poor parents there. He has told me, Jocelin, for I loved him much, that once in his ninth year he had an alarming dream;—as indeed we are all somewhat given to dreaming here. Little Samson, lying uneasily in his crib at Tottington, dreamed that he saw the Arch Enemy in person, just alighted in front of some grand building, with outspread bat-wings, and stretching forth detestable clawed hands to grip him, little Samson, and fly off with him: whereupon the little dreamer shrieked desperate to St. Edmund for help, shrieked and again shrieked; and St. Edmund, a reverend heavenly figure, did come,—and indeed poor little Samson's mother, awakened by his shrieking, did come; and the Devil and the Dream both fled away fruitless. On the morrow, his mother, pondering such an awful dream, thought it were good to take him over to St. Edmund's own Shrine, and pray with him there. See, said little Samson at the sight of the Abbey-Gate, see, mother, this is the building I dreamed of! His poor mother dedicated him to St. Edmund, —left him there with prayers and tears: what better could she do? The exposition of the dream, Brother Samson used to say, was this: *Diabolus* with outspread bat-wings shadowed forth the pleasures of this world, *voluptates hujus saeculi*, which were about to snatch and fly away with me, had not St. Edmund flung his arms round me, that is to say, made me a monk of his. A monk, accordingly, Brother Samson is; and here to this day where his mother left him. A learned man, of devout grave nature; has studied at Paris, has taught in the Town Schools here, and done much else; can preach in three languages, and, like Dr. Caius, [20] 'has had losses' in his time. A thoughtful, firm-standing man; much loved by some, not loved by all; his clear eyes flashing into you, in an almost inconvenient way!

. . . Now, however, come great news to St. Edmundsbury: That there is to be an Abbot elected; that our interlunar obscuration is to cease; St. Edmund's Convent no more to be a doleful widow, but joyous and once again bride! Often in our widowed state had we prayed to the Lord and St. Edmund, singing weekly a matter of 'one-and-twenty penitential Psalms, on our knees in the Choir,' that a fit Pastor might be vouchsafed us.

. . . The Prior, however, as our interim chief, must proceed to work; get ready 'Twelve Monks', and set off with them to his Majesty at Waltham, there shall the election be made. An election, whether managed directly by ballot-box on public hustings, or indirectly by force of public opinion, or were it even by open alehouses, landlords' coercion, popular club-law, or whatever electoral methods, is always an interesting phenomenon. A mountain tumbling in great travail, throwing up dust-clouds and absurd noises is visibly there; uncertain yet what mouse or monster it will give birth to.

Besides, it is a most important social act; nay, at bottom, the one important social act. Given the men a People choose, the People itself, in its exact worth and worthlessness, is given. A heroic people chooses heroes, and is happy; a valet or flunkey people chooses sham-heroes, what are called quacks, thinking them heroes, and is not happy. The grand summary of a man's spiritual condition, what brings out all his herohood and insight, or all his flunkeyhood and horn-eyed dimness, is this question put to him, What man dost thou honour? Which is thy ideal of a man; or nearest that? So too of a People: for a People too, every People, *speaks* its choice,— were it only by silently obeying, and not revolting,—in the course of a century or so. Nor are electoral methods, Reform Bills and suchlike, unimportant. A People's electoral methods are, in the long-run, the express image of its electoral *talent*;

tending and gravitating perpetually, irresistibly, to a conformity with that: and are, at all stages, very significant of the People. Judicious readers, of these times, are not disinclined to see how Monks elect their Abbot in the Twelfth Century; how the St. Edmundsbury mountain manages its midwifery; and what mouse or man the outcome is.

... Our electoral committee, its eye on the Sacrosancta, is soon named, soon sworn; and we, striking up the Fifth Psalm, *Verba mea*,

> 'Give ear unto my words, O Lord,
> My meditation weigh,'

march out chanting, and leave the Six to their work in the Chapter here. Their work, before long, they announce as finished: they, with their eye on the Sacrosancta, imprecating the Lord to weigh and witness their meditation, have fixed on Three Names, and written them in this Sealed Paper. Let Samson Subsacrista, general servant of the party, take charge of it. On the morrow morning, our Prior and his Twelve will be ready to get under way.

This, then, is the ballot-box and electoral winnowing-machine they have at St. Edmundsbury: a mind fixed on the Thrice Holy, an appeal to God on high to witness their meditation; by far the best, and indeed the only good electoral winnowing-machine,—if men have souls in them. Totally worthless, it is true, and even hideous and poisonous, if men have no souls. But without soul, alas, what winnowing-machine in human elections can be of avail? We cannot get along without soul; we stick fast, the mournfullest spectacle; and salt itself will not save us!

... The *Dominus Rex*, benignantly receiving our Thirteen with their obeisance, and graciously declaring that he will strive to act for God's honour and the Church's good, commands, 'by the Bishop of Winchester and Geoffrey the Chancellor,'—*Galfridus Cancellarius*, Henry's and the Fair Rosamond's authentic Son present here!—commands, 'That they, the said Thirteen, do now withdraw, and fix upon Three from their own Monastery.' A work soon done; the Three hanging ready round Samson's neck, in that leather pouch of his. Breaking the seal, we find the names,—what think *ye* of it, ye higher dignitaries, thou indolent Prior, thou Willelmus *Sacrista* with the red bottle-nose?—the names, in this order: of Samson *Subsacrista*, of Roger the distressed Cellarer, of Hugh *Tertius-Prior*.

. . . In short while, they are next ordered, To add yet another three; but not from their own Convent; from other Convents, "for the honour of my kingdom". Here,—what is to be done here? We will demur, if need be! We do name three, however, for the nonce: the Prior of St. Faith's, a good Monk of St. Neot's, a good Monk of St. Alban's; good men all; all made abbots and dignitaries since, at this hour. There are now Nine upon our List. What the thoughts of the Dominus Rex may be farther? The Dominus Rex, thanking graciously, sends out word that we shall now strike off three. The three strangers are instantly struck off. Willelmus Sacrista adds, that he will of his own accord decline,—a touch of grace and respect for the *Sacrosancta*, even in Willelmus! The King then orders us to strike off a couple more; then yet one more: Hugo Third-Prior goes, and Roger *Cellerarius*, and venerable Monk Dennis;—and now there remain on our List two only, Samson Subsacrista and the Prior.

Which of these two? It were hard to say,—by Monks who may get themselves foot-gyved and thrown into limbo, for speaking! We humbly request that the Bishop of Winchester and Geoffrey the Chancellor may again enter, and help us to decide. "Which do you want?" asks the Bishop. Venerable Dennis made a speech, 'commending the persons of the Prior and Samson; but always in the corner of his discourse, *in angulo sui sermonis*, brought Samson in.' "I see!" said the Bishop: "We are to understand that your Prior is somewhat remiss; that you want to have him you call Samson for Abbot." "Either of them is good," said venerable Dennis, almost trembling; "but we would have the better, if it pleased God". "Which of the two *do* you want?" inquires the Bishop pointedly. "Samson!" answered Dennis; "Samson!" echoed all the rest that durst speak or echo anything: and Samson is reported to the King accordingly. His Majesty, advising of it for a moment, orders that Samson be brought in with the other Twelve.

... Thus, then, have the St. Edmundsbury Monks, without express ballot-box or other good winnowing-machine, contrived to accomplish the most important social feat a body of men can do, to winnow-out the man that is to govern them: and truly one sees not that, by any winnowing-machine whatever, they could have done it better. O ye kind Heavens, there is in every Nation and Community a *fittest*, a wisest, bravest, best; whom could we find and make King over us, all were in very truth well; —the best that God and Nature had permitted *us* to make it! By what art discover him? Will the Heavens in their pity teach us no art; for our need of him is great!

Ballot-boxes, Reform Bills, winnowing-machines: all these are good, or are not so good;—alas, brethren, how *can* these, I say, be other than inadequate, be other than failures, melancholy to behold? Dim all souls of men to the divine, the high and awful meaning of Human Worth and Truth, we shall never, by all the machinery in Birmingham, discover the True and Worthy. It is written, 'if we are ourselves valets, there shall exist no hero for us; we shall not know the hero when we see him';—we shall take the quack for a hero; and cry, audibly through all ballot-boxes and machinery whatsoever, Thou art he; be thou King over us!

What boots it? Seek only deceitful Speciosity, money with gilt-carriages, 'fame' with newspaper-paragraphs, whatever name it bear, you will find only deceitful Speciosity; godlike Reality will be forever far from you. The Quack shall be legitimate inevitable King of you; no earthly machinery able to exclude the Quack. Ye shall be born thralls of the Quack, and suffer under him, till your hearts are near broken, and no French Revolution or Manchester Insurrection, or partial or universal volcanic combustions and explosions, never so many, can do more than 'change the *figure* of your Quack'; the essence of him remaining, for a time and times.—"How long, O Prophet?" say some, with a rather melancholy sneer. Alas, ye *un*prophetic, ever till this come about: Till deep misery, if nothing softer will, have driven you out of your Speciosities *into* your Sincerities; and find that there either is a God-like in the world or else ye are an unintelligible madness;

that there is a God, as well as a Mammon and a Devil, and a Genius of Luxuries and canting Dilettantisms and Vain Shows! How long that will be, compute for yourselves. My unhappy brothers!—

. . . How Abbot Samson, giving his new subjects seriatim the kiss of fatherhood in the St. Edmundsbury chapterhouse, proceeded with cautious energy to set about reforming their disjointed distracted way of life; how he managed with his Fifty rough *Milites* (Feudal Knights), with his lazy Farmers, remiss refractory Monks, with Pope's Legates, Viscounts, Bishops, Kings; how on all sides he laid about him like a man, and putting consequence on premiss, and everywhere the saddle on the right horse, struggled incessantly to educe organic method out of lazily fermenting wreck,—the careful reader will discern, not without true interest, in these pages of Jocelin Boswell. In most antiquarian quaint costume, not of garments alone, but of thought, word, action, outlook and position, the substantial figure of a man with eminent nose, bushy brows, and clear-flashing eyes, his russet beard growing daily grayer, is visible, engaged in true governing of men. It is beautiful how the chrysalis governing-soul, shaking off its dusty slough and prison, starts forth winged, a true royal soul! Our new Abbot has a right honest unconscious feeling without insolence as without fear or flutter, of what he is and what others are. A courage to quell the proudest, an honest pity to encourage the humblest. Withal there is a noble reticence in this Lord Abbot: much vain unreason he hears; lays up without response. He is not there to expect reason and nobleness of others; he is there to give them of his own reason and nobleness. Is he not their servant, as we said, who can suffer from them, and for them; bear the burden their poor spindle-limbs totter and stagger under; and, in virtue *thereof* govern them, lead them out of weakness into strength, out of defeat into victory!

One of the first Herculean Labours Abbot Samson undertook, or the very first, was to institute a strenuous review and radical reform of his economics. It is the first labour of every governing man, from *Paterfamilias* to *Dominus Rex*. To get the rain thatched out from you is the preliminary of whatever

farther, in the way of speculation or of action, you may mean
to do. Old Abbot Hugo's budget, as we say, had become empty,
filled with deficit and wind. To see his account-books clear, be
delivered from those ravening flights of Jew and Christian
creditors, pouncing on him like obscene harpies wherever he
shewed face, was a necessity for Abbot Samson.

On the morrow after his instalment, he brings in a load of
money-bonds, all duly stamped, sealed with this or the other
Convent Seal: frightful, unmanageable, a bottomless confusion of Convent finance. There they are;—but there at least
they all are; all that shall be of them. Our Lord Abbot demands
that all the official seals in use among us be now produced and
delivered to him. Three-and-thirty seals turn up; are
straightway broken, and shall seal no more: the Abbot only,
and those duly authorised by him shall seal any bond. There
are but two ways of paying debt: increase of industry in raising
income, increase of thrift in laying it out. With iron energy, in
slow but steady undeviating perseverance, Abbot Samson
sets to work in both directions. His troubles are manifold:
cunning *milites*, unjust bailiffs, lazy sockmen,[21] he an in-
experienced Abbot; relaxed lazy monks, not disinclined to
mutiny in mass: but continued vigilance, rigorous method,
what we call 'the eye of the master,' work wonders. The clear-
beaming eyesight of Abbot Samson, steadfast severe, all-
penetrating,—it is like *Fiat lux*[22] in that inorganic waste
whirlpool; penetrates gradually to all nooks, and of the chaos
makes a *kosmos* or ordered world!

He arranges everywhere, struggles unweariedly to arrange,
and place on some intelligible footing, the 'affairs and dues,
res ac redditus', of his dominion. The Lakenheath eels cease to
breed squabbles between human beings; the penny of
reapsilver[23] to explode into the streets the Female Chartism of
St. Edmundsbury. These and innumerable greater things.
Wheresover Disorder may stand or lie, let it have a care;
here is the man that has declared war with it, that never will
make peace with it. Man is the Missionary of Order; he is the
servant not of the Devil and Chaos, but of God and the
Universe! Let all sluggards and cowards, remiss, false-spoken,
unjust, and otherwise diabolic persons have a care: this is a

dangerous man for them. He has a mild grave face; a thoughtful sternness, a sorrowful pity: but there is a terrible flash of anger in him too; lazy monks often have to murmur, '*Saevit ut lupus*, He rages like a wolf; was not our Dream true!' 'To repress and hold-in such sudden anger he was continually careful,' and succeeded well:—right, Samson; that it may become in thee as noble central heat, fruitful, strong, beneficent; not blaze out, or the seldomest possible blaze out, as wasteful volcanoism to scorch and consume!

'We must first creep, and gradually learn to walk,' had Abbot Samson said of himself, at starting. In four years he has become a great walker; striding prosperously along; driving much before him. In less than four years, says Jocelin, the Convent Debts were all liquidated: the harpy Jews not only settled with, but banished, bag and baggage out of the *Bannaleuca* (Liberties, *Banlieue*) of St. Edmundsbury,—so has the King's Majesty, been persuaded to permit. Farewell to *you*, at any rate; let us, in no extremity, apply again to you! Armed men march them over the borders, dismiss them under stern penalties,—sentence of excommunication on all that shall again harbour them here: there were many dry eyes at their departure.

New life enters everywhere, springs up beneficent, the Incubus of Debt once rolled away. Samson hastes not; but neither does he pause to rest. This of the Finance is a lifelong business with him;—Jocelin's anecdotes are filled to weariness with it. As indeed to Jocelin it was of very primary interest.

But we have to record also, with a lively satisfaction, that spiritual rubbish is as little tolerated in Samson's Monastery as material. With due rigour, Willelmus Sacrista, and his bibations and *tacenda* are, at the earliest opportunity, softly yet irrevocably put an end to. The bibations, namely, had to end; even the building where they used to be carried on was razed from the soil of St. Edmundsbury, and 'on its place grow rows of beans': Willelmus himself, deposed from the Sacristy and all offices, retires into obscurity, into absolute taciturnity unbroken thenceforth to this hour. Whether the poor Willelmus did not still, by secret channels, occasionally get some slight wetting of vinous or alcoholic liquor,—now grown, in a manner, indispensable to the poor man? Jocelin hints not; one knows not how to hope, what to hope! But if he did, it was in silence and darkness; with an ever-present feeling that tee-totalism was his only true course. Drunken dissolute Monks are a class of persons who had better keep out of Abbot Samson's way. *Saevit ut lupus*; was not the Dream true! murmured many a Monk. Nay Ranulf de Glanvill, Justiciary in Chief, took umbrage at him, seeing these strict ways; and watched farther with suspicion: but discerned gradually that there was nothing wrong, that there was much the opposite of wrong.

NOTES

1. No. 33 of Wordsworth's *Miscellaneous Sonnets* opens,
       The world is too much with us; late and soon,
       Getting and spending, we lay waste our powers:
   it was first published in 1807.
2. Thomas Chalmers, D.D. (1780–1847), Scottish theologian and philanthropist. In his *Commercial Discourses* (1820) he encouraged the application of Christian ideals to business life.
3. James Harrington (1611–1677), republican theorist, author of *The Commonwealth of Oceana* (1656).
4. Coleridge's journal *The Friend* appeared in 27 nos. in 1809–1810 and was published in three-volume form in 1818.
5. John De Lolme (1740?–1807), author of *The Constitution of England* (1771).
6. Diogenes, Cynic philosopher, lived from 412 to 323 B.C.
7. *Cf. Paradise Lost*, I, 157.
8. Tophet, burning waste-tip near Jerusalem, which served as a graphic image of Hell.
9. Baphometic, a term evocative of secret worship, or Mahomet.
10. Apage Satanas, get thee behind me, Satan!
11. Ophiuchus, the serpent held by a man in the constellation, Serpentarius.
12. *Cf.* Goethe, *Dichtung und Warheit*, IV, 16, 'alles ruft uns zu: dass wir entsagen sollen'. Renunciation is also a theme of *Wilhelm Meister*.
13. *v.* Goethe's *Wilhelm Meister's Apprenticeship*, Book VII, Ch. 3.

14. Joe Manton (1766–1835), inventive gunmaker.
15. fodercorns, supplies of fodder for horses, given as feudal dues.
16. avragiums, carrying-services due to a feudal lord.
17. *Cf.* B. Jonson, *Timber* (1641); *Scientia*. '*Knowledge* is the action of the Soule', *etc.*
18. *Pitanceria*, office for administering donations to monasteries.
19. *clanculo*, secretly.
20. It is not Dr Caius, but Dogberry (in *Much Ado about Nothing*, Act IV, Sc. 2) who has 'had losses'.
21. sockmen, tenants who owed any service other than knight-service.
22. *Fiat lux*, let there be light.
23. reapsilver, money paid to a tenant in lieu of his or her labour at harvest-time.

The Whig View of History

[Thomas Babington Macaulay (1800–1859), essayist, historian and Whig statesman, wrote confidently in favour of British political and economic achievement. His review of Southey's *Colloquies* is an attack on Romantic Tory criticism of the manufacturing system and on proposals to increase State-power. Macaulay continued the work of the Whig historians associated with Holland House, such as C. J. Fox, H. Hallam and Sir James Mackintosh. (Holland House was the London home of C. J. Fox and of his nephew Lord Holland, and maintained its reputation as an exclusive, Whig literary salon into the 1830s.) Macaulay believed that the 'natural progress of society' worked through the efforts of individuals. The comparison, in his *History of England*, between England in 1685 and England in his own day offers detailed reasons for the pride which many Victorians undoubtedly felt in their continuing prosperity and scientific advancement. Matthew Arnold was to criticise Macaulay's work for its lack of subtlety.]

T. B. MACAULAY

From 'Southey's Colloquies'

[Macaulay's review of Southey's *Colloquies* appeared in *The Edinburgh Review*, XXXI, No. 100 (January, 1830).]

... It is not from bills of mortality and statistical tables that Mr Southey has learned his political creed. He cannot stoop to study the history of the system which he abuses to strike the balance between the good and evil which it has produced to compare district with district, or generation with generation. We will give his own reason for his opinion—the only reason which he gives for it in his own words:—

'We remained awhile in silence, looking upon the assemblage of dwellings below. Here, and in the adjoining hamlet of Millbeck, the effects of manufactures and of agriculture may be seen and compared. The old cottages are such as the poet and the painter equally delight in beholding. Substantially built of the native stone without mortar, dirtied with no white lime, and their long, low roofs covered with slate, if they had been raised by the magic of some indigenous Amphion's music, the materials could not have adjusted themselves more beautifully in accord with the surrounding scene; and time has still further harmonized them with weather—stains, lichens, and moss, short grasses, and short fern, and stone-plants of various kinds. The ornamental chimneys, round or square, less adorned than those which, like little turrets, crest the houses of the Portuguese peasantry; and yet not less happily suited to their place, the hedge of clipt box beneath the windows, the rose-bushes beside the door, the little patch of flower-ground, with its tall hollyhocks in front; the garden beside, the bee-hives, and the orchard with its bank of daffodils and snow-drops, the earliest and the profusest in these parts, indicate in the owners some portion of ease and leisure, some regard to neatness and comfort, some sense of natural, and innocent, and healthful enjoyment. The new cottages of the manufacturers are upon the manufacturing pattern—naked, and in a row.

'How is it,' said I, 'that every thing which is connected with manufactures presents such features of unqualified deformity? From the largest of Mammon's temples down to the poorest hovel in which his helotry are stalled, these edifices have all one character. Time will not mellow them; nature will neither clothe nor conceal them; and they will remain always as offensive to the eye as to the mind'.[1]

Here is wisdom. Here are the principles on which nations are to be governed. Rose-bushes and poor-rates, rather than steam-engines and independence. Mortality and cottages with weather-stains, rather than health and long life with edifices which time cannot mellow. We are told that our age has invented atrocities beyond the imagination of our fathers; that society has been brought into a state, compared with which extermination would be a blessing;—and all because the dwellings of cotton-spinners are naked and rectangular. Mr Southey has found out a way, he tells us, in which the effects of manufactures and agriculture may be compared.

And what is this way? To stand on a hill, to look at a cottage and a manufactory, and to see which is the prettier. Does Mr Southey think that the body of the English peasantry live, or ever lived, in substantial or ornamented cottages, with box-hedges, flower-gardens, bee-hives, and orchards? If not, what is his parallel worth? We despise those *filosofastri*[2] who think that they serve the cause of science by depreciating literature and the fine arts. But if any thing could excuse their narrowness of mind, it would be such a book as this. It is not strange that when one enthusiast makes the picturesque the test of political good, another should feel inclined to proscribe altogether the pleasures of taste and imagination.

... In every season of distress which we can remember, Mr Southey has been proclaiming that it is not from economy, but from increased taxation that the country must expect relief; and he still, we find, places the undoubting faith of a political Diafoirus, in his

'Resaignare, repurgare, et reclysterizare.'[3]

'A people', he tells us, 'may be too rich, but a government cannot be so'.

'A state', says he, 'cannot have more wealth at its command than may be employed for the general good, a liberal expenditure in national works being one of the surest means of promoting national prosperity; and the benefit being still more obvious, of an expenditure directed to the purposes of national improvement. But a people may be too rich.'[4]

We fully admit, that a state cannot have at its command more wealth than *may be* employed for the general good. But neither can individuals, or bodies of individuals, have at their command more wealth than *may be* employed for the general good. If there be no limit to the sum which may be usefully laid out in public works and national improvement, then wealth, whether in the hands of private men or of the government, *may* always, if the possessors choose to spend it usefully, be usefully spent. The only ground, therefore, on which Mr Southey can possibly maintain that a government cannot be too rich, but that a people may be too rich, must be this, that governments are more likely to spend their money on good objects than private individuals.

But what is useful expenditure? 'A liberal expenditure in national works', says Mr Southey, 'is one of the surest means for promoting national prosperity.' What does he mean by national prosperity? Does he mean the wealth of the state? If so, his reasoning runs thus :— The more wealth a state has the better; for the more wealth a state has, the more wealth it will have. This is surely something like that fallacy, which is ungallantly termed a lady's reason. If by national prosperity he means the wealth of the people, of how gross a contradiction is he guilty. A people, he tells us, may be too rich—a government cannot for a government can employ its riches in making the people richer. The wealth of the people is to be taken from them, because they have too much, and laid out in works, which will yield them more.

We are really at a loss to determine whether Mr Southey's reason for recommending large taxation is that it will make the people rich, or that it will make them poor. But we are sure, that if his object is to make them rich, he takes the wrong course. There are two or three principles respecting public works, which, as an experience of vast extent proves, may be trusted in almost every case.

It scarcely ever happens, that any private man, or body of men, will invest property in a canal, a tunnel, or a bridge, but from an expectation that the outlay will be profitable to them. No work of this sort can be profitable to private speculators, unless the public be willing to pay for the use of it. The public will not pay of their own accord for what yields no profit or convenience to them. There is thus a direct and obvious connection between the motive which induces individuals to undertake such a work, and the utility of the work.

Can we find any such connection in the case of a public work executed by a government? If it is useful, are the individuals who rule the country richer? If it is useless, are they poorer? A public man may be solicitous for his credit : but is not he likely to gain more credit by an useless display of ostentatious architecture in a great town, than by the best road or the best canal in some remote province? The fame of public works is a much less certain test of their utility, than the amount of toll collected at them. In the corrupt age, there will be direct embezzlement. In the purest age, there will be abundance of jobbing. Never were the statesmen of any country more sensitive to public opinion, and more spotless in pecuniary transactions, than those who have of late governed England. Yet we have only to look at the buildings recently erected in London for a proof of our rule. In a bad age, the fate of the public is to be robbed. In a good age, it is much milder—merely to have the dearest and the worst of everything.

Buildings for state purposes the state must erect. And here we think that, in general, the state ought to stop. We firmly believe, that five hundred thousand pounds subscribed by individuals for rail-roads or canals would produce more advantage to the public than five millions voted by Parliament for the same purpose. There are certain old saws about the master's eye and about every body's business, in which we place very great faith.

There is, we have said, no consistency in Mr Southey's political system. But if there be in his political system any leading principle, any one error which diverges more widely and variously than any other, it is that of which his theory about national works is a ramification. He conceives that the business of the magistrate is, not merely to see that the persons and property of the people are secure from attack, but that he ought to be a jack-of-all-trades,—architect, engineer, school-master, merchant, theologian,—a Lady Bountiful in every parish,—a Paul Pry in every house, spying, eaves-dropping, relieving, admonishing, spending our money for us, and choosing our opinions for us. His principle is, if we understand it rightly, that no man can do anything so well for himself, as his rulers, be they who they may, can do it for him,—that a government approaches nearer and nearer to perfection, in proportion as it interferes more and more with the habits and notions of individuals.

From *The History of England*
from the Accession of James II
[The text is from Macaulay's *History*, I, 1849, Ch. 3, omitting
Macaulay's footnote-references to his sources.]

. . . If we would study with profit the history of our ancestors,
we must be constantly on our guard against that delusion which
the well known names of families, places, and offices naturally
produce, and must never forget that the country of which we
read was a very different country from that in which we live.
In every experimental science there is a tendency towards
perfection. In every human being there is a wish to ameliorate
his own condition. These two principles have often sufficed,
even when counteracted by great public calamities and by bad
institutions, to carry civilisation rapidly forward. No ordinary
misfortune, no ordinary misgovernment, will do so much to
make a nation wretched, as the constant progress of physical
knowledge and the constant effort of every man to better
himself will do to make a nation prosperous. It has often been
found that profuse expenditure, heavy taxation, absurd
commercial restrictions, corrupt tribunals, disastrous wars,
seditions, persecutions, conflagrations, inundations, have not
been able to destroy capital so fast as the exertions of private
citizens have been able to create it. It can easily be proved
that, in our own land, the national wealth has, during at least
six centuries, been almost uninterruptedly increasing; that it
was greater under the Tudors than under the Plantagenets;
that it was greater under the Stuarts than under the Tudors;
that, in spite of battles, sieges, and confiscations, it was greater
on the day of the Restoration than on the day when the Long
Parliament met; that, in spite of maladministration, of extrava-
gance, of public bankruptcy, of two costly and unsuccessful
wars, of the pestilence and of the fire, it was greater on the
day of the death of Charles the Second than on the day of his
Restoration. This progress, having continued during many
ages, became at length, about the middle of the eighteenth
century, portentously rapid, and has proceeded, during the

nineteenth, with accelerated velocity. In consequence, partly of our geographical and partly of our moral position, we have, during several generations, been exempt from evils which have elsewhere impeded the efforts and destroyed the fruits of industry. While every part of the Continent, from Moscow to Lisbon, has been the theatre of bloody and devastating wars, no hostile standard has been seen here but as a trophy. While revolutions have taken place all around us, our government has never once been subverted by violence. During more than a hundred years there has been in our island no tumult of sufficient importance to be called an insurrection. The law has never been borne down either by popular or by regal tyranny. Public credit has been held sacred. The administration of justice has been pure. Even in times which might by Englishmen be justly called evil times, we have enjoyed what almost every other nation in the world would have considered as an ample measure of civil and religious freedom. Every man has felt entire confidence that the state would protect him in the possession of what had been earned by his diligence and hoarded by his self-denial. Under the benignant influence of peace and liberty, science has flourished, and has been applied to practical purposes on a scale never before known. The consequence is that a change to which the history of the old world furnishes no parallel has taken place in our country. Could the England of 1685 be, by some magical process, set before our eyes, we should not know one landscape in a hundred or one building in ten thousand. The country gentleman would not recognise his own fields. The inhabitant of the town would not recognise his own street. Everything has been changed, but the great features of nature, and a few massive and durable works of human art. We might find out Snowdon and Windermere, the Cheddar Cliffs and Beachy Head. We might find out here and there a Norman minster, or a castle which witnessed the wars of the Roses. But, with such rare exceptions, everything would be strange to us. Many thousands of square miles which are now rich corn land and meadow, intersected by green hedgerows, and dotted with villages and pleasant country seats, would appear as moors overgrown with furze, or fens abandoned to wild ducks. We should see straggling huts built of wood and covered with thatch, where we now see manufacturing towns and seaports renowned to the farthest ends of the world. The capital itself would shrink to dimensions not much exceeding those of its present suburb on the south of the Thames. Not less strange to us would be the garb and manners of the people, the furniture and the equipages, the interior of the shops and dwellings. Such a change in the state of a nation seems to be at least as well entitled to the notice of a historian as any change of dynasty or of the ministry.

. . . The chief cause which made the fusion of the different elements of society so imperfect was the extreme difficulty which our ancestors found in passing from place to place. Of all inventions, the alphabet and the printing press alone excepted, those inventions which abridge distance have done most for the civilisation of our species. Every improvement of the means of locomotion benefits mankind morally and intellectually as well as materially, and not only facilitates the interchange of the various productions of nature and art, but tends to remove national and provincial antipathies, and to bind together all the branches of the great human family. In the seventeenth century the inhabitants of London were, for almost every practical purpose, farther from Reading than they now are from Edinburgh, and farther from Edinburgh than they now are from Vienna.

The subjects of Charles the Second were not, it is true, quite unacquainted with that principle which has, in our own time, produced an unprecedented revolution in human affairs, which has enabled navies to advance in face of wind and tide, and battalions, attended by all their baggage and artillery, to traverse kingdoms at a pace equal to that of the fleetest race horse. The Marquess of Worcester had recently observed the expansive power of moisture rarefied by heat. After many experiments he had succeeded in constructing a rude steam engine, which he called a fire water work, and which he pronounced to be an admirable and most forcible instrument of propulsion. But the Marquess was suspected to be a madman, and known to be a Papist. His inventions, therefore, found no favourable reception. His fire water work might, perhaps, furnish matter for conversation at a meeting of the Royal Society, but was not applied to any practical purpose. There were no railways, except a few made of timber, on which coals were carried from the mouths of the Northumbrian pits to the banks of the Tyne. There was very little internal communication by water. A few attempts had been made to deepen and embank the natural streams, but with slender success. Hardly a single navigable canal had been even projected. The English of that day were in the habit of talking with mingled admiration and despair of the immense trench by which Lewis the Fourteenth had made a junction between the Atlantic and the Mediterranean. They little thought that their country would, in the course of a few generations, be intersected, at the cost of private adventurers, by artificial rivers making up more than four times the length of the Thames, the Severn, and the Trent together.

It was by the highways that both travellers and goods generally passed from place to place. And those highways appear to have been far worse than might have been expected from the degree of wealth and civilisation which the nation had even then attained. On the best lines of communication the ruts were deep, the descents precipitous, and the way often such as it was hardly possible to distinguish, in the dusk, from the unenclosed heath and fen which lay on both sides.

. . . In some parts of Kent and Sussex none but the strongest horses could, in winter, get through the bog, in which, at every step, they sank deep. The markets were often inaccessible during several months. It is said that the fruits of the earth were sometimes suffered to rot in one place, while in another place, distant only a few miles, the supply fell far short of the demand. The wheeled carriages were, in this district, generally pulled by oxen. When Prince George of Denmark visited the stately mansion of Petworth in wet weather, he was six hours in going nine miles; and it was necessary that a body of sturdy hinds should be on each side of his coach, in order to prop it. Of the carriages which conveyed his retinue several were upset and injured. A letter from one of his gentlemen in waiting has been preserved, in which the unfortunate courtier complains that, during fourteen hours, he never once alighted, except when his coach was overturned or stuck fast in the mud.

... In one respect it must be admitted that the progress of civilisation has diminished the physical comforts of a portion of the poorest class. It has already been mentioned that, before the Revolution, many thousands of square miles, now enclosed and cultivated, were marsh, forest, and heath. Of this wild land much was, by law, common, and much of what was not common by law was worth so little that the proprietors suffered it to be common in fact. In such a tract, squatters and trespassers were tolerated to an extent now unknown. The peasant who dwelt there could, at little or no charge, procure occasionally some palatable addition to his hard fare, and provide himself with fuel for the winter. He kept a flock of geese on what is now an orchard rich with apple blossoms. He snared wild fowl on the fen which has long since been drained and divided into corn fields and turnip fields. He cut turf among the furze bushes on the moor which is now a meadow bright with clover and renowned for butter and cheese. The progress of agriculture and the increase of population necessarily deprived him of these privileges. But against this disadvantage a long list of advantages is to be set off. Of the blessings which civilisation and philosophy bring with them, a large proportion is common to all ranks, and would, if withdrawn, be missed as painfully by the labourer as by the peer. The market place which the rustic can now reach with his cart in an hour was, a hundred and sixty years ago, a day's journey from him. The street which now affords to the artisan, during the whole night, a secure, a convenient, and a brilliantly lighted walk was, a hundred and sixty years ago, so dark after sunset that he would not have been able to see his hand, so ill paved that he would have run constant risk of breaking his neck, and so ill watched that he would have been in imminent danger of being knocked down and plundered of his small earnings. Every bricklayer who falls from a scaffold, every sweeper of a crossing who is run over by a carriage, may now have his wounds dressed and his limbs set with skill such as, a hundred and sixty years ago, all the wealth of a great lord like Ormond, or of a merchant prince like Clayton, could not have purchased. Some frightful diseases have been extirpated by science; and some have been banished by police. The term of human life has been lengthened over the whole kingdom, and especially in the towns. The year 1685 was not accounted sickly; yet in the year 1685 more than one in twenty-three of the inhabitants of the capital died. At present only one inhabitant of the capital in forty dies annually. The difference in salubrity between the London of the nineteenth century and the London of the seventeenth century is very far greater than the difference between London in an ordinary season and London in the cholera.

Still more important is the benefit which all orders of society and especially the lower orders, have derived from the mollifying influence of civilisation on the national character. The groundwork of that character has indeed been the same through many generations, in the sense in which the groundwork of the character of an individual may be said to be the same when he is a rude and thoughtless schoolboy and when he is a refined and accomplished man. It is pleasing to reflect that the public mind of England has softened while it has ripened, and that we have, in the course of ages, become, not only a wiser, but also a kinder people. There is scarcely a page of the history or lighter literature of the seventeenth century which does not contain some proof that our ancestors were less humane than their posterity. The discipline of workshops, of schools, of private families, though not more efficient than at present, was infinitely harsher. Masters, well born and bred, were in the habit of beating their servants. Pedagogues knew no way of imparting knowledge but by beating their pupils. Husbands, of decent station, were not ashamed to beat their wives. The implacability of hostile factions was such as we can scarcely conceive. Whigs were disposed to murmur because Stafford was suffered to die without seeing his bowels burned before his face. Tories reviled and insulted Russell as his coach passed from the Tower to the scaffold in Lincoln's Inn Fields. As little mercy was shown by the populace to sufferers of a humbler rank. If an offender was put into the pillory, it was well if he escaped with life from the shower of brickbats and paving stones. If he was tied to the cart's tail,

the crowd pressed round him, imploring the hangman to give
it the fellow well, and make him howl. Gentlemen arranged
parties of pleasure to Bridewell on court days for the purpose
of seeing the wretched women who beat hemp there whipped.
A man pressed to death for refusing to plead, a woman burned
for coining, excited less sympathy than is now felt for a galled
horse or an overdriven ox. Fights compared with which a
boxing match is a refined and humane spectacle were among
the favourite diversions of a large part of the town. Multitudes
assembled to see gladiators hack each other to pieces with
deadly weapons, and shouted with delight when one of the
combatants lost a finger or an eye. The prisons were hells on
earth, seminaries of every crime and of every disease. At the
assizes the lean and yellow culprits brought with them from
their cells to the dock an atmosphere of stench and pestilence
which sometimes avenged them signally on bench, bar and
jury. But on all this misery society looked with profound indifference. Nowhere could be found that sensitive and restless
compassion which has, in our time, extended a powerful
protection to the factory child, to the Hindoo widow, to the
negro slave, which pries into the stores and watercasks of every
emigrant ship, which winces at every lash laid on the back of
a drunken soldier, which will not suffer the thief in the hulks
to be ill fed or overworked, and which has repeatedly endeavoured to save the life even of the murderer. It is true that
compassion ought, like all other feeling, to be under the
government of reason, and has, for want of such government,
produced some ridiculous and some deplorable effects. But the
more we study the annals of the past, the more shall we
rejoice that we live in a merciful age, in an age in which
cruelty is abhorred, and in which pain, even when deserved, is
inflicted reluctantly and from a sense of duty. Every class
doubtless has gained largely by this great moral change: but
the class which has gained most is the poorest, the most
dependent, and the most defenceless.

The general effect of the evidence which has been sub-
mitted to the reader seems hardly to admit of doubt. Yet, in
spite of evidence, many will still image to themselves the
England of the Stuarts as a more pleasant country than the

England in which we live. It may at first sight seem strange that society, while constantly moving forward with eager speed, should be constantly looking backward with tender regret. But these two propensities, inconsistent as they may appear, can easily be resolved into the same principle. Both spring from our impatience of the state in which we actually are. That impatience, while it stimulates us to surpass preceding generations, disposes us to overrate their happiness. It is, in some sense, unreasonable and ungrateful in us to be constantly discontented with a condition which is constantly improving. But in truth, there is constant improvement precisely because there is constant discontent. If we were perfectly satisfied with the present, we should cease to contrive, to labour, and to save with a view to the future. And it is natural that, being dissatisfied with the present, we should form a too favourable estimate of the past.

In truth we are under a deception similar to that which misleads the traveller in the Arabian desert. Beneath the caravan all is dry and bare: but far in advance, and far in the rear, is the semblace of refreshing waters. The pilgrims hasten forward and find nothing but sand where, an hour before, they had seen a lake. They turn their eyes and see a lake where, an hour before, they were toiling through sand. A similar illusion seems to haunt nations through every stage of the long progress from poverty and barbarism to the highest degrees of opulence and civilisation. But, if we resolutely chase the mirage backward, we shall find it recede before us into the regions of fabulous antiquity. It is now the fashion to place the golden age of England in times when noblemen were destitute of comforts the want of which would be intolerable to a modern footman, when farmers and shopkeepers breakfasted on loaves the very sight of which would raise a riot in a modern workhouse, when men died faster in the purest country air than they now die in the most pestilential lanes of our towns, and when men died faster in the lanes of our towns than they now die on the coast of Guiana. We too shall, in our turn, be outstripped, and in our turn be envied. It may well be, in the twentieth century, that the peasant of Dorsetshire may think himself miserably paid with fifteen shillings a week;

that the carpenter at Greenwich may receive ten shillings a day; that labouring men may be as little used to dine without meat as they now are to eat rye bread; that sanitary police and medical discoveries may add several more years to the average length of human life; that numerous comforts and luxuries which are now unknown, or confined to a few, may be within the reach of every diligent and thrifty working man. And yet it may then be the mode to assert that the increase of wealth and the progress of science have benefited the few at the expense of the many, and to talk of the reign of Queen Victoria as the time when England was truly merry England, when all classes were bound together by brotherly sympathy, when the rich did not grind the faces of the poor, and when the poor did not envy the splendour of the rich.

NOTES

1. R. Southey, *Sir Thomas More: or Colloquies on the Progress and Prospects of Society* (1829), I, 173–4.
2. filosofastri, pseudo-philosophers.
3. Diafoirus is the doctor in Molière's *Le malade imaginaire* (1673). It is, however, the hypochondriac himself, Argan, who in the burlesque-finale attains his doctor's degree by answering, correctly, that the treatment for an incurable disease is to bleed again, purge again, apply a clyster again.
4. Southey, *Colloquies*, I, 193.

Social Problems in Fiction

[Benjamin Disraeli (1804–1881), in his trilogy, *Coningsby*, *Sybil* and *Tancred* (1844–1847), largely initiated the treatment of the Condition-of-England Question in the novel-form, a debate to which Mrs Gaskell, Kingsley, Dickens and George Eliot also contributed. *Coningsby* was the book which did most to fire the imaginations of the 'Young England' group of Tory reformers who accepted Disraeli as their spokesman and leader. Its emphasis on the power of youth, its appeal to new religious energies and to revitalised traditional feudal relationships offered them a political faith: the Carlylean 'great man', sage, statesman or monarch, could heal the proliferating divisions of modern life by a combination of imaginative vision and a reorganisation of political structures.

To the Rev. Charles Kinglsey (1819–1875), a Christian socialist influenced by Carlyle and F. D. Maurice, as to many other sympathetic observers, the recalcitrance of sordid material conditions gave little hope of peaceful amelioration, while violence, which was suspected of the Trades Unions and the Chartists, was unacceptable. The only answer seemed to be a reliance on 'the kingdom which is not of this world', or emigration. In *Yeast* Kingsley's perception of pervasive social injustice is expressed pugnaciously, in an attempt to shake people's weary acquiescence in evil.]

BENJAMIN DISRAELI

From *Coningsby, or the New Generation*

[The text is from the first edition, 1844. In the first extract, from Book IV, Ch. 13, Coningsby is sitting at the feet of the Jewish sage, Sidonia; in the second, from Book VII, Ch. 2, he is developing Sidonia's ideas in conversation with a college friend.]

. . . "Do you think then there is a wild desire for extensive political change in the country?"

49

"Hardly that: England is perplexed at the present moment, not inventive. That will be the next phasis in her moral state, and to that I wish to draw your thoughts. For myself while I ascribe little influence to physical causes for the production of this perplexity, I am still less of opinion that it can be removed by any new disposition of political power. It would only aggravate the evil. That would be recurring to the old error of supposing you can necessarily find national content in political institutions. A political institution is a machine; the motive power is the national character. With that it rests, whether the machine will benefit society, or destroy it. Society in this country is perplexed, almost paralysed; in time it will move, and it will devise. How are the elements of the nation to be blended again together? In what spirit is that reorganisation to take place?"

"To know that would be to know every thing".

"At least let us free ourselves from the double ignorance of the Platonists. Let us not be ignorant that we are ignorant".

"I have emancipated myself from that darkness for a long time", said Coningsby. "Long has my mind been musing over these thoughts, but to me all is still obscurity".

"In this country", said Sidonia, "since the peace, there has been an attempt to advocate a reconstruction of society on a purely rational basis. The principle of Utility has been powerfully developed. I speak not with lightness of the labours of the disciples of that school. I bow to intellect in every form: and we should be grateful to any school of philosophers even if we disagree with them; doubly grateful in this country, where for so long a period our statesmen were in so pitiable an arrear of public intelligence. There has been an attempt to reconstruct society on a basis of material motives and calculations. It has failed. It must ultimately have failed under any circumstances; its failure in an ancient and densely peopled kingdom was inevitable. How limited is human reason, the profoundest inquirers are most conscious. We are not indebted to the Reason of man for any of the great achievements which are the landmarks of human action and human progress. It was not Reason that besieged Troy; it was not Reason that sent forth the Saracen from the

Desert to conquer the world; that inspired the Crusades; that instituted the Monastic orders; it was not Reason that produced the Jesuits; above all, it was not reason that created the French Revolution. Man is only truly great when he acts from the passions; never irresistible but when he appeals to the Imagination. Even Mormon counts more votaries than Bentham."

"And you think then that as Imagination once subdued the State, Imagination may now save it?"

"Man is made to adore and to obey: but if you will not command him; if you give him nothing to worship; he will fashion his own divinities, and find a chieftain in his own passions."

". . . We should now so act, that when the occasion arrives, we should clearly comprehend what we want, and have formed an opinion as to the best means by which that want can be supplied.

"For this purpose, I would accustom the public mind to the contemplation of an existing though torpid power in the constitution; capable of removing our social grievances were we to transfer to it those prerogatives which the Parliament has gradually usurped, and used in a manner which has produced the present material and moral disorganisation. The House of Commons is the house of a few; the Sovereign is the Sovereign of all. The proper leader of the people is the individual who sits upon the throne."

"Then you abjure the Representative principle?"

"Why so? Representation is not necessarily, or even in a principal sense, Parliamentary. Parliament is not sitting at this moment, and yet the nation is represented in its highest as well as in its most minute interests. Not a grievance escapes notice and redress. I see in the newspaper this morning that a pedagogue has brutally chastised his pupil. It is a fact known over all England. We must not forget that a principle of government is reserved for our days, that we shall not find in our Aristotles, or even in the forests of Tacitus, not in our Saxon Wittenagemotes, nor in our Plantagenet Parliaments. Opinion now is supreme, and opinion speaks in print. The representation of the press is far more complete than the representation of Parliament. Parliamentary representation was the happy device of a ruder age, to which it was admirably adapted; an age of semi-civilisation, when there was a leading class in the community; but it exhibits many symptoms of desuetude. It is controlled by a system of representation more vigorous and comprehensive; which absorbs its duties and fulfils them efficiently; and in which discussion is pursued on fairer terms, and often with more depth and information."

"And to what power would you intrust the function of Taxation".

"To some power that would employ it more discreetly than in creating our present amount of debt, and in establishing our present system of imposts.

"In a word, true wisdom lies in the policy that would effect its end by the influence of opinion, and yet by the means of existing forms. Nevertheless if we are forced to revolutions, let us propose to our consideration the idea of free monarchy, established on fundamental laws, itself the apex of a vast pile of municipal and local government, ruling an educated people, represented by a free and intellectual press. Before such a royal authority, supported by such a national opinion, the sectional anomalies of our country would disappear. Under such a system, where qualification would not be parliamentary, but personal, even statesmen would be educated; we should have no more diplomatists who could not speak French; no more bishops ignorant of theology; no more generals-in-chief who never saw a field.

"Now there is a polity adapted to our laws, our institutions, our feelings, our manners, our traditions; a polity capable of great ends, and appealing to high sentiments; a polity which in my opinion would render government an object of national affection; which would terminate sectional anomalies, assuage religious heats, and extinguish Chartism."

CHARLES KINGSLEY

From 'Yeast, a Problem'

[The text is from *Fraser's Magazine*, XXXVIII (December, 1848).

In this extract, from Ch. 14, Lancelot Smith learns that his fortune has disappeared in the failure of his uncle's bank. *Yeast* appeared in book-form in 1851.]

. . . 'If I were a Christian', said Lancelot, 'like you, I would call this credit system of yours the devil's selfish counterfeit of God's order of love and faith, the child of that miserable dream which, as Dr. Chalmers well said, expects universal selfishness to do the work of universal love. Look at your credit system; how—not in abuse, but in its very essence—it carries the seeds of self-destruction. In the first place, a man's credit depends, not upon his real worth and property, but upon his reputation for property; daily and hourly he is tempted; he is forced, to puff himself, to pretend to be richer than he is'.

The banker sighed and shrugged his shoulders. 'We all do it, my dear boy'.

'I know it. You must do it, or be more than human. There is lie the first, and look at lie the second. This credit system is founded on the universal faith and honour of men towards men. But do you think faith and honour can be the children of selfishness? Men must be chivalrous and disinterested to be honourable. And you expect them all to join in universal faith—each for his own selfish interest! You forget that if that is the prime motive, men will be honourable only as long as it suits that same self-interest.'

The banker shrugged his shoulders again.

'Yes, my dear uncle', said Lancelot, 'you all forget it though you suffer for it daily and hourly; though the honourable men among you complain of the stain which has fallen on the old chivalrous good faith of English commerce, and say that now, abroad as well as at home, an Englishman's word is no longer worth other men's bonds. You see the evil, and you deplore it in disgust. Ask yourself honestly, how can you strive against it, while you allow in practice, and in theory too, except in church on Sundays, the very falsehood from which it all springs?—that a man is bound to get wealth, not for his country, but no, for himself; that, in short, not patriotism, but selfishness, is the bond of all society. Selfishness can collect, not unite, a herd of cowardly wild cattle, that they may feed together, breed together, keep off the wolf and bear together. But when one of your wild cattle falls sick, what becomes of the corporate feelings of the herd then? For one man of your class who is nobly helped by his fellows, are not the thousand left behind to perish? Your Bible talks of society, not as a herd, but as a living tree, an organic individual body, a holy brotherhood, and kingdom of God. And here is an idol which you have set up instead of it!'

But the Banker was deaf to all arguments. No doubt he had plenty, for he was himself a just and a generous, aye, and a God-fearing man, only he regarded Lancelot's young fancies as too visionary to deserve an answer; which they most probably are, else, having been broached as often as they have been, they would surely, ere now, have provoked the complete refutation which can, no doubt, be given to them by hundreds of learned votaries of commerce. And here I beg my readers to recollect, that I am in no way answerable for the speculations either of Lancelot or any of his acquaintances; and that these papers have been, from beginning to end, as in name so in nature, Yeast—an honest sample of the questions which, good or bad, are fermenting in the minds of the young of this day, and are rapidly leavening the minds of the rising generation. No doubt they are all as full of fallacies as possible, but as long as the saying of the German sage stands true, that 'the destiny of any nation, at any given moment, depends on the opinions of its young men under five-and-twenty,' so long it must be worth while for those who wish to preserve the present order of society to justify its acknowledged evils somewhat, not only to the few young men who are interested in preserving them, but also to the many who are not.

Though, therefore, I am neither Plymouth Brother nor Communist, and as thoroughly convinced as the newspapers can make me that to assert the duties of property is only to plot its destruction, and that a community of goods (as every one knows was the case with the apostolic Christians), must needs imply a community of wives, I shall take the liberty of narrating Lancelot's fanatical conduct, without execratory comment, certain that he will still receive his just reward of condemnation; and that, if I find facts, a sensible public will find abhorrence for them. His behaviour was, indeed, most singular; he absolutely refused a good commercial situation which his uncle procured him. He did not believe in being 'cured by a hair of the dog that bit him'; and he refused, also, the really generous offers of the creditors, to allow him a sufficient maintenance.

The Rise of Sociology

[John Stuart Mill (1806–1873) was intensively educated by his father, James Mill, for the furtherance of Utilitarian ideas. He wrote for the *Westminster Review* as a Philosophic Radical, believing in the efficacy of representative government, the economic principles of Ricardo and the psychology of Hartley. In his *Autobiography* he describes how he came to doubt the adequacy of this Benthamism, with its central goal of self-interest, and to turn to other ideas, notably those of Coleridge and Comte. In 'The Spirit of the Age' Mill analyses society in a Comtean fashion as being in a 'transitional' or 'critical' condition between the older 'metaphysical' and the new 'positive' stages. Mill's concern for stable authority is also Comtean, but the tendency to assimilate social progress to the spread of sound opinion through free discussion is his own. The *System of Logic* and the *Principles of Political Economy* gave Mill his dominating stature in Victorian intellectual liberalism. Though Mill had recognised that the wealth-motive was not a sufficient guide to all the affairs of society, he was convinced of its adequacy in the economic field. In the *Principles*, generally, he separated the production of wealth from its distribution, touching also on wider principles which he foresaw would be of concern to highly industrialised societies approaching the stationary state. Here capital is stationary, and the primary purpose of political economy is equity of distribution, which, embracing education, abridgement of labour and the provision of cultural amenities, eventually becomes one with the 'Art of Living'. Mill also made a well-known contribution to the cause of feminine emancipation.

A vaguer prospect on the future is opened by George Henry Lewes (1817–1878), who is chiefly known for his association with George Eliot. Lewes popularised many scientific and philosophical ideas, and in his exposition of the place of spiritual values in Comte's system he sustains a mood of exalted optimism. In the extract chosen he speculates on the effects of the universal recognition of Positivist ideas, the consequent hierarchical structuring of classes according to the degree of generality and abstraction of their functions, and the 'spontaneous' emergence of a speculative and spiritual *élite* which would control education and promulgate the 'final systematisation of human ethics'.

Frederic Harrison (1831–1923), a Positivist and supporter of working-class and Trade Union causes, was a far less complacent figure than appears in Arnold's satire. Greatly influenced by Ruskin, and aware of the menace of pollution, he vehemently denounced the injustices of Victorian society, yet he was also impressed with its energy and trusted to the Religion of Humanity to inspire its re-organisation.]

JOHN STUART MILL

From *Autobiography*

[The extracts from Ch. 5, 'A Crisis in my Mental History. One Stage Onward', are taken from the first edition, 1873.]

... From the winter of 1821, when I first read Bentham, and especially from the commencement of the Westminster Review, I had what might truly be called an object in life; to be a reformer of the world. My conception of my own happiness was entirely identified with this object. The personal sympathies I wished for were those of fellow labourers in this enterprise. I endeavoured to pick up as many flowers as I could by the way; but as a serious and permanent personal satisfaction to rest upon, my whole reliance was placed on this; and I was accustomed to felicitate myself on the certainty of a happy life which I enjoyed, through placing my happiness in something durable and distant, in which some progress might be always making, while it could never be exhausted by complete attainment. This did very well for several years, during which the general improvement going on in the world and the idea of myself as engaged with others in struggling to promote it seemed enough to fill up an interesting and animated existence. But the time came when I awakened from this as from a dream. It was in the autumn of 1826. I was in a dull state of nerves, such as everybody is occasionally liable to; unsusceptible to enjoyment or pleasurable excitement; one of those moods when what is pleasure at other times, becomes insipid or indifferent; the state, I should think, in which converts to Methodism usually are, when smitten by their first "conviction of sin". In this frame of mind it occurred to me to put the question directly to myself: "Suppose that all your objects in life were realized; that all the changes in institutions and opinions which you are looking forward to, could be completely effected at this very instant: would this be great joy and happiness to you?" And an irrepressible self-consciousness distinctly answered, "No!" At this my heart sank within me: the whole foundation on which my life was constructed fell down. All my happiness was to have been found in the continual pursuit of this end. The end had ceased to charm, and how could there ever again be any interest in the means? I seemed to have nothing left to live for.

At first I hoped that the cloud would pass away of itself; but it did not. A night's sleep, the sovereign remedy for the smaller vexations of life, had no effect on it. I awoke to a renewed consciousness of the woful fact. I carried it with me into all companies, into all occupations. Hardly anything had power to cause me even a few minutes' oblivion of it. For some months the cloud seemed to grow thicker and thicker. The lines in Coleridge's "Dejection"—I was not then acquainted with them—exactly describe my case:

> A grief without a pang, void, dark and drear,
> A drowsy, stifled, unimpassioned grief,
> Which finds no natural outlet or relief
> In word, or sigh, or tear.

In vain I sought relief from my favourite books; those memorials of past nobleness and greatness from which I had always hitherto drawn strength and animation. I read them now without feeling or with the accustomed feeling minus all its charm; and I became persuaded, that my love of mankind, and of excellence for its own sake, had worn itself out. I sought no comfort by speaking to others of what I felt. If I had loved any one sufficiently to make confiding my griefs a necessity, I should not have been in the condition I was. I felt, too, that mine was not an interesting, or in any way respectable distress. There was nothing in it to attract sympathy. Advice, if I had known where to seek it, would have been most precious. The words of Macbeth to the physician often occurred to my thoughts. But there was no one on whom I could build the faintest hope of such assistance. My father, to whom it would have been natural to me to have recourse in any practical difficulties, was the last person to whom, in such a case as this, I looked for help. Everything convinced me that he had no knowledge of any such mental state as I was suffering from, and that even if he could be made to understand it, he was not the physician who could heal it. My education, which was wholly his work, had been conducted without any regard to the possibility of its ending in this result: and I saw no use in giving him the pain of thinking that his plans had failed, when the failure was probably irremediable, and, at all events, beyond the power of *his* remedies. Of other friends, I had at that time none to whom I had any hope of making my condition intelligible. It was however abundantly intelligible to myself; and the more I dwelt upon it, the more hopeless it appeared.

My course of study had led me to believe, that all mental and moral feelings and qualities, whether of a good or of a bad kind, were the results of association; that we love one thing, and hate another, take pleasure in one sort of action or contemplation, and pain in another sort, through the clinging of pleasurable or painful ideas to those things, from the effect of education or of experience. As a corollary from this, I had always heard it maintained by my father, and was myself convinced, that the object of education should be to form the strongest possible associations of the salutary class; associations of pleasure with all things beneficial to the great whole, and of pain with all things hurtful to it. This doctrine appeared inexpugnable; but it now seemed to me, on retrospect, that my teachers had occupied themselves but superficially with the means of forming and keeping up these salutary associations. They seemed to have trusted altogether to the old familiar instruments, praise and blame, reward and punishment. Now, I did not doubt that by these means, begun early, and applied unremittingly, intense associations of pain and pleasure, especially of pain, might be created, and might produce desires and aversions capable of lasting undiminished to the end of life. But there must always be something artificial and casual in associations thus produced. The pains and pleasures thus forcibly associated with things, are not connected with them by any natural tie; and it is therefore, I thought, essential to the durability of these associations, that they should have become so intense and inveterate as to be practically indissoluble, before the habitual exercise of the power of analysis had commenced. For I now saw, or thought I saw, what I had always before received with incredulity— that the habit of analysis has a tendency to wear away the feelings: as indeed it has, when no other mental habit is cultivated, and the analysing spirit remains without its natural complements and correctives. The very excellence of analysis (I argued) is that it tends to weaken and undermine whatever is the result of prejudice; that it enables us mentally to separate ideas which have only casually clung together: and no associations whatever could ultimately resist this dissolving force, were it not that we owe to analysis our clearest knowledge of the permanent sequences in nature; the real connexions between Things, not dependent on our will and feelings; natural laws, by virtue of which, in many cases, one thing is inseparable from another in fact; which laws, in proportion as they are clearly perceived and imaginatively realized, cause our ideas of things which are always joined together in Nature, to cohere more and more closely in our thoughts. Analytic habits may thus even strengthen the associations between causes and effects, means and ends, but tend altogether to weaken those which are, to speak familiarly, a *mere* matter of feeling. They are therefore (I thought) favourable to prudence and clear-sightedness, but a perpetual worm at the root both of the passions and of the virtues; and above all, fearfully undermine all desires, and all pleasures, which are the effects of association, that is, according to the theory held, all except the purely physical and organic; of the entire insufficiency of which to make life desirable, no one had a stronger conviction than I had. These were the laws of human nature, by which, as it seemed to me, I had been brought to my present state. All those to whom I looked up, were of opinion that the pleasure of sympathy with human beings, and the feelings which made the good of others, and especially of mankind on a large scale, the object of existence, were the greatest and surest sources of happiness. Of the truth of this I was convinced, but to know that a feeling would make me happy if I had it, did not give me the feeling. My education, I thought, had failed to create these feelings in sufficient strength to resist the dissolving influence of analysis, while the whole course of my intellectual cultivation had made precocious and premature analysis the inveterate habit of my mind. I was thus, as I said to myself, left stranded at the commencement of my voyage, with a well-equipped ship and a rudder, but no sail; without any real desire for the ends which I had been so carefully fitted out to work for: no delight in virtue, or the general good, but also just as little in anything else. The fountains of vanity and ambition seemed to have dried up within me, as completely as those of benevolence. I had had (as I reflected) some gratification of vanity at too early an age: I had obtained some distinction, and felt myself of some importance, before the desire of distinction and of importance had grown into a passion: and little as it was which I had attained, yet having been attained too early, like all pleasures enjoyed too soon, it had made me *blasé* and indifferent to the pursuit. Thus neither selfish nor unselfish pleasures were pleasures to me. And there seemed no power in nature sufficient to begin the formation of my character anew, and create in a mind now irretrievably analytic, fresh associations of pleasure with any of the objects of human desire.

These were the thoughts which mingled with the dry heavy dejection of the melancholy winter of 1826–7. During this time I was not incapable of my usual occupations. I went on with them mechanically, by the mere force of habit. I had been so drilled in a certain sort of mental exercise, that I could still carry it on when all the spirit had gone out of it. I even composed and spoke several speeches at the debating society, how, or with what degree of success, I know not. Of four years continual speaking at that society, this is the only year of which I remember next to nothing. Two lines of Coleridge's, in whom alone of all writers I have found a true description of what I felt, were often in my thoughts, not at this time (for I had never read them), but in a later period of the same mental malady:

> Work without hope draws nectar in a sieve,
> And hope without an object cannot live.

In all probability my case was by no means so peculiar as I fancied it, and I doubt not that many others have passed through a similar state; but the idiosyncrasies of my education had given to the general phenomenon a special character, which made it seem the natural effect of causes that it was hardly possible for time to remove. I frequently asked myself, if I could, or if I was bound to go on living, when life must be passed in this manner. I generally answered to myself, that I did not think I could possibly bear it beyond a year. When, however, not more than half that duration of time had elapsed, a small ray of light broke in upon my gloom. I was reading, accidentally, Marmontel's "Memoires",[1] and came to the passage which relates his father's death, the distressed position of the family and the sudden inspiration by which he, then a mere boy, felt and made them feel that he would be everything to them—would supply the place of all that they had lost. A vivid conception of that scene and its feelings came over me, and I was moved to tears. From this moment my burden grew lighter. The oppression of the thought that all feeling was dead within me, was gone. I was no longer hopeless: I was not a stock or a stone. I had still, it seemed, some of the material out of which all worth of character, and all capacity for happiness, are made. Relieved from my ever present sense of irremediable wretchedness, I gradually found that the ordinary incidents of life could again give some pleasure; that I could again find enjoyment, not intense, but sufficient for cheerfulness, in sunshine and sky, in books, in conversations, in public affairs; and that there was, once more, excitement, though of a moderate kind, in exerting myself for opinions, and for the public good. Thus the cloud gradually drew off, and I again enjoyed life: and though I had several relapses, some of which lasted many months, I never again was as miserable as I had been.

The experiences of this period had two very marked effects on my opinions and character. In the first place, they led me to adopt a theory of life, very unlike that on which I had before acted, and having much in common with what at that time I certainly had never heard of, the anti-self-consciousness theory of Carlyle. I never, indeed, wavered in the conviction that happiness is the test of all rules of conduct, and the end of life. But I now thought that this end was only to be attained by not making it the direct end. Those only are happy (I thought) who have their minds fixed on some object other than their own happiness; on the happiness of others, on the improvement of mankind, even on some art or pursuit, followed not as a means, but as itself an ideal end. Aiming thus at something else they find happiness by the way. The enjoyments of life (such was now my theory) are sufficient to make it a pleasant thing, when they are taken *en passant*, without being made a principal object. Once make them so, and they are immediately felt to be insufficient. They will not bear a scrutinizing examination. Ask yourself whether you are happy, and you cease to be so. The only chance is to treat, not happiness, but some end external to it, as the purpose of life. Let your self-consciousness, your scrutiny, your self-interrogation, exhaust themselves on that; and if otherwise fortunately circumstanced you will inhale happiness with the air you breathe, without dwelling on it or thinking about it, without either forestalling it in imagination, or putting it to flight by fatal questioning. This theory now became the basis of my philosophy of life. And I still hold to it as the best theory for all those who have but a moderate degree of sensibility and of capacity for enjoyment, that is, for the great majority of mankind.

The other important change which my opinions at this time underwent, was that I, for the first time, gave its proper place, among the prime necessities of human well-being, to the internal culture of the individual. I ceased to attach almost exclusive importance to the ordering of outward circumstances, and the training of the human being for speculation and for action.

I had now learnt by experience that the passive susceptibilities needed to be cultivated as well as the active capacities,
and required to be nourished and enriched as well as guided.
I did not, for an instant, lose sight of, or undervalue, that part
of the truth which I had seen before; I never turned recreant
to intellectual culture, or ceased to consider the power and
practice of analysis as an essential condition both of individual
and of social improvement. But I thought that it had consequences which required to be corrected, by joining other
kinds of cultivation with it. The maintenance of a due balance
among the faculties, now seemed to me of primary importance.
The cultivation of the feelings became one of the cardinal
points in my ethical and philosophical creed. And my thoughts
and inclinations turned in an increasing degree towards
whatever seemed capable of being instrumental to that object.

I now began to find meaning in the things which I had read
or heard about the importance of poetry and art as instruments of human culture. But it was some time longer before I
began to know this by personal experience. The only one of the
imaginative arts in which I had from childhood taken great
pleasure, was music; the best effect of which (and in this it
surpasses perhaps every other art) consists in exciting enthusiasm; in winding up to a high pitch those feelings of an
elevated kind which are already in the character, but to which
this excitement gives a glow and a fervour, which, though
transitory at its utmost height, is precious for sustaining them
at other times. This effect of music I had often experienced;
but like all my pleasurable susceptibilities it was suspended
during the gloomy period. I had sought relief again and again
from this quarter, but found none. After the tide had turned,
and I was in process of recovery, I had been helped forward
by music, but in a much less elevated manner. I at this time
first became acquainted with Weber's Oberon, and the
extreme pleasure which I drew from its delicious melodies
did me good, by showing me a source of pleasure to which I
was as susceptible as ever. The good, however, was much
impaired by the thought, that the pleasure of music (as is
quite true of such pleasures as this was, that of mere tune)
fades with familiarity, and requires either to be revived by

intermittence, or fed by continual novelty. And it is very characteristic both of my then state, and of the general tone of my mind at this period of my life, that I was seriously tormented by the thought of the exhaustibility of musical combinations. The octave consists only of five tones and two semitones, which can be put together in only a limited number of ways, of which but a small proportion are beautiful: most of these, it seemed to me, must have been already discovered and there could not be room for a long succession of Mozarts and Webers, to strike out, as these had done, entirely new and surpassingly rich veins of musical beauty. This source of anxiety may, perhaps, be thought to resemble that of the philosophers of Laputa, who feared lest the sun should be burnt out. It was, however, connected with the best feature in my character, and the only good point to be found in my very unromantic and in no way honourable distress. For though my dejection, honestly looked at, could not be called other than egotistical, produced by the ruin, as I thought, of my fabric of happiness, yet the destiny of mankind in general was ever in my thoughts and could not be separated from my own. I felt that the flaw in my life, must be a flaw in life itself: that the question was, whether, if the reformers of society and government could succeed in their objects, and every person in the community were free and in a state of physical comfort, the pleasures of life, being no longer kept up by struggles and privation, would cease to be pleasures. And I felt that unless I could see my way to some better hope than this for human happiness in general, my dejection must continue; but that if I could see such an outlet, I should then look on the world with pleasure; content as far as I was myself concerned, with any fair share of the general lot.

This state of my thoughts and feelings made the fact of my reading Wordsworth for the first time (in the autumn of 1828), an important event in my life. I took up the collection of his poems from curiosity, with no expectation of mental relief from it, though I had before resorted to poetry with that hope. In the worst period of my depression, I had read through the whole of Byron (then new to me), to try whether a poet, whose peculiar department was supposed to be that of the intenser

feelings, could rouse any feelings in me. As might be expected,
I got no good from this reading, but the reverse. The poet's
state of mind was too like my own. His was the lament of
a man who had worn out all pleasures, and who seemed to
think that life, to all who possess the good things of it, must
necessarily be the vapid, uninteresting thing which I found it.
His Harold and Manfred had the same burden on them which I
had; and I was not in a frame of mind to desire any comfort
from the vehement sensual passion of his Giaours, or the
sullenness of his Laras. But while Byron was exactly what did
not suit my condition, Wordsworth was exactly what did.
I had looked into the Excursion two or three years before,
and found little in it; and I should probably have found as
little, had I read it at this time. But the miscellaneous poems,
in the two-volume edition of 1815 (to which little of value
was added in the latter part of the author's life), proved to
be the precise thing for my mental wants at that particular
juncture.

In the first place, these poems addressed themselves powerfully to one of the strongest of my pleasurable susceptibilities,
the love of rural objects and natural scenery; to which I had
been indebted not only for much of the pleasure of my life,
but quite recently for relief from one of my longest relapses into
depression. In this power of rural beauty over me, there was
a foundation laid for taking pleasure in Wordsworth's poetry;
the more so, as his scenery lies mostly among mountains, which,
owing to my early Pyrenean excursion, were my ideal of natural
beauty. But Wordsworth would never have had any great
effect on me, if he had merely placed before me beautiful
pictures of natural scenery. Scott does this still better than
Wordsworth, and a very second-rate landscape does it more
effectually than any poet. What made Wordsworth's poems
a medicine to my state of mind was that they expressed, not
mere outward beauty, but states of feeling, and of thought
coloured by feeling, under the excitement of beauty. They
seemed to be the very culture of the feelings which I was in
quest of. In them I seemed to draw from a source of inward
joy, of sympathetic and imaginative pleasure, which could be
shared by all human beings; which had no connexion with

struggle or imperfection, but would be made richer by every improvement in the physical or social condition of mankind. From them I seemed to learn what would be the perennial sources of happiness, when all the greater evils of life shall have been removed. And I felt myself at once better and happier as I came under their influence. There have certainly been, even in our own age, greater poets than Wordsworth; but poetry of deeper and loftier feeling could not have done for me at that time what his did. I needed to be made to feel that there was real permanent happiness in tranquil contemplation. Wordsworth taught me this, not only without turning away from, but with a greatly increased interest in the common feelings and common destiny of human beings. And the delight which these poems gave me, proved that with culture of this sort, there was nothing to dread from the most confirmed habit of analysis. At the conclusion of the Poems came the famous Ode, falsely called Platonic, "Intimations of Immortality"; in which, along with more than his usual sweetness of melody and rhythm, and along with the two passages of grand imagery but bad philosophy so often quoted, I found that he too had had similar experience to mine; that he also had felt that the first freshness of youthful enjoyment of life was not lasting; but that he had sought for compensation, and found it, in the way in which he was now teaching me to find it. The result was that I gradually, but completely, emerged from my habitual depression, and was never again subject to it. I long continued to value Wordsworth less according to his intrinsic merits, than by the measure of what he had done for me. Compared with the greatest poets, he may be said to be the poet of unpoetical natures, possessed of quiet and contemplative tastes. But unpoetical natures are precisely those which require poetic cultivation. This cultivation Wordsworth is much more fitted to give, than poets who are intrinsically far more poets than he.

. . . though I ceased to consider representative democracy as an absolute principle, and regarded it as a question of time, place, and circumstance; though I now looked upon the choice of political institutions as a moral and educational question more than one of material interests, thinking that it ought to

be decided mainly by the consideration, what great improvement in life and culture stands next in order for the people
concerned, as the condition of their further progress, and what
institutions are most likely to promote that; nevertheless, this
change in the premises of my political philosophy did not alter
my practical political creed as to the requirements of my own
time and country. I was as much as ever a Radical and
Democrat for Europe, and especially for England. I thought
the predominance of the aristocratic classes, the noble and the
rich, in the English constitution, an evil worth any struggle to
get rid of; not on account of taxes, or any such comparatively
small inconvenience, but as the great demoralizing agency in
the country. Demoralizing, first, because it made the conduct
of the Government an example of gross public immorality,
through the predominance of private over public interests in
the State, and the abuse of the powers of legislation for the
advantage of classes. Secondly, and in a still greater degree,
because the respect of the multitude always attaching itself
principally to that which, in the existing state of society, is the
chief passport to power; and under English institutions, riches,
hereditary or acquired, being the almost exclusive source of
political importance; riches, and the signs of riches, were
almost the only things really respected, and the life of the
people was mainly devoted to the pursuit of them. I thought,
that while the higher and richer classes, held the power of
government, the instruction and improvement of the mass of
the people were contrary to the self-interest of those classes,
because tending to render the people more powerful for throwing off the yoke: but if the democracy obtained a large, and
perhaps the principal share, in the governing power, it would
become the interest of the opulent classes to promote their
education, in order to ward off really mischievous errors, and
especially those which would lead to unjust violations of
property. On these grounds I was not only as ardent as ever
for democratic institutions, but earnestly hoped that Owenite,
St. Simonian, and all other anti-property doctrines might
spread widely among the poorer classes; not that I thought
those doctrines true, or desired that they should be acted on,
but in order that the higher classes might be made to see that

they had more to fear from the poor when uneducated, than when educated.

... I attempted, in the beginning of 1831, to embody in a series of articles, headed "The Spirit of the Age", some of my new opinions, and especially to point out in the character of the present age, the anomalies and evils characteristic of the transition from a system of opinions which had worn out, to another only in process of being framed. These articles were, I fancy, lumbering in style, and not lively or striking enough to be, at any time, acceptable to newspaper readers; but had they been far more attractive, still, at that particular moment, when great political changes were impending, and engrossing all minds, these discussions were ill-timed, and missed fire altogether. The only effect which I know to have been produced by them, was that Carlyle, then living in a secluded part of Scotland, read them in his solitude, and saying to himself (as he afterwards told me) "Here is a new Mystic", inquired on coming to London that autumn respecting their authorship; an inquiry which was the immediate cause of our becoming personally acquainted.

I have already mentioned Carlyle's earlier writings as one of the channels through which I received the influence which enlarged my early narrow creed; but I do not think that those writings, by themselves, would ever have had any effect on my opinions. What truths they contained, though of the very kind which I was already receiving from other quarters, were presented in a form and vesture less suited than any other to give them access to a mind trained as mine had been. They seemed a haze of poetry and German metaphysics, in which almost the only clear thing was a strong animosity to most of the opinions which were the basis of my mode of thought; religious scepticism, utilitarianism, the doctrine of circumstances, and the attaching any importance to democracy, logic, or political economy. Instead of my having been taught anything, in the first instance, by Carlyle, it was only in proportion as I came to see the same truths through media more suited to my mental constitution, that I recognised them in his writings. Then, indeed, the wonderful power with which he put them forth made a deep impression upon me, and I was during a long period one of his most fervent admirers; but the good his writings did me, was not as philosophy to instruct, but as poetry to animate. Even at the time when our acquaintance commenced, I was not sufficiently advanced in my new modes of thought, to appreciate him fully; a proof of which is, that on his showing me the manuscript of Sartor Resartus, his best and greatest work, which he had just then finished, I made little of it; though when it came out about two years afterwards in Fraser's Magazine I read it with enthusiastic admiration and the keenest delight. I did not seek and cultivate Carlyle less on account of the fundamental differences in our philosophy. He soon found out that I was not "another mystic," and when for the sake of my own integrity I wrote to him a distinct profession of those of my opinions which I knew he most disliked, he replied that the chief difference between us was that I "was as yet consciously nothing of a mystic". I do not know at what period he gave up the expectation that I was destined to become one; but though both his and my opinions underwent in subsequent years considerable changes, we never approached much nearer to each other's modes of thought than we were in the first years of our acquaintance. I did not, however, deem myself a competent judge of Carlyle. I felt that he was a poet and that I was not; that he was a man of intuition, which I was not; and that as such, he not only saw many things long before me, which I could only when they were pointed out to me, hobble after and prove, but that it was highly probable he could see many things which were not visible to me even after they were pointed out. I knew that I could not see round him, and could never be certain that I saw him; and I never presumed to judge him with any definiteness, until he was interpreted to me by one greatly the superior of us both—who was more a poet than he, and more a thinker than I—whose own mind and nature included his, and infinitely more.

From 'The Spirit of the Age'

[The extracts, from the first two parts, are taken from *The Examiner*, 9 and 23 January, 1831. The seventh part appeared in May of that year, still leaving the series unfinished.]

THE "SPIRIT OF THE AGE" is in some measure a novel expression. I do not believe that it is to be met with in any work exceeding fifty years in antiquity. The idea of comparing one's own age with former ages, or with our notion of those which are yet to come, had occurred to philosophers; but it never before was itself the dominant idea of any age.

It is an idea essentially belonging to an age of change. Before men begin to think much and long on the peculiarities of their own times, they must have begun to think that those times are, or are destined to be, distinguished in a very remarkable manner from the times which preceded them. Mankind are then divided, into those who are still what they were, and those who have changed: into the men of the present age, and the men of the past. To the former, the spirit of the age is a subject of exultation; to the latter, of terror; to both, of eager and anxious interest. The wisdom of ancestors, and the march of intellect, are bandied from mouth to mouth; each phrase originally an expression of respect and homage, each ultimately usurped by the partisans of the opposite catchword, and in the bitterness of their spirit, turned into the sarcastic gibe of hatred and insult.

The present times possess this character. A change has taken place in the human mind; a change which, being effected by insensible gradations, and without noise, had already proceeded far before it was generally perceived. When the fact disclosed itself, thousands awoke as from a dream. They knew not what processes had been going on in the minds of others, or even in their own, until the change began to invade outward objects; and it became clear that those were indeed new men, who insisted upon being governed in a new way.

But mankind are now conscious of their new position. The conviction is already not far from being universal, that the

times are pregnant with change; and that the nineteenth
century will be known to posterity as the era of one of the
greatest revolutions of which history has preserved the remem-
brance, in the human mind, and in the whole constitution of
human society. Even the religious world teems with new
interpretations of the Prophecies, foreboding mighty changes
near at hand. It is felt that men are henceforth to be held
together by new ties, and separated by new barriers; for the
ancient bonds will now no longer unite, nor the ancient boun-
daries confine. Those men who carry their eyes in the back of
their heads and can see no other portion of the destined track
of humanity than that which it has already travelled, imagine
that because the old ties are severed mankind henceforth are
not to be connected by any ties at all; and hence their affliction, and their awful warnings. For proof of this assertion, I
may refer to the gloomiest book ever written by a cheerful
man—SOUTHEY'S "Colloquies on the Progress and
Prospects of Society"; a very curious and not uninstructive
exhibition of one of the points of view from which the spirit
of the age may be contemplated. They who prefer the ravings
of a party politician to the musings of a recluse, may consult
a late article in Blackwood's Magazine,[2] under the same title
which I have prefixed to this paper. For the reverse of the
picture, we have only to look into any popular newspaper or
review.

Amidst all this indiscriminate eulogy and abuse, these
undistinguishing hopes and fears, it seems to be a very fit
subject for philosophical inquiry, what the spirit of the age
really is; and how or wherein it differs from the spirit of any
other age. The subject is deeply important: for, whatever we
may think or affect to think of the present age, we cannot get
out of it; we must suffer with its sufferings, and enjoy with its
enjoyments; we must even partake its character. No man whose
good qualities were mainly those of another age, ever had much
influence on his own. And since every age contains in itself the
germ of all future ages as surely as the acorn contains the
future forest, a knowledge of our own age is the fountain of
prophecy—the only key to the history of posterity. It is only
in the present that we can know the future; it is only through

the present that it is in our power to influence that which is to come.

Yet, because our own age is *familiar* to us, we are presumed, if I may judge from appearances, to know it by nature. A statesman, for example, if it be required of him to have studied anything at all (which, however, is more than I would venture to affirm) is supposed to have studied history—which is at best the spirit of ages long past, and more often the mere inanimate carcass without the spirit : but is it ever asked (or to whom does the question ever occur?) whether he understands his own age? Yet that also is history, and the most important part of history, and the only part which a man may know and understand, with absolute certainty, by using the proper means. He may learn in a morning's walk through London more of the history of England during the nineteenth century, than all the professed English histories in existence will tell him concerning the other eighteen : for, the obvious and universal facts, which every one sees and no one is astonished at, it seldom occurs to any one to place upon record; and posterity if it learn the rule, learns it, generally, from the notice bestowed by contemporaries on some accidental exception. Yet are politicians and philosophers perpetually exhorted to judge of the present by the past, when the present alone affords a fund of materials for judging, richer than the whole stores of the past, and far more accessible.

But it is unadvisable to dwell longer on this topic, lest we should be deemed studiously to exaggerate that want, which we desire that the reader should think ourselves qualified to supply. It were better, without further preamble, to enter upon the subject, and be tried by our ideas themselves, rather than by the need of them.

The first of the leading peculiarities of the present age is, that it is an age of transition. Mankind have outgrown old institutions and old doctrines, and have not yet acquired new ones. When we say outgrown, we intend to prejudge nothing. A man may not be either better or happier at six-and-twenty, than he was at six years of age : but the same jacket which fitted him then, will not fit him now.

The prominent trait just indicated in the character of the

present age, was obvious a few years ago only to the more discerning: at present it forces itself upon the most inobservant. Much might be said, and shall be said on a fitting occasion, of the mode in which the old order of things has become unsuited to the state of society and of the human mind. But when almost every nation on the continent of Europe has achieved, or is in the course of rapidly achieving, a change in its form of government; when our own country, at all former times the most attached in Europe to its old institutions, proclaims almost with one voice that they are vicious both in the outline and in the details, and that they *shall* be renovated, and purified, and made fit for civilized man, we may assume that a part of the effects of the cause just now pointed out, speak sufficiently loudly for themselves. To him who can reflect, even these are but indications which tell of a more vital and radical change. Not only, in the conviction of almost all men, things as they are, are wrong—but, according to that same conviction, it is not by remaining in the old ways that they can be set right. Society demands, and anticipates, not merely a new machine. but a machine constructed in another manner. Mankind will not be led by their old maxims, nor by their old guides; and they will not choose either their opinions or their guides as they have done heretofore. The ancient constitutional texts were formerly spells which would call forth or allay the spirit of the English people at pleasure: what has become of the charm? Who can hope to sway the minds of the public by the old maxims of law, or commerce, or foreign policy, or ecclesiastical policy? Whose feelings are now roused by the mottoes and watch-words of Whig and Tory? And what Whig or Tory could command ten followers in the warfare of politics by the weight of his own personal authority? Nay, what landlord could call forth his tenants, or what manufacturer his men? Do the poor respect the rich, or adopt their sentiments? Do the young respect the old, or adopt their sentiments? Of the feelings of our ancestors it may almost be said that we retain only such as are the natural and necessary growth of a state of human society, however constituted; and I only adopt the energetic expression of a member of the House of Commons, less than two years ago, in saying of the young men, even of that rank in society, that they are ready to advertise for opinions.

Since the facts are so manifest, there is the more chance that a few reflections on their causes, and on their probable consequences, will receive whatever portion of the reader's attention they may happen to deserve.

With respect, then, to the discredit into which old institutions and old doctrines have fallen, I may premise, that this discredit is, in my opinion, perfectly deserved. Having said this, I may perhaps hope, that no perverse interpretation will be put upon the remainder of my observations, in case some of them should not be quite so conformable to the sentiments of the day as my commencement might give reason to expect. The best guide is not he who, when people are in the right path, merely praises it, but he who shows them the pitfalls and the precipices by which it is endangered; and of which, as long as they were in the wrong road, it was not so necessary that they should be warned.

There is one very easy, and very pleasant way of accounting for this general departure from the modes of thinking of our ancestors: so easy, indeed, and so pleasant, especially to the hearer, as to be very convenient to such writers for hire or for applause, as address themselves not to the men of the age that is gone by, but to the men of the age which has commenced. This explanation is that which ascribes the altered state of opinion and feeling to the growth of the human understanding. According to this doctrine, we reject the sophisms and prejudices which misled the uncultivated minds of our ancestors, because we have learned too much, and have become too wise, to be imposed upon by such sophisms and such prejudices. It is our knowledge and our sagacity which keep us free from these gross errors. We have now risen to the capacity of perceiving our true interests; and it is no longer in the power of impostors and charlatans to deceive us.

I am unable to adopt this theory. Though a firm believer in the improvement of the age, I do not believe that its improvement has been of this kind. The grand achievement of the present age is the *diffusion* of *superficial* knowledge; and that surely is no trifle, to have been accomplished by a single generation. The persons who are in possession of knowledge adequate to the formation of sound opinions by their own lights, form also a constantly increasing number, but hitherto at all times a small one. It would be carrying the notion of the march of intellect too far, to suppose that an average man of the present day is superior to the greatest men of the beginning of the eighteenth century; yet they *held* many opinions which we are fast renouncing. The intellect of the age, therefore, is not the cause which we are in search of. I do not perceive that, in the mental training which has been received by the immense majority of the reading and thinking part of my countrymen, or in the kind of knowledge and other intellectual aliment which has been supplied to them, there is anything likely to render them much less accessible to the influence of imposture and charlatanerie than there ever was.

. . . The intellectual tendencies of the age, considered both on the favourable and on the unfavourable side, it will be necessary, in the prosecution of the present design, to review and analyse in some detail. For the present it may be enough to remark, that it is seldom safe to ground a positive estimate of a character upon mere negatives: and that the faults or the prejudices, which a person, or an age, or a nation *has not*, go but a very little way with a wise man towards forming a high opinion of them. A person may be without a single prejudice, and yet utterly unfit for every purpose in nature. To have erroneous convictions is one evil; but to have not strong or deep-rooted convictions at all, is an enormous one. Before I compliment either a man or a generation upon having got rid of their prejudices, I require to know what they have substituted in lieu of them.

Now, it is self-evident that no fixed opinions have yet generally established themselves in the place of those which we have abandoned; that no new doctrines, philosophical or social, as yet command, or appear likely soon to command, an assent at all comparable in unanimity to that which the ancient doctrines could boast of while they continued in vogue. So long as this intellectual anarchy shall endure, we may be warranted in believing that we are in a fair way to become wiser than our forefathers; but it would be premature to affirm that we are already wiser. We have not yet advanced beyond the unsettled state, in which the mind is, when it has recently found itself out in a grievous error, and has not yet satisfied itself of the truth. The men of the present day rather incline to an opinion than embrace it; few, except the very penetrating, or the very presumptuous, have full confidence in their own convictions. This is not a state of health, but, at the best, of convalescence. It is a necessary stage in the progress of civilization, but it is attended with numerous evils; as one part of a road may be rougher or more dangerous than another, although every step brings the traveller nearer to his desired end.

Not increase of wisdom, but a cause of the reality of which we are better assured, may serve to account for the decay of prejudices; and this is, increase of discussion. Men may not reason better, concerning the great questions in which human nature is interested, but they reason more. Large subjects are discussed more, and longer, and by more minds. Discussion has penetrated deeper into society; and if no greater numbers than before have attained the higher degrees of intelligence, fewer grovel in that state of abject stupidity, which can only co-exist with utter apathy and sluggishness.

The progress which we have made, is precisely that sort of progress which increase of discussion suffices to produce, whether it be attended with increase of wisdom or no. To discuss, and to question established opinions, are merely two phrases for the same thing. When all opinions are questioned, it is in time found out what are those which will not bear a close examination. Ancient doctrines are then put upon their proofs; and those which were originally errors, or have become so by change of circumstances, are thrown aside. Discussion does this. It is by discussion, also, that true opinions are discovered and diffused. But this is not so certain a consequence of it as the weakening of error. To be rationally assured that a given doctrine is *true*, it is often necessary to examine and weigh an immense variety of facts. One single well-established fact, clearly irreconcilable with a doctrine, is sufficient to prove that it is *false*. Nay, opinions often upset themselves by their own incoherence; and the impossibility of their being well-founded may admit of being brought home to a mind not possessed of so much as one positive truth. All the inconsistencies of an opinion with itself, with obvious facts, or even with other prejudices, discussion evolves and makes manifest: and indeed this mode of refutation, requiring less study and less real knowledge than any other, is better suited to the inclination of most disputants. But the moment, and the mood of mind, in which men break loose from an error, is not, except in natures very happily constituted, the most favourable to those mental processes which are necessary to the investigation of truth. What led them wrong at first, was generally nothing else but the incapacity of seeing more than one thing at a time; and that incapacity is apt to stick to them when they have turned their eyes in an altered direction. They usually resolve that the new light which has broken in upon them shall be the sole light; and they wilfully and passionately blew out the ancient lamp, which, though it did not show them what they now see, served very well to enlighten the objects in its immediate neighbourhood. Whether men adhere to old opinions or adopt new ones, they have in general an invincible propensity to split the truth, and take half, or less than half of it; and a habit of erecting their quills and bristling up like a porcupine against anyone who brings them the other half, as if he were attempting to deprive them of the portion which they have.

I am far from denying, that, besides getting rid of error, we are also continually enlarging the stock of positive truth. In physical science and art, this is too manifest to be called in question; and in the moral and social sciences, I believe it to be as undeniably true. The wisest men in every age generally surpass in wisdom the wisest of any preceding age, because the wisest men possess and profit by the constantly increasing accumulation of the ideas of all ages: but the multitude (by which I mean the majority of all ranks) have the ideas of their own age, and no others: and if the multitude of one age are nearer to the truth than the multitude of another, it is only in so far as they are guided and influenced by the authority of the wisest among them.

This is connected with certain points which, as it appears to me, have not been sufficiently adverted to by many of those who hold, in common with me, the doctrine of the indefinite progressiveness of the human mind; but which must be understood, in order correctly to appreciate the character of the present age, as an age of moral and political transition. These, therefore, I shall attempt to enforce and illustrate in the next paper.

... I have said that the present age is an age of transition: I shall now attempt to point out one of the most important consequences of this fact. In all other conditions of mankind, the uninstructed have faith in the instructed. In an age of transition, the divisions among the instructed nullify their authority, and the uninstructed lose their faith in them. The multitude are without a guide; and society is exposed to all the errors and dangers which are to be expected when persons who have never studied any branch of knowledge comprehensively and as a whole attempt to judge for themselves upon particular parts of it.

That this is the condition we are really in, I may spare myself the trouble of attempting to prove: it has become so habitual, that the only difficulty to be anticipated is in persuading anyone that this is not our natural state, and that it is consistent with any good wishes towards the human species, to pray that we may come safely out of it. The longer anyone observes and meditates, the more clearly he will see, that even wise men are apt to mistake the almanac of the year for a treatise on chronology; and as in an age of transition the source of all improvement is the exercise of private judgment, no wonder that mankind should attach themselves to that, as to the ultimate refuge, the last and only resource of humanity. In like manner, if a caravan of travellers had long been journeying in an unknown country under a blind guide, with what earnestness would the wiser among them exhort the remainder to use their own eyes, and with what disfavour would anyone be listened to who should insist upon the difficulty of finding their way, and the necessity of procuring a guide after all. He would be told with warmth, that they had hitherto missed their way solely from the fatal weakness of allowing themselves to be guided, and that they never should reach their journey's end until each man dared to think and see for himself. And it would perhaps be added (with a smile of contempt), that if he were sincere in doubting the capacity of his fellow-travellers to see their way, he might prove his sincerity by presenting each person with a pair of spectacles, by means whereof their powers of vision might be strengthened, and, all indistinctness removed.

The men of the past, are those who continue to insist upon our still adhering to the blind guide. The men of the present, are those who bid each man look about for himself, with or without the promise of spectacles to assist him.

While these two contending parties are measuring their sophistries against one another, the man who is capable of other ideas than those of his age, has an example in the present state of physical science, and in the manner in which men shape their thoughts and their actions within its sphere, of what is to be hoped for and laboured for in all other departments of human knowledge; and what, beyond all possibility of doubt, will one day be attained.

We never hear of the right of private judgment in physical science; yet it exists; for what is there to prevent anyone from denying every proposition in natural philosophy, if he be so minded? The physical sciences however have been brought to so advanced a stage of improvement by a series of great men, and the methods by which they are cultivated so entirely preclude the possibility of material error when due pains are taken to arrive at the truth, that all persons who have studied those subjects have come to a nearly unanimous agreement upon them. . . . The physical sciences, therefore (speaking of them generally), are continually *growing*, but never *changing*: in every age they receive indeed mighty improvements, but for them the age of transition is past.

It is almost unnecessary to remark in how very different a condition from this, are the sciences which are conversant with the moral nature and social condition of man. In those sciences, this imposing unanimity among all who have studied the subject does not exist; and every dabbler, consequently, thinks his opinion as good as another's. Any man who has eyes and ears shall be judge whether, in point of fact, a person who has never studied politics, for instance, or political economy systematically, regards himself as any way precluded thereby from promulgating with the most unbounded assurance the crudest opinions, and taxing men who have made those sciences the occupation of a laborious life, with the most contemptible ignorance and imbecility. It is rather the person who *has* studied the subject systematically that is regarded as disqualified. He is a *theorist*: and the word which expresses the highest and noblest effort of human intelligence is turned into a byword of derision. . . . Men form their opinions according to natural shrewdness, without any of the advantages of study. Here and there a hardheaded man, who sees farther into a mill-stone than his neighbours, and takes it into his head that thinking on a subject is one way of understanding it, excogitates an entire science, and publishes his volume; in utter unconsciousness of the fact, that a tithe of his discoveries were known a century ago, and the remainder (supposing them not too absurd to have occurred to anybody before) have been refuted in any year which you can mention, from that time to the present.

This is the state we are in; and the question is, how we are to get out of it. As I am unable to take the view of this matter which will probably occur to most persons as being the most simple and natural, I shall state in the first instance what this is, and my reasons for dissenting from it.

A large portion of the talking and writing common in the present day, respecting the instruction of the people, and the diffusion of knowledge, appears to me to conceal, under loose and vague generalities, notions at bottom altogether fallacious and visionary.

I go, perhaps, still further than most of those to whose language I so strongly object, in the expectations which I entertain of vast improvements in the social condition of man, from the growth of intelligence among the body of the people; and I yield to no one in the degree of intelligence of which I believe them to be capable. But I do not believe that, along with this intelligence, they will ever have sufficient opportunities of study and experience, to become themselves familiarly conversant with all the inquiries which lead to the truths by which it is good that they should regulate their conduct, and to receive into their own minds the whole of the evidence from which those truths have been collected, and which is necessary for their establishment. If I thought all this indispensable, I should despair of human nature. As long as the day consists but of twenty-four hours, and the age of man extends but to threescore and ten, so long (unless we expect improvements in the arts of production sufficient to restore the golden age) the great majority of mankind will need the far greater part of their time and exertions for procuring their daily bread. Some few remarkable individuals will attain great eminence under every conceivable disadvantage; but for men in general, the principal field for the exercise and display of their intellectual faculties is, and ever will be, no other than their own particular calling or occupation. This does not place any limit to their possible intelligence; since the mode of learning, and the mode of practising, that occupation itself, might be made one of the most valuable of all exercises of intelligence: especially when, in all the occupations in which man is a mere machine, his agency is so rapidly becoming superseded by real machinery. But what sets no limit to the *powers* of the mass of mankind, nevertheless limits greatly their possible *acquirements*. Those persons whom the circumstances of society, and their own position in it, permit to dedicate themselves to the investigation and study of physical, moral, and social truths, as their peculiar calling, can alone be expected to make the evidences of such truths a subject of profound meditation, and to make themselves thorough masters of the philosophical grounds of those opinions of which it is desirable that all should be firmly *persuaded*, but which they alone can entirely and philosophically *know*. The remainder of mankind must, and, except in periods of transition like the present, always do, take the far greater part of their opinions on all extensive subjects upon the authority of those who have studied them.

It does not follow that all men are not to inquire and investigate. The only complaint is, that most of them are precluded by the nature of things from ever inquiring and investigating enough. It is right that they should acquaint themselves with the evidence of the truths which are presented to them, to the utmost extent of each man's intellect, leisure, and inclination. Though a man may never be able to understand Laplace, that is no reason he should not read Euclid. But it by no means follows that Euclid is a blunderer, or an arrant knave, because a man who begins at the forty-seventh proposition cannot understand it : and even he who begins at the beginning and is stopped by the *pons asinorum*, is very much in the wrong if he swears he will navigate his vessel himself, and not trust to the nonsensical calculations of mathematical land-lubbers. Let him learn what he can, and as well as he can—still however bearing in mind, that there are others who probably know much with which he not only is unacquainted, but of the evidence of which, in the existing state of his knowledge, it is impossible that he should be a competent judge.

It is no answer to what has just been observed, to say that the grounds of the most important moral and political truths are simple and obvious, intelligible to persons of the most limited faculties, with moderate study and attention; that all mankind, therefore, may master the evidences, and none need take the doctrines upon trust. The matter of fact upon which this objection proceeds, is happily true. The proofs of the moral and social truths of greatest importance to mankind, are few, brief, and easily intelligible; and happy will be the day on which these shall begin to be circulated among the people, instead of second-rate treatises on the Polarization of Light, and on the Rigidity of Cordage. But, in the first place, it is not everyone—and there is no one at a very early period of life— who has had sufficient experience of mankind in general, and has sufficiently reflected upon what passes in his own mind to be able to appreciate the force of the reasons when laid before him. There is, however, a great number of important truths, especially in Political Economy, to which, from the particular nature of the evidence on which they rest, this difficulty does not apply. The proofs of these truths may be brought down to the level of even the uninformed multitude, with the most complete success. But, when all is done, there still remains something which they must always and inevitably take upon trust : and this is, that the arguments really *are* as conclusive as they appear; that there exist no considerations relevant to the subject which have been kept back from them; that every objection which can suggest itself has been duly examined by competent judges, and found immaterial. It is easy to say that the truth of certain propositions is obvious to *common sense*. It may be so: but how am I assured that the conclusions of common sense are confirmed by accurate knowledge? Judging by common sense is merely another phrase for judging by first appearances; and everyone who has mixed among mankind with any capacity for observing them, knows that the men who place implicit faith in their own common sense are, without any exception, the most wrong-headed and impracticable persons with whom he has ever had to deal. The maxim of pursuing truth without being biassed by authority, does not state the question fairly; there is no person who does not prefer truth to authority—for authority is only appealed to as a voucher for truth. The real question, to be determined by each man's own judgment, is, whether most confidence is due in the particular case, to his own understanding, or to the opinion of his authority? It is therefore obvious, that there are some persons in whom disregard of authority is a virtue, and others in whom it is both an absurdity and a vice. The presumptuous man needs authority to restrain him from error: the modest man needs it to strengthen him in the right. What truths, for example, can be more obvious, or can rest upon considerations more simple and familiar, than the first principles of morality? Yet we know that extremely ingenious things may be said in opposition to the plainest of them—things which the most highly instructed men, though never for a single moment misled by them, have had no small difficulty in satisfactorily answering. Is it to be imagined that if these sophisms had been referred to the verdict of the half-instructed—and we cannot expect the majority of every class to be anything more—the solution of the fallacy would always have been found and understood? notwithstanding which, the fallacy would not, it is most probable, have made the slightest impression upon them:—and why? Because the judgment of the multitude would have told them, that their own judgment was not a decision in the last resort; because the conviction of their understandings going along with the moral truth, was sanctioned by the authority of the best-informed; and the objection, though insoluble by their own understandings, was not supported but contradicted by the same imposing authority. But if you once persuade an ignorant or a half-instructed person, that he ought to assert his liberty of thought, discard all authority, and—I do not say *use* his own judgment, for that he never can do too much—but *trust* solely to his own judgment, and receive or reject opinions according to his own views of the evidence;—if, in short, you teach to all the lesson of *indifferency*, so carnestly, and with such admirable effect, inculcated by Locke upon *students*, for whom alone that great man wrote, the merest trifle will suffice to unsettle and perplex their minds. There is not a truth in the whole range of human affairs, however obvious and simple, the evidence of which an ingenious and artful sophist may not succeed in rendering doubtful to minds not very highly cultivated, if those minds insist upon judging of all things exclusively by their own lights. The presumptuous man will dogmatize, and rush headlong into opinions, always shallow, and as often wrong as right; the man who sets only the just value upon his own moderate powers, will scarcely ever feel more than a half-conviction. You may prevail on them to repudiate the authority of the best instructed, but each will full surely be a mere slave to the authority of the person next to him, who has greatest facilities for continually forcing upon his attention considerations favourable to the conclusion he himself wishes to be drawn.

It is, therefore, one of the necessary conditions of humanity, that the majority must either have wrong opinions, or no fixed opinions, or must place the degree of reliance warranted by reason, in the authority of those who have made moral and social philosophy their peculiar study. It is right that every man should attempt to understand his interest and his duty. It is right that he should follow his reason as far as his reason will carry him, and cultivate the faculty as highly as possible. But reason itself will teach most men that they must, in the last resort, fall back upon the authority of still more cultivated minds, as the ultimate sanction of the convictions of their reason itself.

But where is the authority which commands this confidence,

or deserves it? Nowhere: and here we see the peculiar character, and at the same time the peculiar inconvenience, of a period of moral and social transition. At all other periods there exists a large body of received doctrine, covering nearly the whole field of the moral relations of man, and which no one thinks of questioning, backed as it is by the authority of all, or nearly all, persons, supposed to possess knowledge enough to qualify them for giving an opinion on the subject. This state of things does not now exist in the civilized world—except, indeed, to a certain limited extent in the United States of America. The progress of inquiry has brought to light the insufficiency of the ancient doctrines; but those who have made the investigation of social truths their occupation, have not yet sanctioned any new body of doctrine with their unanimous, or nearly unanimous, consent. The true opinion is recommended to the public by no greater weight of authority than hundreds of false opinions; and, even at this day, to find anything like a united body of grave and commanding authority, we must revert to the doctrines from which the progressiveness of the human mind, or, as it is more popularly called, the improvement of the age, has set us free.

In the meantime, as the old doctrines have gone out, and the new ones have not yet come in, everyone must judge for himself as he best may. Learn, and think for yourself, is reasonable advice for the day: but let not the business of the day be so done as to prejudice the work of the morrow. "Les supériorités morales," to use the words of Fievée,[3] "finiront par s'entendre"; the first men of the age will one day join hands and be agreed: and then there is no power in itself, on earth or in hell, capable of withstanding them.

But ere this can happen there must be a change in the whole framework of society, as at present constituted. Worldly power must pass from the hands of the stationary part of mankind into those of the progressive part. There must be a moral and social revolution, which shall, indeed, take away no men's lives or property, but which shall leave to no man one fraction of unearned distinction or unearned importance.

That man cannot achieve his destiny but through such a transformation, and that it will and *shall* be effected, is the conclusion of every man who can *feel the wants of his own age*, without hankering after past ages.

... For mankind to change their institutions while their minds are unsettled, without fixed principles, and unable to trust either themselves or other people, is, indeed, a fearful thing. But a bad way is often the best, to get out of a bad position. Let us place our trust for the future, not in the wisdom of mankind, but in something far surer—the force of circumstances—which makes men see that, when it is near at hand, which they could not foresee when it was at a distance and which so often and so unexpectedly makes the right course, in a moment of emergency, at once the easiest and the most obvious.

From *The Principles of Political Economy*

[The extract, Book IV, Ch. 6, 'Of the Stationary State', is taken from the first edition, 1848.]

1. The preceding chapters comprise the general theory of the economical progress of society, in the sense in which those terms are commonly understood; the progress of capital, of population, and of the productive arts. But in contemplating any progressive movement, not in its nature unlimited, the mind is not satisfied with merely tracing the laws of the movement; it cannot but ask the further question, to what goal? Towards what ultimate point is society tending by its industrial progress? When the progress ceases, in what condition are we to expect that it will leave mankind?

It must always have been seen, more or less distinctly, by political economists, that the increase of wealth is not boundless; that at the end of what they term the progressive state lies the stationary state, that all progress in wealth is but a postponement of this, and that each step in advance is an approach to it. We have now been led to recognize that this ultimate goal is at all times near enough to be fully in view, that we are always on the verge of it, and that if we have not reached it long ago, it is because the goal itself flies before us.

The richest and most prosperous countries would very soon attain the stationary state, if no further improvements were made in the productive arts, and if there were a suspension of the overflow of capital from those countries into the uncultivated or ill-cultivated regions of the earth.

This impossibility of ultimately avoiding the stationary state—this irresistible necessity that the stream of human industry should finally spread itself out into an apparently stagnant sea—must have been, to the political economists of the last two generations, an unpleasing and discouraging prospect; for the tone and tendency of their speculations goes completely to identify all that is economically desirable with the progressive state, and with that alone. With Mr. M'Culloch,[4] for example, prosperity does not mean a large production and a good distribution of wealth, but a rapid increase of it; his test of prosperity is high profits; and as the tendency of that very increase of wealth, which he calls prosperity, is towards low profits, economical progress, according to him, must tend to the extinction of prosperity. Adam Smith always assumes that the condition of the mass of the people, though it may not be positively distressed, must be pinched and stinted in a stationary condition of wealth, and can only be satisfactory in a progressive state. The doctrine that, to however distant a time incessant struggling may put off our doom, the progress of society must 'end in shallows and in miseries', far from being, as many people still believe, a wicked invention of Mr. Malthus, was either expressly or tacitly affirmed by his most distinguished predecessors, and can only be successfully combated on his principles. Before attention had been directed to the principle of population as the active force in determining the remuneration of labour, the increase of mankind was virtually treated as a constant quantity; it was, at all events, assumed that in the natural and normal state of human affairs population must constantly increase, from which it followed that a constant increase of the means of support was essential to the physical comfort of the mass of mankind. The publication of Mr. Malthus' Essay is the era from which better views of this subject must be dated; and notwithstanding the acknowledged errors of his first edition, few writers have done more than himself, in the subsequent editions, to promote these juster and more hopeful anticipations.

Even in a progressive state of capital, in old countries, a conscientious or prudential restraint on population is indispensable, to prevent the increase of numbers from outstripping the increase of capital, and the condition of the classes who are at the bottom of society from being deteriorated. Where there is not, in the people, or in some very large proportion of them, a resolute resistance to this deterioration— a determination to preserve an established standard of comfort —the condition of the poorest class sinks, even in a progressive state, to the lowest point which they will consent to endure. The same determination would be equally effectual to keep up their condition in the stationary state, and would be quite as likely to exist. Indeed, even now, the countries in which the greatest prudence is manifested in the regulating of population, are often those in which capital increases least rapidly. Where there is an indefinite prospect of employment for increased numbers, there is apt to appear less necessity for prudential restraint. If it were evident that a new hand could not obtain employment but by displacing, or succeeding to, one already employed, the combined influences of prudence and public opinion might generally be relied on for restricting the coming generation within the numbers necessary for replacing the present.

2. I cannot, therefore, regard the stationary state of capital and wealth, with the unaffected aversion so generally manifested towards it by political economists of the old school. I am inclined to believe that it would be, on the whole, a very considerable improvement on our present condition. I confess I am not charmed with the ideal of life held out by those who think that the normal state of human beings is that of struggling to get on; that the trampling, crushing, elbowing, and treading on each other's heels, which form the existing type of social life, are the most desirable lot of human kind, or anything but the disagreeable symptoms of one of the phases of industrial progress. The northern and middle states of America are a specimen of this stage of civilization in very favourable circumstances; having, apparently, got rid of all social

injustices and inequalities that affect persons of Caucasian race and of the male sex, while the proportion of population to capital and land is such as to ensure abundance to every able-bodied member of the community who does not forfeit it by misconduct. They have the six points of Chartism, and they have no poverty: and all that these advantages do for them is that the life of the whole of one sex is devoted to dollar-hunting, and of the other to breeding dollar-hunters. This is not a kind of social perfection which philanthropists to come will feel any very eager desire to assist in realizing. Most fitting, indeed, is it, that while riches are power, and to grow as rich as possible the universal object of ambition, the path to its attainment should be open to all, without favour or partiality. But the best state for human nature is that in which, while no one is poor, no one desires to be richer, nor has any reason to fear being thrust back, by the efforts of others to push themselves forward.

That the energies of mankind should be kept in employment by the struggle for riches, as they were formerly by the struggle of war, until the better minds succeed in educating the others into better things, is undoubtedly more desirable than that they should rust and stagnate. While minds are coarse they require coarse stimuli, and let them have them. In the meantime, those who do not accept the present very early stage of human improvement as its ultimate type, may be excused for being comparatively indifferent to the kind of economical progress which usually excites the congratulations of politicians; the mere increase of production and accumulation. For the safety of national independence it is essential that a country should not fall much behind its neighbours in these things. But in themselves they are of little importance, so long as either the increase of population or anything else prevents the mass of the people from reaping any part of the benefit of them. I know not why it should be matter of congratulation that persons who are already richer than any one needs to be, should have doubled their means of consuming things which give little or no pleasure except as representative of wealth; or that numbers of individuals should pass over, every year, from the middle classes into a richer class, or from the class of the occupied rich to that of the unoccupied. It is only in the backward countries of the world that increased production is still an important object : in those most advanced, what is economically needed is a better distribution, of which an indispensable means is a stricter restraint on population. Levelling institutions, either of a just or of an unjust kind, cannot alone accomplish it ; they may lower the heights of society, but they cannot raise the depths.

On the other hand, we may suppose this better distribution of property attained, by the joint effect of the prudence and frugality of individuals, and of a system of legislation favouring equality of fortunes, so far as is consistent with the just claim of the individual to the fruits, whether great or small, of his or her own industry. We may suppose, for instance (according to the suggestion thrown out in a former chapter), a limitation of the sum which any one person may acquire by gift or inheritance, to the amount sufficient to constitute a moderate independence. Under this twofold influence, society would exhibit these leading features : a well-paid and affluent body of labourers ; no enormous fortunes, except what were earned and accumulated during a single lifetime ; but a much larger body of persons than at present, not only exempt from the coarser toils, but with sufficient leisure, both physical and mental, from mechanical details, to cultivate freely the graces of life, and afford examples of them to the classes less favourably circumstanced for their growth. This state of things which seems, economically considered, to be the most desirable condition of society, is not only perfectly compatible with the stationary state, but, it would seem, more naturally allied with that state than with any other.

There is room in the world, no doubt, and even in old countries, for an immense increase of population, supposing the arts of life to go on improving, and capital to increase. But although it may be innocuous, I confess I see very little reason for desiring it. The density of population necessary to enable mankind to obtain, in the greatest degree, all the advantages both of co-operation and of social intercourse, has, in all the most populous countries, been attained. A population may be too crowded, though all be amply supplied with food and raiment. It is not good for man to be kept perforce at all times in the presence of his species. A world from which solitude is extirpated, is a very poor ideal. Solitude, in the sense of being often alone, is essential to any depth of meditation or of character; and solitude in the presence of natural beauty and grandeur, is the cradle of thoughts and aspirations which are not only good for the individual, but which society could ill do without. Nor is there much satisfaction in contemplating the world with nothing left to the spontaneous activity of nature; with every rood of land brought into cultivation which is capable of growing food for human beings; every flowery waste or natural pasture ploughed up, all quadrupeds or birds which are not domesticated for man's use exterminated as his rivals for food, every hedgerow or superfluous tree rooted out, and scarcely a place left where a wild shrub or flower could grow without being eradicated as a weed in the name of improved agriculture. If the earth must lose that great portion of its pleasantness which it owes to things that the unlimited increase of wealth and population would extirpate from it, for the mere purpose of enabling it to support a larger, but not a better or a happier population, I sincerely hope, for the sake of posterity, that they will be content to be stationary, long before necessity compels them to it.

It is scarcely necessary to remark that a stationary condition of capital and population implies no stationary state of human improvement. There would be as much scope as ever for all kinds of mental culture, and moral and social progress; as much room for improving the Art of Living, and much more likelihood of its being improved, when minds ceased to be engrossed by the art of getting on. Even the industrial arts might be as earnestly and as successfully cultivated, with this sole difference, that instead of serving no purpose but the increase of wealth, industrial improvements would produce their legitimate effect, that of abridging labour. Hitherto it is questionable if all the mechanical inventions yet made have lightened the day's toil of any human being. They have enabled a greater population to live the same life of drudgery, and imprisonment, and an increased number of manufacturers and others to make large fortunes. They have increased the comforts of the middle classes. But they have not yet begun to effect those great changes in human destiny, which it is in their nature and in their futurity to accomplish. Only when, in addition to just institutions, the increase of mankind shall be under the deliberate guidance of a judicious foresight, can the conquests made from the powers of nature by the intellect and energy of scientific discoverers, become the common property of the species, and the means of improving and elevating the universal lot.

From *The Subjection of Women*
[The extract, from Ch. 2, is taken from the first edition, 1869.]

The equality of married persons before the law, is not only the sole mode in which that particular relation can be made consistent with justice to both sides, and conducive to the happiness of both, but it is the only means of rendering the daily life of mankind, in any high sense, a school of moral cultivation. Though the truth may not be felt or generally acknowledged for generations to come, the only school of genuine moral sentiment is society between equals. The moral education of mankind has hitherto emanated chiefly from the law of force, and is adapted almost solely to the relations which force creates. In the less advanced states of society, people hardly recognise any relation with their equals. To be an equal is to be an enemy. Society, from its highest place to its lowest, is one long chain, or rather ladder, where every individual is either above or below his nearest neighbour, and wherever he does not command he must obey. Existing moralities, accordingly, are mainly fitted to a relation of command and obedience. Yet command and obedience are but unfortunate necessities of human life: society in equality is its normal state. Already in modern life, and more and more as it progressively improves, command and obedience become exceptional facts in life, equal association its general rule. The morality of the first ages rested on the obligation to submit to power; that of the ages next following, on the right of the weak to the forbearance and protection of the strong. How much longer is one form of society and life to content itself with the morality made for another? We have had the morality of submission, and the morality of chivalry and generosity; the time is now come for the morality of justice. Whenever, in former ages, any approach has been made to society in equality, Justice has asserted its claims as the foundation of virtue. It was thus in the free republics of antiquity. But even in the best of these, the equals were limited to the free male citizens; slaves, women, and the unenfranchised residents were under the law of force. The joint influence of Roman civilization and of Christianity obliterated these distinctions, and in theory (if only partially in practice) declared the claims of the human being, as such, to be paramount to those of sex, class, or social position. The barriers which had begun to be levelled were raised again by the northern conquests; and the whole of modern history consists of the slow process by which they have since been wearing away. We are entering into an order of things in which justice will again be the primary virtue; grounded as before on equal, but now also on sympathetic association; having its root no longer in the instinct of equals for self-protection, but in a cultivated sympathy between them; and no one being now left out, but an equal measure being extended to all. It is no novelty that mankind do not distinctly foresee their own changes, and that their sentiments are adapted to past, not to coming ages. To see the futurity of the species has always been the privilege of the intellectual élite, or of those who have learnt from them; to have the feelings of that futurity has been the distinction, and usually the martyrdom, of a still rarer élite. Institutions, books, education, society, all go on training human beings for the old, long after the new has come; much more when it is only coming. But the true virtue of human beings is fitness to live together as equals; claiming nothing for themselves but what they as freely concede to every-one else; regarding command of any kind as an exceptional necessity, and in all cases a temporary one; and preferring, whenever possible, the society of those with whom leading and following can be alternate and reciprocal. To these virtues, nothing in life as at present constituted gives cultivation by exercise. The family is a school of despotism, in which the virtues of despotism, but also its vices, are largely nourished. Citizenship, in free countries, is partly a school of society in equality; but citizenship fills only a small place in modern life, and does not come near the daily habits or inmost sentiments. The family, justly constituted, would be the real school of the virtues of freedom. It is sure to be a sufficient one of everything else. It will always be a school of obedience for the children, of command for the parents. What is needed is, that it should be a school of sympathy in equality, of living together in love, without power on one side or obedience on the other. This it ought to be between the parents. It would then be an exercise of those virtues which each requires to fit them for all other association, and a model to the children of the feelings and conduct which their temporary training by means of obedience is designed to render habitual, and therefore natural, to them. The moral training of mankind will never be adapted to the conditions of the life for which all other human progress is a preparation, until they practise in the family the same moral rule which is adapted to the normal constitution of human society. Any sentiment of freedom which can exist in a man whose nearest and dearest intimacies are with those of whom he is absolute master, is not the genuine or Christian love of freedom, but, what the love of freedom generally was in the ancients and in the middle ages—an intense feeling of the dignity and importance of his own personality; making him disdain a yoke for himself, of which he has no abhorrence whatever in the abstract, but which he is abundantly ready to impose on others for his own interest or glorification.

G. H. LEWES

From *Comte's Philosophy of the Sciences*
[The extract, from Part II, Section 12, 'The Future', is taken from the first edition, 1853.]

Let us now consider the great spiritual reorganization of modern society, pointing out its intimate connection with the just social reclamations of the lower classes. Every spiritual power should be essentially popular, since its most extended sphere of duty relates to the constant protection of the most numerous classes, habitually the most exposed to oppression, and with which the education common to all leads it into daily contact. In the final state the spiritual class will be connected with the popular mass by common sympathies, consequent upon a certain similitude of situation, and parallel habits of material improvidence, as well as by analogous interests with regard to the temporal chiefs, necessarily possessors of the principal wealth.

But we must especially remark the extreme popular efficacy of speculative authority, whether by reason of its office of universal education, or because of the regular interference which, according to our previous indications, it will always exercise in the different conflicts of society : thereby developing suitably the mediatory influence habitually attendant on the elevation of its views, and the generosity of its inclinations. Narrow views and malignant passions will in vain attempt to institute legally laborious hindrances against the accumulation of capital, at the risk of paralyzing directly all real social activity. It is clear that these tyrannical proceedings will have much less real efficacy than the universal reprobation applied by the positive ethics to any utterly selfish use of the wealth possessed.

When the new speculative class shall have arisen, the great practical collisions continually becoming more numerous in the total absence of any industrial systematization, will doubtless constitute the principal occasions of its social development, by making apparent to all classes the increasing utility of its active moral intervention, alone capable of sufficiently tempering material antagonism, and of habitually modifying the opposing sentiments of envy and disdain inspired on either hand. The classes most disposed at present to recognize the real ascendancy which wealth enjoys, will then be led by decisive and probably melancholy experience to implore the necessary protection of that very spiritual power which they now look upon as essentially chimerical.

It is in this manner that a power which by its nature can

rest on no other foundation than that of its universal free recognition, will be gradually established on the ground of the services rendered by it. The popular point of view is henceforward the only one which can spontaneously offer at once sufficient grandeur and distinctness to be able to place the minds of men in a truly organic direction.

The unavailing changes of individuals, ministerial or even royal, which appear of so much importance to the various present factions, will naturally become quite indifferent to the people, whose own social interests can in no wise be affected thereby.

The assurance of education and work to every one will always constitute the sole essential object of popular policy properly so called: now this great end, perfectly separated from constitutional discussions and combinations, can never be adequately attained but by a real reorganization; first and foremost spiritual; afterwards necessarily temporal.

Such is the connection which the entire situation of modern society instituted between popular necessities and philosophical tendencies, and according to which the true social point of view will gradually prevail in proportion as the active intervention of the People, speaking in their name, begins to characterize more and more the grand political problem.

FREDERIC HARRISON

From 'A Few Words about the Nineteenth Century'
[The text is from *The Fortnightly Review*, XXXI, N.S., 411–26 (April, 1882).]

Robert Lowe,[5] the Society of British Engineers, and the British Association itself, hardly ever pretended that this Victorian age is so incalculably wiser, better, more beautiful, than any other in recorded history. What they say is that it has incalculably more good things, incredibly greater opportunities than any other. Quite so! It has a thousand times the resources of any other age. Permit us to ask—Does it use them

to a thousand times better purpose? I am no detractor of our
own age. I do not know if there is any in which I would rather
have lived, take it all round. We all feel, in spite of a want of
beauty, of rest, of completeness, which sits heavy on our souls
and frets the thoughtful spirit—we all feel a-tiptoe with hope
and confidence. We *are* on the threshold of a great time, even
if our time is not great itself. In science, in religion, in social
organisation, we all know what great things are in the air.
"We shall see it, but not *now*"—or our children and our children's children will see it. The Vatican with its syllabus, the
Mediaevalists-at-all-costs, Mr. Carlyle, Mr. Ruskin, the
Æsthetes, are all wrong about the nineteenth century. It is
not the age of money-bags and cant, soot, hubbub, and ugliness.
It is the age of great expectation and unwearied striving after
better things. Still, is it the Millennium foretold by the
prophets, by civil engineers and railway kings?

. . . To bury Middlesex and Surrey under miles of flimsy
houses, crowd into them millions and millions of over-worked,
underfed, half-taught, and often squalid men and women; to
turn the silver Thames into the biggest sewer recorded in
history; to leave us all to drink the sewerage water, to breathe
the carbonised air; to be closed up in a labyrinth of dull,
sooty, unwholesome streets; to leave hundreds and thousands
confined there, with gin, and bad air, and hard work, and low
wages, breeding contagious diseases, and sinking into despair
of soul and feebler condition of body; and then to sing
paeans and shout, because the ground shakes and the air is
shrill with the roar of infinite engines and machines, because
the blank streets are lit up with garish gas-lamps, and more
garish electric lamps, and the Post Office carries billions of
letters, and the railways every day carry 100,000 persons in
and out of the huge factory we call the greatest metropolis of
the civilised world—this is surely not the last word in civilisation.

. . . But amidst all the dangers of these material appliances
flung random upon a society unprepared for them, let us
beware how we join in the impatience which protests that we
are better without them. Let Mr. Carlyle pronounce anathemas
on steam-engines, and Mr. Ruskin seek by the aid of St.

George to abolish factories from England; all this is permitted to a man of genius, for all is permitted to genius, and it is perhaps a grim way of giving us ample warning. But men of practical purpose have a different aim. The railways, the factories, the telegraphs, the gas, the electric wonders of all kinds, are here. No latter-day sermons or societies of St. George can get rid of them, or persuade men to give up what they find so enormously convenient. Nay, the case is far stronger than this. These things are amongst the most precious achievements of the human race, or rather, they will be, when we have learned how to use them without all the evils they bring with them. Man, in his desperate struggle with the forces of nature, is far too slightly armed to dispense with any one of the appliances that the genius of man can discover. He needs them all to get nearer to the mystery of the world, to furnish his material wants, to raise and beautify his personal and social life. There is one way in which they may be made a curse, not a blessing, and that is to exaggerate their value, to think that new material appliances to life form a truly higher life; that a man is *ipso facto* a nobler being because he can travel a thousand miles in twenty-four hours, and hear the words that a man is speaking in New York. What has happened to the nineteenth century is what happens to a country when a gold-field is suddenly discovered. Civilised life for the time seems dancing mad; and though men will give a hundred dollars for a glass of champagne, degradation and want are commoner even than nuggets. It is significant that the most powerful pictures of degradation which the American continent has produced were drawn in the Western goldfields, and the most serious scheme of modern communism has been thought out in the same ground. But the nugget (the sudden acquisition of vast material resources) makes havoc in London and Manchester as much as in San Francisco or Melbourne. It does not follow, as some prophets tell us, that gold is not a useful metal, only we may buy gold too dear.

Society, to use Mr. Herbert Spencer's profound suggestion, is a continual action and reaction between the forces that divide it into new forms of life, and those which reunite these new forms in harmony. Or, to use Comte's still more abstract

theory, society is the result of the equilibrium between progress and order, or new phases and old types. But in an age of
sudden material expansion, the forces that drive on the new
phases in special lines are abnormally raised to fever heat,
whilst those which in ordinary times are active to preserve
the type are routed, abashed, and bewildered. In the long
run the course of Order will rally again; but for the moment
it is asked to do its work in what is something like an invasion
or an earthquake. We have hardly yet got so far as to recognise
that the sudden acquisition of vast material resources is not
only a great boon to humanity, but also a tremendous moral,
social, and even physical and intellectual experiment. Society
is a most subtle organisation; and we are apt to lose sight of the
fact that an unlimited supply of steam power, or electric power,
is not necessarily pure gain. The progress achieved in the
external conditions of life within the last hundred years is no
doubt greater than any recorded in human history. It is
obvious that other kinds of progress have advanced at no
such express speed. But, until all kinds of human energy get
into more harmonious proportion, cantatas to the nineteenth
century will continue to pall upon the impartial mind.

Socially, morally, and intellectually speaking, an era of
extraordinary changes is an age that has cast on it quite
exceptional duties. A child might as well play with a steam-
engine or an electric machine, as we could prudently accept
our material triumphs with a mere "rest and be thankful".
To decry steam and electricity, inventions and products, is
hardly more foolish than to deny the price which civilisation
itself has to pay for the use of them. There are forces at work
now, forces more unwearied than steam, and brighter than
the electric arc, to rehumanise the dehumanised members of
society; to assert the old immutable truths; to appeal to the
old indestructible instinct; to recall beauty; forces yearning
for rest, grace, and harmony; rallying all that is organic in
man's social nature, and proclaiming the value of spiritual
life over material life. But there never was a century in human
history when these forces had a field so vast before them, or
issues so momentous on their failure or their success. There
never was an age when the need was so urgent for synthetic

habits of thought, systematic education, and a common moral and religious faith.

NOTES

1. Mormontel's *Mémoires d'un père pour servir à l'instruction de ses enfants* (Paris, 1804).
2. A late article; 'A letter to Christopher North Esquire on the Spirit of the Age' by 'One of the Democracy'; *Blackwood's Magazine*, XXVIII (December, 1830). The article foresees approaching revolutions in 'institution and law, class and property, accomplished through anarchy, blood, rapine and misery'.
3. Jean Fievée (1767–1839), French political writer and journalist.
4. John Ramsay McCulloch (1789–1864), contributor to the *Encyclopædia Britannica* on economic subjects and author of *The Principles of Political Economy* (Edinburgh, 1825).
5. Robert Lowe (1811–1892) Minister of Education, who introduced the system of 'payment by results' and who led Whig opposition to the extension of the franchise in 1866.

The Religious Dilemma

[Dr Thomas Arnold (1795–1842), the headmaster of Rugby, took up, in his *Principles of Church Reform*, the idea of a tolerant and comprehensive Church Establishment put forward by Coleridge. The secular tendency of Arnold's practical proposals, together with his adverse comments on sectarianism, reveals his Broad Church influence upon his son's idea of culture. However, all such liberal Protestantism was opposed by the Anglo-Catholics, the most prominent writer among whom was John Henry Newman (1801–1890), later Cardinal Newman. The story of Newman's conversion from Anglicanism to Roman Catholicism is told in his autobiographical *Apologia*. In his account of his religious opinions since his conversion Newman puts the classic Victorian case for dogmatism, expressing the need for an infallible authority in an age of honest doubt. The later *Essay in Aid of a Grammar of Assent* argues for religious and moral commitment. The emphasis is Coleridgean; the practical imagination is explored as superior to mere reasoning in stimulating men to worthwhile action.

The new agnostic camp, influenced by Darwin, is represented by Leslie Stephen (1832–1904), critic and editor, the father of Virginia Woolf. He had relinquished his Anglican orders in 1875. Stephen asserts the empirical conclusion that morality does not require a theological foundation. He holds that moral truth evolves as does scientific truth, a view which is hopeful rather than assured, yet preferable, in his opinion, to a commitment to revealed religion which involves one in the strain of hostility to new ideas. It was Stephen who familiarised the public with the word 'agnostic', which T. H. Huxley had coined in 1870.]

THOMAS ARNOLD

From *Principles of Church Reform*
[The extracts are from the first edition of 1833, pp. 69–70, 73–7, 79–80, 81 and 82–4.]

It may appear to some a point of small importance, but I believe that it would go a long way towards producing a kindly and united feeling amongst all the inhabitants of the parish, that the parish church should, if possible be the only place of public worship; and that the different services required, should rather be performed at different times in the same spot than at the same time in different places. In this respect, the spirit of the Mosaic law may be most usefully followed, which forbade the multiplication of temples and altars, but fixed on one spot to become endeared and hallowed to the whole people as the scene of their common worship. Besides, the parish church has a sacredness which no other place of worship can boast of, in its antiquity, and in its standing amidst the graves of so many generations of our fathers. It is painful to think that any portion of the people should have ever broken their connexion with it; it would be equally delightful to see them again assembled within its walls, without any base compromise of opinion on either side, but because we had learned a better wisdom than to deprive it of its just claim to the affections of all our countrymen, or to exclude any portion of our countrymen from the happiness of loving it as it deserves. Nor is it a light thing in the judgements of those who understand the ennobling effects of a quick perception of what is beautiful and venerable, that some of the most perfect specimens of architecture in existence should no longer be connected, in any man's mind, with the bitterness of sectarian hostility; that none should be forced to associate, with their most solemn and dearest recollections, such utter coarseness and deformity as characterize the great proportion of the Dissenting chapels throughout England.

. . . suppose Tithes to be commuted,—the revenues of the Clergy equalized,—residence universally enforced,—and pluralities done away with, the efficiency of the Establishment, as a great social engine of intellectual, moral, and religious good, will still be incomplete,—and for this very reason its stability will be precarious. There will still remain that vast mass of the dissenting and of the godless population, who, not sharing in its benefits, will labour to effect its destruction. These two parties are leagued together; and unless their league can be dissolved, the long continuance of a national Church in this country is a thing impossible. The cry which is destroying the Protestant Establishment in Ireland is already beginning to be echoed here: the Dissenters repeat the complaint of the Catholics,—"Why should we be obliged to contribute towards the maintenance of a Church which is not ours?" All the inherent evils of our destestable sectarian system will presently be brought to light, and will derange the very frame of society. Church rates have been already resisted;—that is to say, the noblest and most useful of all our public buildings will be suffered to go to ruin, or to be maintained by private munificence. Marriage, the most important of all social ordinances, will be made a private ceremony;—for such must be the character of a rite performed without the intervention of any public officer; whether that officer be a magistrate or a clergyman, may be a question of comparative indifference; for in either case society sanctions, and in a manner presides at the celebration of its holiest contract; but a Dissenting minister is a mere private individual, or rather an alien from the national society, to whose acts society lends no authority. The registration of births, marriages, and deaths, a thing essentially of national concern, and to be placed under the control of public officers, is already claimed by the Dissenters as a right to be enjoyed by their own communities separately. Our universities, the great seats of public education, are in danger of becoming odious, because they are practically closed against so large a portion of the community;—while the evils of Dissenting colleges, pledged by their very name to narrow-mindedness, will continue to multiply.

The end of all this will be, what the godless party are earnestly labouring to effect, the dissolution of the Establishment altogether;—that is, in other words, the public renouncing of our allegiance to God; for, without an establishment, although it may happen that the majority of Englishmen may still be Christians, yet England will not be a Christian nation;—its government will be no Christian government;— we shall be wholly a kingdom of the world, and ruled according to none but worldly principles. In such a state the establishment of paganism would be an absolute blessing; any thing would be better than a national society, formed for no higher than physical ends;—to enable men to eat, drink, and live luxuriously;—acknowledging no power greater than its own, and by consequence, no law higher than its own municipal enactments. Let a few generations pass over in such a state, and the missionary, who should preach the worship of Ceres, or set up an oracle of Apollo, or teach the people to kindle the eternal fire of Vesta on the common altar hearth of their country, would be to that degraded society as life from the dead.*

But we are told to look at America; the United States have no national religion; but yet we are assured that they are as religious a people as ourselves. When a man of science hears a fact asserted in direct contradiction to the known laws of

---

* [Arnold's note.]

I cannot resist the pleasure of copying here the beautiful lines in which Mr. Wordsworth sympathizes so entirely with the feeling expressed in the text:

> "The world is too much with us; late and soon,
>   Getting and spending, we lay waste our powers;
>   Little we see in nature that is ours;
>   We have given our hearts away, a sordid boon!
>   This sea, that bares her bosom to the moon;
>   The winds, that will be howling at all hours,
>   And are up-gathered now like sleeping flowers;
>   For this, for every thing, we are out of tune;
>   It moves us not. Great God! I'd rather be
>   A pagan suckled in a creed outworn;
>   So might I, standing on this pleasant lea,
>   Have glimpses that would make me less forlorn;
>   Have sight of Proteus rising from the sea,
>   Or hear old Triton blow his wreathed horn."

nature, he cannot but suspect some misrepresentation or confusion in the statement. To assert that the irregular efforts of individual zeal and courage will oppose an invading enemy as effectually as a good regular army, would be little better than insanity; and yet it may be true, that in the last war the Spanish guerillas did more service to their country than the Spanish regular armies. We know, however, that the guerillas did not, and could not deliver Spain; it was an efficient regular army which achieved that work. So, if it could be shown that under any circumstances Christianity was flourishing as much without an establishment as with one, it would merely prove that the particular establishment in question was in a state of deplorable corruption, as it had so completely forfeited its inherent advantages.

. . . Crowded together as we are, we cannot afford to be disorderly; it is well if, with all the aid of the most powerful and the purest institutions we can organize and keep from taint the unwieldy masses of our population. And as the best of all institutions, I am anxious to secure a truly national Church, which, uniting within itself all Christians who deserve the name, except perhaps the mere handful of the Quakers and Roman Catholics, would leave without its pale nothing but voluntary or involuntary godlessness.

We should hear no complaints then of the burden of supporting a church to which men do not belong. Such language in a Dissenter's mouth is forcible; but who would heed it from a man who belonged to no church, who paid no minister of his own,—but hating God altogether, was consistently averse to contributing towards his service? Truly we may wait a long time before we shall find the thieves of a country willing to pay for the building of gaols, or the maintenance of an efficient police.

But, it may be said, admitting the soundness of the principles put forward in these pages, that the National Church should be rendered thoroughly comprehensive in doctrine, in government, and in ritual, by what power are they to be carried into effect? To whose hands, in particular, should be committed the delicate task of remodelling the Articles, a measure obviously essential to the proposed comprehension, yet presenting the greatest practical difficulty? It seems to me, that this is a question more properly to be answered by the Government, than by an individual; only, I may be allowed to express an earnest hope, that if ever an union with Dissenters be attempted, and it should thus become necessary to alter our present terms of communion, the determining on the alterations to be made should never be committed to a convocation, or to any commission consisting of clergymen alone.

. . . Layman have no right to shift from their own shoulders an important part of Christian responsibility; and as no educated layman individually is justified in taking his own faith upon trust from a clergyman, so neither are the laity, as a body, warranted in taking the national faith in the same way.

. . . In venturing even to suggest so great a change in the constitution of our Church, I may probably expose myself to a variety of imputations. Above all, whoever pleads in favour of a wide extension of the terms of communion, is immediately apt to be accused of latitudinarianism, or as it is now called, of liberalism. Such a charge in the mouths of men at once low principled and ignorant, is of no importance whatever; neither should I regard it if it proceeded from the violent fanatical party, to whom truth must ever remain unknown, as it is unsought after. But in the Church of England even bigotry often wears a softer and a nobler aspect; and there are men at once pious, high minded, intelligent, and full of all kindly feelings, whose intense love for the forms of the Church, fostered as it has been by all the best associations of their pure and holy lives, has absolutely engrossed their whole nature; they have neither eyes to see of themselves any defect in the Liturgy or Articles, nor ears to hear of such when alleged by others. It can be no ordinary church to have inspired such a devoted adoration in such men;—nor are they ordinary men over whom the sense of high moral beauty has obtained so complete a mastery. They will not, I fear, be willing to believe how deeply painful it is to my mind, to know that I am regarded by them as an adversary; still more to feel that I am associated in their judgments with principles and with a party which I abhor as deeply as they do. But while I know the devotedness of their admiration for the Church of England, as it is now constituted, I cannot but wish that they would regard those thousands and ten thousands of their countrymen, who are excluded from its benefit; that they would consider the wrong done to our common country by these unnatural divisions among her children. *The Church of Christ* is indeed far beyond all human ties; but of all human ties, that to our country is the highest and most sacred: and *England*, to a true Englishman, ought to be dearer than the peculiar forms of *The Church of England*.

For the sake, then, of our country, and to save her from the greatest possible evils,—from evils far worse than any loss of territory, or decline of trade,—from the sure moral and intellectual degradation which will accompany the unchristianizing of the nation, that is, the destroying of its national religious Establishment, is it too much to ask of good men, that they should consent to unite themselves with other good men, without requiring them to subscribe to their own opinions, or to conform to their own ceremonies? They are not asked to surrender or compromise the smallest portion of their own faith, but simply to forbear imposing it upon their neighbours. They are not called upon to give up their own forms of worship, but to allow the addition of others; not for themselves to join in it, if they do not like to do so, but simply to be celebrated in the same church, and by ministers, whom they shall acknowledge to be their brethren, and members no less than themselves of the National Establishment.

JOHN HENRY NEWMAN

From *Apologia Pro Vita Sua*

[Newman's *Apologia* was issued in eight weekly parts from April to June, 1864, and in a single volume later that year. This text is an extract from Part VII of the first volume-edition.]

. . . Starting then with the being of a God, (which, as I have said, is as certain to me as the certainty of my own existence, though when I try to put the grounds of that certainty into logical shape I find a difficulty in doing so in mood and figure to my satisfaction,) I look out of myself into the world of men, and there I see a sight which fills me with unspeakable distress. The world seems simply to give the lie to that great truth, of which my whole being is so full; and the effect upon me is, in consequence, as a matter of necessity, as confusing as if it denied that I am in existence myself. If I looked into a mirror, and did not see my face, I should have the sort of feeling which actually comes upon me, when I look into this living busy world, and see no reflexion of its Creator. This is, to me, one of the great difficulties of this absolute primary truth, to which I referred just now. Were it not for this voice, speaking so clearly in my conscience and my heart, I should be an atheist, or a pantheist, or a polytheist when I looked into the world. I am speaking for myself only; and I am far from denying the real force of the arguments in proof of a God, drawn from the general facts of human society, but these do not warm me or enlighten me; they do not take away the winter of my desolation, or make the buds unfold and the leaves grow within me, and my moral being rejoice. The sight of the world is nothing else than the prophet's scroll, full of "lamentations, and mourning, and woe".[1]

To consider the world in its length and breadth, its various history, and the many races of man, their starts, their fortunes, their mutual alienation, their conflicts; and then their ways, habits, governments, forms of worship; their enterprises, their aimless courses, their random achievements and acquirements, the impotent conclusion of long-standing facts, the tokens so faint and broken, of a superintending design, the blind evolution of what turn out to be great powers or truths, the progress of things, as if from unreasoning elements, not towards final causes, the greatness and littleness of man, his far-reaching aims, his short duration, the curtain hung over his futurity, the disappointments of life, the defeat of good, the success of evil, physical pain, mental anguish, the prevalence and intensity of sin, the pervading idolatries, the corruptions, the dreary hopeless irreligion, that condition of the whole race, so fearfully yet exactly described in the Apostle's words, "having no

hope and without God in the world,"[2]—all this is a vision to
dizzy and appal; and inflicts upon the mind the sense of a
profound mystery, which is absolutely beyond human solution.

What shall be said to this heart-piercing, reason-bewildering
fact? I can only answer, that either there is no Creator, or this
living society of men is in a true sense discarded from His
presence. Did I see a boy of good make and mind, with the
tokens on him of a refined nature, cast upon the world without
provision, unable to say whence he came, his birth-place or his
family connexions, I should conclude that there was some
mystery connected with his history, and that he was one, of
whom, from one cause or other, his parents were ashamed.
Thus only should I be able to account for the contrast between
the promise and condition of his being. And so I argue about
the world;—*if* there be a God, *since* there is a God, the human
race is implicated in some terrible aboriginal calamity. It is
out of joint with the purposes of its Creator. This is a fact,
a fact as true as the fact of its existence; and thus the doctrine
of what is theologically called original sin becomes to me
almost as certain as that the world exists, and as the existence
of God.

And now, supposing it were the blessed and loving will of the
Creator to interfere in this anarchical condition of things, what
are we to suppose would be the methods which might be
necessarily or naturally involved in His object of mercy?
Since the world is in so abnormal a state, surely it would be
no surprise to me, if the interposition were of necessity
equally extraordinary—or what is called miraculous. But that
subject does not directly come into the scope of my present
remarks. Miracles as evidence, involve an argument; and of
course I am thinking of some means which does not immediately
run into argument. I am rather asking what must be the
face-to-face antagonist, by which to withstand and baffle
the fierce energy of passion and the all-corroding, all-dissolving
scepticism of the intellect in religious inquiries? I have no
intention at all to deny, that truth is the real object of our
reason, and that, if it does not attain to truth, either the
premiss or the process is in fault; but I am not speaking of
right reason, but of reason as it acts in fact and concretely

in fallen man. I know that even the unaided reason, when correctly exercised, leads to a belief in God, the immortality of the soul, and in a future retribution; but I am considering it actually and historically; and in this point of view, I do not think I am wrong in saying that its tendency is towards a simple unbelief in matters of religion. No truth, however sacred, can stand against it, in the long run; and hence it is that in the pagan world, when our Lord came, the last traces of the religious knowledge of former times were all but disappearing from those portions of the world in which the intellect had been active and had had a career.

And in these latter days, in like manner, outside the Catholic Church things are tending, with far greater rapidity than in that old time from the circumstance of the age, to atheism in one shape or other. What a scene, what a prospect, does the whole of Europe present at this day! and not only Europe, but every government and every civilization through the world, which is under the influence of the European mind! Especially, for it most concerns us, how sorrowful, in the view of religion, even taken in its most elementary, most attenuated form, is the spectacle presented to us by the educated intellect of England, France, and Germany! Lovers of their country and of their race, religious men, external to the Catholic Church, have attempted various expedients to arrest fierce wilful human nature in its onward course, and to bring it into subjection. The necessity of some form of religion for the interests of humanity, has been generally acknowledged: but where was the concrete representative of things invisible, which would have the force and the toughness necessary to be a breakwater against the deluge? Three centuries ago the establishment of religion, material, legal, and social, was generally adopted as the best expedient for the purpose, in those countries which separated from the Catholic Church; and for a long time it was successful; but now the crevices of those establishments are admitting the enemy. Thirty years ago, education was relied upon: ten years ago there was a hope that wars would cease for ever, under the influence of commercial enterprise and the reign of the useful and fine arts; but will any one venture to say that there is any thing any where on this earth, which will afford a fulcrum for us, whereby to keep the earth from moving onwards?

The judgment, which experience passes on establishments or education, as a means of maintaining religious truth in this anarchical world, must be extended even to Scripture, though Scripture be divine. Experience proves surely that the Bible does not answer a purpose, for which it was never intended. It may be accidentally the means of the conversion of individuals; but a book, after all, cannot make a stand against the wild living intellect of man, and in this day it begins to testify, as regards its own structure and contents, to the power of that universal solvent, which is so successfully acting upon religious establishments.

Supposing then it to be the Will of the Creator to interfere in human affairs, and to make provisions for retaining in the world a knowledge of Himself, so definite and distinct as to be proof against the energy of human scepticism, in such a case,— I am far from saying that there was no other way,—but there is nothing to surprise the mind, if He should think fit to introduce a power into the world, invested with the prerogative of infallibility in religious matters. Such a provision would be a direct, immediate, active, and prompt means of withstanding the difficulty; it would be an instrument suited to the need; and, when I find that this is the very claim of the Catholic Church, not only do I feel no difficulty in admitting the idea, but there is a fitness in it, which recommends it to my mind. And thus I am brought to speak of the Church's infallibility, as a provision, adapted by the mercy of the Creator, to preserve religion in the world, and to restrain that freedom of thought, which of course in itself is one of the greatest of our natural gifts, and to rescue it from its own suicidal excesses. And let it be observed that, neither here nor in what follows, shall I have occasion to speak directly of the revealed body of truths, but only as they bear upon the defence of natural religion. I say, that a power, possessed of infallibility in religious teaching, is happily adapted to be a working instrument, in the course of human affairs, for smiting hard and throwing back the immense energy of the aggressive intellect:—and in saying this, as in the other things that I have to say, it must still be recollected that I am all along bearing in mind my main purpose, which is a defence of myself.

I am defending myself here from a plausible charge brought against Catholics, as will be seen better as I proceed. This charge is this:—that I, as a Catholic, not only make profession to hold doctrines which I cannot possibly believe in my heart, but that I also believe in the existence of a power on earth, which at its own will imposes upon men any new set of *credenda*, when it pleases, by a claim to infallibility; in consequence, that my own thoughts are not my own property; that I cannot tell that to-morrow I may not have to give up what I hold to-day, and that the necessary effect of such a condition of mind must be a degrading bondage, or a bitter inward rebellion relieving itself in secret infidelity, or the necessity of ignoring the whole subject of religion in a sort of disgust, and of mechanically saying every thing that the Church says, and leaving to others the defence of it. As then I have above spoken of the relation of my mind towards the Catholic Creed, so now I shall speak of the attitude which it takes up in the view of the Church's infallibility.

And first, the initial doctrine of the infallible teacher must be an emphatic protest against the existing state of mankind. Man had rebelled against his Maker. It was this that caused the divine interposition: and the first act of the divinely accredited messenger must be to proclaim it. The Church must denounce rebellion as of all possible evils the greatest. She must have no terms with it; if she would be true to her Master, she must ban and anathematize it. This is the meaning of a statement,[3] which has furnished matter for one of those special accusations to which I am present replying: I have, however, no fault at all to confess in regard to it; I have nothing to withdraw, and in consequence I here deliberately repeat it. I said, "The Catholic Church holds it better for the sun and moon to drop from heaven, for the earth to fail, and for all the many millions on it to die of starvation in extremest agony, as far as temporal affliction goes, than that one soul, I will not say, should be lost, but should commit one single venial sin, should tell one wilful untruth, or should steal one poor farthing without excuse." I think the principle here enunciated to be the mere preamble in the formal credentials of the Catholic Church, as an Act of Parliament might begin with a "*Whereas*". It is because of the intensity of the evil which has possession of mankind, that a suitable antagonist has been provided against it, and the initial act of that divinely-commissioned power is of course to deliver her challenge and to defy the enemy. Such a preamble then gives a meaning to her position in the world, and an interpretation to her whole course of teaching and action.

In like manner she has ever put forth, with most energetic distinctness, those other great elementary truths, which either are an explanation of her mission or give a character to her work. She does not teach that human nature is irreclaimable, else wherefore should she be sent? not that it is to be shattered and reversed, but to be extricated, purified, and restored; not that it is a mere mass of evil, but that it has the promise of great things, and even now has a virtue and a praise proper to itself. But in the next place she knows and she preaches that such a restoration, as she aims at effecting in it, must be brought about, not simply through any outward provision of preaching and teaching, even though it be her own, but from a certain inward spiritual power or grace imparted directly from above, and which is in her keeping. She has it in charge to rescue human nature from its misery, but not simply by raising it upon its own level, but by lifting it up to a higher level than its own. She recognizes in it real moral excellence though degraded, but she cannot set it free from earth except by exalting it towards heaven. It was for this end that a renovating grace was put into her hands; and therefore from the nature of the gift, as well as from the reasonableness of the case, she goes on, as a further point, to insist, that all true conversion must begin with the first springs of thought, and to teach that each individual man must be in his own person one whole and perfect temple of God, while he is also one of the living stones which build up a visible religious community. And thus the distinctions between nature and grace, and between outward and inward religion, become two further articles in what I have called the preamble of her divine commission.

Such truths as these she vigorously reiterates, and pertinaciously inflicts upon mankind; as to such she observes no half-measures, no economical reserve, no delicacy or prudence. "Ye must be born again," is the simple, direct form of words which she uses after her Divine Master: "your whole nature must be re-born; your passions, and your affections, and your aims, and your conscience, and your will must all be bathed in a new element, and reconsecrated to your Maker, and, the last not the least, your intellect." It was for repeating these points of her teaching in my own way, that certain passages of one of my Volumes have been brought into the general accusation which has been made against my religious opinions. The writer has said that I was demented if I believed, and unprincipled if I did not believe, my statement that a lazy, ragged, filthy, story-telling beggar-woman, if chaste, sober, cheerful, and religious, had a prospect of heaven, which was absolutely closed to an accomplished statesman, or lawyer, or noble, be he ever so just, upright, generous, honourable and conscientious, unless he had also some portion of the divine Christian grace; yet I should have thought myself defended from criticism by the words which our Lord used to the chief priests, "The publicans and harlots go into the kingdom of God before you."[4] And I was subjected again to the same alternative of imputations, for having ventured to say that consent to an unchaste wish was indefinitely more heinous than any lie viewed apart from its causes, its motives, and its consequences: though a lie, viewed under the limitation of these conditions, is a random utterance, an almost outward act, not directly from the heart, however disgraceful it may be, whereas we have the express words of our Lord to the doctrine that "whoso looketh on a woman to lust after her, hath committed adultery with her already in his heart."[5] On the strength of these texts I have surely as much right to believe in these doctrines as to believe in the doctrine of original sin, or that there is a supernatural revelation, or that a Divine Person suffered, or that punishment is eternal.

Passing now from what I have called the preamble of that grant of power, with which the Church is invested, to that power itself, Infallibility, I make two brief remarks: on the one hand, I am not here determining anything about the essential seat of that power, because that is a question doctrinal, not historical and practical; nor, on the other hand, an I extending the direct subject-matter, over which that power has jurisdiction, beyond religious opinion:—and now as to the power itself.

This power, viewed in its fulness, is as tremendous as the giant evil which has called for it. It claims, when brought into exercise in the legitimate manner, for otherwise of course it is but dormant, to have for itself a sure guidance into the very meaning of every portion of the Divine Message in detail, which was committed by our Lord to His Apostles. It claims to know its own limits, and to decide what it can determine absolutely and what it cannot. It claims moreover, to have a hold upon statements not directly religious, so far as this, to determine whether they indirectly relate to religion, and, according to its own definitive judgment, to pronounce whether or not, in a particular case, they are consistent with revealed truth. It claims to decide magisterially, whether infallibly or not, that such and such statements are or are not prejudicial to the Apostolic *depositum* of faith, in their spirit or in their consequences, and to allow them, or condemn and forbid them, accordingly. It claims to impose silence at will on any matters, or controversies, of doctrine, which on its own *ipse dixit*, it pronounces to be dangerous, or inexpedient, or inopportune. It claims that whatever may be the judgment of Catholics upon such acts, these acts should be received by them with those outward marks of reverence, submission and loyalty, which Englishmen, for instance, pay to the presence of their sovereign, without public criticism on them, as being in their matter inexpedient, or in their manner violent or harsh. And lastly, it claims to have the right of inflicting spiritual punishment, of cutting off from the ordinary channels of the divine life, and of simply excommunicating, those who refuse to submit themselves to its formal declarations. Such is the infallibility lodged in the Catholic Church, viewed in the concrete, as clothed and surrounded by the appendages of its high sovereignty: it is, to repeat what I said above, a supereminent prodigious power sent upon earth to encounter and master a giant evil.

And now, having thus described it, I profess my own absolute submission to its claim.

From *An Essay in Aid of a Grammar of Assent*

[Newman's *Grammar of Assent* was published in 1870. The text is from Ch. 4, paras. 2 and 3.]

... In comparison of the directness and force of the apprehension, which we have of an object, when our assent is to be called real, Notional Assent and Inference seem to be thrown back into one and the same class of intellectual acts, though the former of the two is always an unconditional acceptance of a proposition, and the latter is an acceptance on the condition of an acceptance of its premisses. In Notional Assents as well as in inferring, the mind contemplates its own creations instead of things; in Real, it is directed towards things, represented by the impressions which they have left on the imagination. These images, when assented to, have an influence both on the individual and on society, which mere notions cannot exert.

... I think it best here to confine myself to some instances of the change of Notional Assent into Real.

1. For instance: boys at school look like each other, and pursue the same studies, some of them with greater success than others; but it will sometimes happen, that those who acquitted themselves but poorly in class, when they come into the action of life, and engage in some particular work, which they have already been learning in its theory and with little promise of proficiency, are suddenly found to have what is called an eye for that work—an eye for trade matters, or for engineering, or again for literature—which no one expected from them at school, while they were engaged on notions. Minds of this stamp not only know the received rules of their profession, but enter into them, and even anticipate them, or dispense with them, or substitute other rules instead. And when new questions are opened, and arguments are drawn up on one side and the other in long array, they with a natural ease and promptness form their views and give their decision, as if they had no need to reason, from their clear apprehension of the lie and issue of the whole matter in dispute, as if it were drawn out in a map

before them. These are the reformers, systematizers, inventors, in various departments of thought, speculative and practical; in education, in administration, in social and political matters, in science. Such men are not infallible; however great their powers, they sometimes fall into great errors, in their own special department, while the second-rate men who go by rule come to sound and safe conclusions. Images need not be true; but I am illustrating what vividness of apprehension is, and what is the strength of belief consequent upon it.

2. Again:—twenty years ago the Duke of Wellington wrote his celebrated letter on the subject of the national defences.[6] His authority gave it an immediate circulation among all classes of the community; none questioned what he said, nor as if taking his words on faith merely, but as intellectually recognizing their truth; yet so few could be said to see or feel that truth. His letter lay, so to say, upon the pure intellect of the national mind, and nothing for a time came of it. But eleven years afterwards, after his death, the anger of the French colonels with us, after the attempt upon Louis Napoleon's life, transferred its facts to the charge of the imagination. Then forthwith the national assent became in various ways an operative principle, especially in its promotion of the volunteer movement. The Duke, having a special eye for military matters, had realized the state of things from the first; but it took a course of years to impress upon the public mind an assent to his warning deeper and more energetic than the reception it is accustomed to give to a clever article in a newspaper or a review.

3. And so generally: great truths, practical or ethical, float on the surface of society, admitted by all, valued by few, exemplifying the poet's adage, "Probitas laudatur et alget,"[7] until changed circumstances, accident, or the continual pressure of their advocates, force them upon its attention. The iniquity, for instance, of the slave-trade ought to have been acknowledged by all men from the first; it was acknowledged by many, but it needed an organized agitation, with tracts and speeches innumerable, so to affect the imagination of men as to make their acknowledgment of that iniquitousness operative.

In like manner, when Mr. Wilberforce, after succeeding in the slave question, urged the Duke of Wellington to use his great influence in discountenancing duelling, he could only get from him in answer, "A relic of barbarism, Mr. Wilberforce;" as if he accepted a notion without realizing a fact: at length, the growing intelligence of the community, and the shock inflicted upon it by the tragical circumstances of a particular duel,[8] were fatal to that barbarism. The governing classes were roused from their dreamy acquiescence in an abstract truth, and recognized the duty of giving it practical expression.

4. Let us consider, too, how differently young and old are affected by the words of some classic author, such as Homer or Horace. Passages, which to a boy are but rhetorical commonplaces, neither better nor worse than a hundred others which any clever writer might supply, which he gets by heart and thinks very fine, and imitates, as he thinks, successfully, in his own flowing versification, at length come home to him, when long years have passed, and he has had experience of life, and pierce him, as if he had never before known them, with their sad earnestness and vivid exactness. Then he comes to understand how it is that lines, the birth of some chance morning or evening at an Ionian festival, or among the Sabine hills, have lasted generation after generation, for thousands of years, with a power over the mind, and a charm, which the current literature of his own day, with all its obvious advantages, is utterly unable to rival. Perhaps this is the reason of the medieval opinion about Virgil, as if a prophet or magician; his single words and phrases, his pathetic half lines, giving utterance, as the voice of Nature herself, to that pain and weariness, yet hope of better things, which is the experience of her children in every time.

5. And what the experience of the world effects for the illustration of classical authors, that office the religious sense, carefully cultivated, fulfils towards Holy Scripture. To the devout and spiritual, the Divine Word speaks of things, not merely of notions. And, again, to the disconsolate, the tempted, the perplexed, the suffering, there comes, by means of their very trials, an enlargement of thought, which enables them to

see in it what they never saw before. Henceforth there is to them a reality in its teachings, which they recognize as an argument, and the best of arguments, for its divine origin. Hence the practice of meditation on the Sacred Text, so highly thought of by Catholics. Reading, as we do, the Gospels from our youth up, we are in danger of becoming so familiar with them as to be dead to their force, and to view them as a mere history. The purpose, then, of meditation is to realize them; to make the facts which they relate stand out before our minds as objects, such as may be appropriated by a faith as living as the imagination which apprehends them.

It is obvious to refer to the unworthy use made of the more solemn parts of the sacred volume by the mere popular preacher. His very mode of reading, whether warnings or prayers, is as if he thought them to be little more than fine writing, poetical in sense, musical in sound, and worthy of inspiration. The most awful truths are to him but sublime or beautiful conceptions, and are adduced and used by him, in season and out of season, for his own purposes, for embellishing his style or rounding his periods. But let his heart at length be ploughed by some keen grief or deep anxiety, and Scripture is a new book to him. This is the change which so often takes place in what is called religious conversion, and it is a change so far simply for the better, by whatever infirmity or error it is in the particular case accompanied. And it is strikingly suggested to us, to take a saintly example, in the confession of the patriarch Job, when he contrasts his apprehension of the Almighty before and after his afflictions. He says he had indeed a true apprehension of the Divine Attributes before them as well as after, but with the trial came a great change in the character of that apprehension:—"With the hearing of the ear," he says, "I have heard Thee, but now mine eye seeth Thee; therefore I reprehend myself and do penance in dust and ashes."[9]

Let these instances suffice of Real Assent in its relation to Notional; they lead me to make three remarks in further illustration of its character.

1. The fact of the distinctness of the images which are required for real assent, is no warrant for the existence of the

objects which those images represent. A proposition, be it ever so keenly apprehended, may be true or may be false. If we simply put aside all inferential information, such as is derived from testimony, from general belief, from the concurrence of the senses, from common sense, or otherwise, we have no right to consider a fact guaranteed to us by the mere strength of our mental impression of it. Hence the proverb, "Fronti nulla fides."[10] An image, with the characters of perfect veracity and faithfulness, may indeed be as a distinct, eloquent object presented before the mind (or, as it is sometimes called, the "objectum internum", or the "subject-object"); but, nevertheless, there may be no external reality in the case, corresponding to it, in spite of its impressiveness. One of the most remarkable instances of this fallacious impressiveness is the illusion which possesses the minds of able men, those especially who are exercised in physical investigations, in favour of the inviolability of the laws of nature. Philosophers of the school of Hume discard the very supposition of miracles, and scornfully refuse to hear evidence in their behalf in given instances, from their intimate experience of physical order and of the ever-recurring sequence of cause and effect. Their imagination usurps the functions of reason, and they cannot bring themselves even to entertain as a notion (and this is all that they are asked to do) a thought contrary to that vivid impression which the hourly sight of uniformity in nature has so deeply fixed in their minds.

Yet it is plain, and I shall take it for granted here, that when I assent to a proposition, I ought to have some more legitimate reason for doing so, than the brilliancy of the image of which that proposition is the expression. That I have no experience of a thing happening except in one way, is a cause of the intensity of my assent, if I assent, but not the reason of my assenting. In saying this, I am not disposed to deny the presence in some men of an idiosyncratic sagacity, which really and rightly sees reasons in impressions which common men cannot see, and is secured from the peril of confusing truth with make-believe; but this is genius, and beyond rule. I grant too, of course, that accidentally impressiveness does in matter of fact, as in the instance which I have been giving, constitute the motive principle of belief; for the mind is ever exposed to the danger of being carried away by the liveliness of its conceptions, to the sacrifice of good sense and conscientious caution, and the greater and the more rare are its gifts, the greater is the risk of swerving from the line of reason and duty; but here I am not speaking of transgressions of rule any more than of exceptions to it, but of the normal constitution of our minds, and of the natural and rightful effect of acts of the imagination upon us, and this is, not to create assent, but to intensify it.

2. Next, Assent, however strong, and accorded to images however vivid, is not therefore necessarily practical. Strictly speaking, it is not imagination that causes action; but hope and fear, likes and dislikes, appetite, passion, affection, the stirrings of selfishness and self-love. What imagination does for us is to find a means of stimulating those motive powers: and it does so by providing a supply of objects strong enough to stimulate them. The thought of honour, glory, duty, self-aggrandisement, gain, or on the other hand of the Divine Goodness, future reward, eternal life, perseveringly dwelt upon, leads us along a course of action corresponding to itself, but only in case there be that in our minds which is congenial to it. However, when there is that preparation of mind, the thought does lead to the act. Hence it is that the fact of a proposition being accepted with a real assent is accidentally an earnest of that proposition being carried out into effect, and the imagination may be said in some sense to be of a practical nature, inasmuch as it leads to practice indirectly by the action of its object upon the affections.

3. There is a third remark suggested by the view which I have been taking of real assents, viz. that they are of a personal character, each individual having his own, and being known by them. It is otherwise with notions; notional apprehension is in itself an ordinary act of our common nature. All of us have the power of abstraction, and can be taught either to make or to enter into the same abstractions; and thus to co-operate in the establishment of a common measure between mind and mind. And, though for one and all of us to assent to the same notions is a further step, as requiring the adoption of a common stand-point of principle and judgment, yet this too depends in

good measure on certain logical processes of thought, with which we are all familiar, and on facts which we all take for granted. But we cannot make sure, for ourselves or others, of real apprehension and assent, because we have to secure first the images which are their objects, and these are often peculiar and special. They depend on personal experience; and the experience of one man is not the experience of another. Real assent, then, as the experience which it presupposes, is an act of the individual, and, as such, thwarts rather than promotes the intercourse of man with man. It shuts itself up, as it were in its own home, or at least it is its own witness and its own standard; and, as in the instances above given, it cannot be reckoned on, anticipated, accounted for, inasmuch as it is the accident of the individual.

... Real Assents ... are sometimes called beliefs, convictions, certainties; and, as given to moral objects, they are perhaps as rare as they are powerful. Till we have them, in spite of a full apprehension and assent in the field of notions, we have no intellectual moorings, and are at the mercy of impulses, fancies, and wandering lights, whether as regards personal conduct, social and political action, or religion. These beliefs, be they true or false in the particular case, form the mind out of which they grow, and impart to it a seriousness and manliness which inspires in other minds a confidence in its views, and is one secret of persuasiveness and influence in the public stage of the world. They create, as the case may be, heroes and saints, great leaders, statesmen, preachers, and reformers, the pioneers of discovery in science, visionaries, fanatics, knight-errants, demagogues, and adventurers. They have given to the world men of one idea, of immense energy, of adamantine will, of revolutionary power. They kindle sympathies between man and man, and knit together the innumerable units which constitute a race and a nation. They become the principle of its political existence; they impart to it homogeneity of thought and fellowship of purpose. They have given form to the medieval theocracy and to the Mahometan superstition; they are now the life both of "Holy Russia", and of that freedom of speech and action which is the special boast of Englishmen.

It appears from what has been said, that, though Real
Assent is not intrinsically operative, it accidentally and
indirectly affects practice. It is in itself an intellectual act,
of which the object is presented to it by the imagination; and
though the pure intellect does not lead to action, nor the
imagination either, yet the imagination has the means, which
pure intellect has not, of stimulating those powers of the mind
from which action proceeds. Real Assent, then, or Belief, as it
may be called, viewed in itself, that is, simply as Assent, does
not lead to action; but the images in which it lives, representing as they do the concrete, have the power of the concrete
upon the affections and passions, and by means of these
indirectly become operative. Still this practical influence is not
invariable, nor to be relied on; for, in a particular case, given
images may have no tendency to affect given minds, or to
excite them to action. Thus, a philosopher or a poet may
vividly realize the brilliant rewards of military genius or of
eloquence, without wishing either to be a commander or an
orator. However, on the whole, broadly contrasting Belief
with Notional Assent and with Inference, we shall not be very
wrong, with this explanation, in pronouncing that acts of
Notional Assent and of Inference do not affect our conduct,
and acts of Belief, that is, of Real Assent, do (not necessarily,
but do) affect it.

. . . Let me . . . be allowed here to say, that, while Assent, or
Belief, presupposes some apprehension of the things believed,
Inference requires no apprehension of the things inferred;
that in consequence, Inference is necessarily concerned with
surfaces and aspects; that it begins with itself, and ends with
itself; that it does not reach as far as facts; that it is employed
upon formulas; that, as far as it takes real objects of whatever
kind into account, such as motive and actions, character and
conduct, art, science, taste, morals, religion, it deals with
them, not as they are, but simply in its own line, as materials
of argument or inquiry, that they are to it nothing more than
major and minor premisses and conclusions. Belief, on the other
hand, being concerned with things concrete, not abstract,
which variously excite the mind from their moral and imaginative properties, has for its object, not only directly what is true,

but inclusively what is beautiful, useful, admirable, heroic; objects which kindle devotion, rouse the passions, and attach the affections; and thus it leads the way to actions of every kind, to the establishment of principles, and the formation of character, and is thus again intimately connected with what is individual and personal.

I insisted on this marked distinction between Beliefs on the one hand, and Notional Assents and Inferences on the other, many years ago in words which it will be to my purpose to use now. I quote them, because, over and above their appositeness in this place, they present the doctrine which I have been enforcing, from a second point of view, and with a freshness and force which I cannot now command, and, moreover, (though they are my own, nevertheless, from the length of time which has elapsed since their publication) almost with the cogency of an independent testimony.

They occur in a protest which I was asked to write in February, 1841, in the form of letters addressed to the Editor of the *Times* Newspaper, against a dangerous doctrine maintained, as I considered, by two very eminent men of that day, now no more—Lord Brougham and Sir Robert Peel.[11] That doctrine was to the effect that the claims of religion could be secured and sustained in the mass of men, and in particular in the lower classes of society, by acquaintance with literature and physical science, and that, through the instrumentality of Mechanics' Institutes and Reading Rooms, to the serious disparagement, as it seemed to me, of direct Christian instruction. In one of these letters is found the passage which follows, and which, with whatever differences in terminology, and hardihood of assertion, befitting the circumstances of its publication, nay, as far as words go, inaccuracy of theological statement, suitably illustrates the subject here under discussion. It runs thus:—

"People say to me, that it is but a dream to suppose that Christianity should regain the organic power in human society which once it possessed. I cannot help that; I never said it could. I am not a politician; I am proposing no measures, but exposing a fallacy and resisting a pretence. Let Benthamism reign, if men have no aspirations; but do not tell them to be romantic and then solace them with 'glory': do not attempt by philosophy what once was done by religion. The ascendancy of faith may be impracticable, but the reign of knowledge is incomprehensible. The problem for statesmen of this age is how to educate the masses, and literature and science cannot give the solution.

"Science gives us the grounds or premises from which religious truths are to be inferred; but it does not set about inferring them, much less does it reach the inference—that is not its province. It brings before us phenomena, and it leaves us, if we will, to call them works of design, wisdom, or benevolence; and further still, if we will, to proceed to confess an Intelligent Creator. We have to take its facts, and to give them a meaning, and to draw our own conclusions from them.

"First comes knowledge, then a view, then reasoning, and then belief. This is why science has so little of a religious tendency; deductions have no power of persuasion. The heart is commonly reached, not through the reason, but through the imagination, by means of direct impressions, by the testimony of facts and events, by history, by description. Persons influence us, voices melt us, looks subdue us, deeds inflame us. Many a man will live and die upon a dogma: no man will be a martyr for a conclusion. A conclusion is but an opinion; it is not a thing which *is*, but which we are '*quite sure about*'; and it has often been observed, that we never say we are sure and certain without implying that we doubt. To say that a thing *must* be, is to admit that it *may not* be. No one, I say, will die for his own calculations; he dies for realities. This is why a literary religion is so little to be depended upon; it looks well in fair weather; but its doctrines are opinions, and, when called to suffer for them, it slips them between its folios, or burns them at its hearth. And this again is the secret of the distrust and raillery with which moralists have been so commonly visited. They say and do not. Why? Because they are contemplating the fitness of things, and they live by the square, when they should be realizing their high maxims in the concrete. Now Sir Robert Peel thinks better of natural history, chemistry, and astronomy than of such ethics; but these too, what are they more than divinity *in posse*? He protests against '*controversial divinity*': is *inferential* much better?

"I have no confidence, then, in philosophers who cannot help being religious, and are Christians by implication. They sit at home, and reach forward to distances which astonish us; but they hit without grasping, and are sometimes as confident about shadows as about realities. They have worked out by a calculation the lie of a country which they never saw, and mapped it by means of a gazetteer; and, like blind men, though they can put a stranger on his way, they cannot walk straight themselves, and do not feel it quite their business to walk at all.

"Logic makes but a sorry rhetoric with the multitude; first shoot round corners, and you may not despair of converting by a syllogism. Tell men to gain notions of a Creator from His works, and, if they were to set about it (which nobody does) they would be jaded and wearied by the labyrinth they were tracing. Their minds would be gorged and surfeited by the logical operation. Logicians are more set upon concluding rightly, than on right conclusions. They cannot see the end for the process. Few men have that power of mind which may hold fast and firmly a variety of thoughts. We ridicule 'men of one idea'; but a great many of us are born to be such, and we should be happier if we knew it. To most men argument makes the point in hand only more doubtful, and considerably less impressive. After all, man is not a reasoning animal; he is a seeing, feeling, contemplating, acting animal. He is influenced by what is direct and precise. It is very well to freshen our impressions and convictions from physics, but to create them we must go elsewhere. Sir Robert Peel 'never can think it possible that a mind can be so constituted, that, after being familiarized with the wonderful discoveries which have been made in every part of experimental science, it can retire from such contemplations without more enlarged conceptions of God's providence, and a higher reverence for His Name.' If he speaks of religious mind, he perpetrates a truism; if of irreligious, he insinuates a paradox.

"Life is not long enough for a religion of inferences; we shall never have done beginning, if we determine to begin with proof. We shall ever be laying our foundations; we shall turn theology into evidences, and divines into textuaries. We shall never get at our first principles. Resolve to believe nothing, and you must prove your proofs and analyze your elements, sinking farther and farther, and finding 'in the lowest depth a lower deep,' till you come to the broad bosom of scepticism. I would rather be bound to defend the reasonableness of assuming that Christianity is true, than to demonstrate a moral governance from the physical world. Life is for action. If we insist on proofs for every thing, we shall never come to action: to act you must assume, and that assumption is faith.

"Let no one suppose, that in saying this I am maintaining that all proofs are equally difficult, and all propositions equally debatable. Some assumptions are greater than others, and some doctrines involve postulates larger than others, and more numerous. I only say, that impressions lead to action, and that reasonings lead from it. Knowledge of premises, and inferences upon them,—this is not to *live*. It is very well as a matter of liberal curiosity and of philosophy to analyze our modes of thought: but let this come second, and when there is leisure for it, and then our examinations will in many ways even be subservient to action. But if we commence with scientific knowledge and argumentative proof, or lay any great stress upon it as the basis of personal Christianity, or attempt to make man moral and religious by libraries and museums, let us in consistency take chemists for our cooks, and mineralogists for our masons.

"Now I wish to state all this as matter of fact, to be judged by the candid testimony of any persons whatever. Why we are so constituted that faith, not knowledge or argument, is our principle of action, is a question with which I have nothing to do; but I think it is a fact, and, if it be such, we must resign ourselves to it as best we may, unless we take refuge in the intolerable paradox, that the mass of men are created for nothing, and are meant to leave life as they entered it.

"So well has this practically been understood in all ages of the world, that no religion yet has been a religion of physics or of philosophy. It has ever been synonymous with revelation. It never has been a deduction from what we know; it has ever been an assertion of what we are to believe. It has never lived in a conclusion; it has ever been a message, a history, or a vision. No legislator or priest ever dreamed of educating our moral nature by science or by argument. There is no difference here between true religion and pretended. Moses was instructed not to reason from the creation, but to work miracles. Christianity is a history supernatural, and almost scenic: it tells us what its Author is, by telling us what He has done . . .

"Lord Brougham himself has recognized the force of this principle. He has not left his philosophical religion to argument; he has committed it to the keeping of the imagination. Why should he depict a great republic of letters, and an intellectual pantheon, except that he feels that instances and patterns, not logical reasonings, are the living conclusions which alone have a hold over the affections or can form the character?"

LESLIE STEPHEN

From *An Agnostic's Apology and other Essays*

[The text is from Stephen's 'The Scepticism of Believers', the second essay in his *An Agnostic's Apology*, 1893, which is a revised and expanded version of his essay, 'The Scepticism of Believers', in *The Fortnightly Review*, N.S., XXII (September, 1877).]

. . . Somehow or other, metaphysicians have a wonderful facility for deducing the same conclusions from the most opposite premisses. That is, perhaps, because metaphysics is not really what it professes to be, the exposition of first principles, from which the inferior truths are deducible, but an attempt to give explicitly the logic of the processes already employed by the commonsense of mankind. Professing to make no assumption, it really assumes all previous knowledge. At any rate, we have the comfort of believing that ethical rules have little dependence upon theories of moral philosophy. I only mean to urge that the assumptions of theology in general, even if they be granted, land us in inextricable labyrinths of dialectics. No doctrine seems to me to be less tenable than that which asserts that morality requires a theological foundation. To connect ethics with theology of the lower type is, in fact, to define it as obedience to the will of an arbitrary being, who may be the reflection of some barbarous ideal, or who may be a metaphysical entity indistinguishable from the abstract Nature. It is a long way from crude anthropomorphism to that bloodless spectre of a theological morality which appears, for example, in the 'categorical imperative' of Kant. Kant's moral law is a command which survives mysteriously when the giver of the command has evaporated. In their anxiety to get rid of the 'expedient' and 'empirical', philosophers remove the law to a region where it has no relation to facts. It becomes mere 'law' in the abstract, of which it is the only condition that it shall not be self-contradictory, and which is, therefore, equally applicable to any set of rules whatever. The essence of morality becomes merely a logical formula, and is fit only for a state of things in which fact can be woven out of syllogism, and the loom at which the universe is wrought can be worked in a professor's lecture-room. Such philosophy, though it still calls itself theistic, is the very antithesis of the old doctrine which goes by the same name. In the primitive stage, morality is the law given by a particular being known under definite historical conditions. To get rid of the arbitrary and empirical element we substitute a being who inhabits the region of the inconceivable, and of whom we cannot think directly without falling into hopeless antinomies. Instead of the arbitrary and particular, we have the hopelessly vague and unintelligible. The true method of escape is surely different. Morality must be represented as dependent, not upon the authority of a particular person, invisible or otherwise, nor relegated to the region where we are hopelessly suspended in the inane, but based upon a knowledge of the concrete constitution of human nature and society.

To make a moral law otherwise than from a study of human life will be possible when it is possible on the same terms to construct a physiology and a system of therapeutics; and meanwhile it remains in ethics what the attempt to square the circle is in the history of mathematics. The charge against the Agnostic, that he weakens his belief in morality because he brings it within the sphere of experience, is just as true as would be the same charge against the man of science, who appeals to facts instead of evolving the facts from the depths of his consciousness.

The theologian occasionally shows a leaning to such transcendental theories, though he ought to know that their inevitable catastrophe is in a reduction of theology to pantheism. But the theology which can appeal to the imagination remains at some intermediate stage between the purely anthropomorphic and the purely metaphysical. The doctrine of another world of which, as of all matters of fact, the absolute system of morality must be independent is still for him the pivot of morals. It is in rejecting this part of the doctrine that the 'scepticism' or positive unbelief of the Agnostic is most keenly denounced. Once more, which is the sceptic? The early Christians, like the modern Socialists, dreamed of a speedy advent of the millennium; a faith flushed with excessive confidence, and capable of transforming, if not of regenerating, society, naturally generates such visions. Modern Socialists generally assign the next century as the period at which we shall all have achieved Utopia. The Christian held that his generation would not pass away before the Messiah was revealed in supernatural glory. The belief was in harmony with his whole theory of the world. His hopes naturally pointed to dreamland—to a world of catastrophes and surprises Everything was to be changed in a moment, in the twinkling of an eye, at the sound of a supernatural trumpet. The true believers were to be caught up into heaven, and set upon the thrones provided for them, and the unbelievers to be cast into the sea of fire and brimstone. The world had been, and might be again, the scene of tremendous and spasmodic convulsions, to be anticipated only in virtue of supernatural revelation. God had sent His Son upon earth to reveal the one true light and suddenly to establish a Divine kingdom. Ages have passed, and faith has grown dim, and the prophecies and revelations have had to be twisted and spiritualised, and have slowly sunk into enigmas to exercise the fertile ingenuity of learned folly. The belief in the Second Advent has faded into inanity, although, like certain men of Galilee, some may still stand gazing into heaven, forgetting the solid earth at their feet. If by the faith which is to save the world you still mean faith in the supernatural, you still hold that faith comes by revelation, or by an inexplicable means upon incalculable occasions. And if the only light which can lighten the world shines at the arbitrary bidding of an inscrutable Being, its occultations are equally mysterious. They are workings of the Devil, whose very existence in a God-governed world is a mystery. Friday asked Robinson Crusoe, why does not God kill the Devil? and neither Robinson Crusoe nor anybody else has hitherto been able to answer the question. The spread of infidel opinions is, more or less, supposed to be the work of the Devil. But why the Devil should suddenly get into the pulpit, and why his preaching should be so successful, are still inscrutable mysteries. The showing forth of the light and its obscuration equally belong to the region where the human intellect has no footing. To the Agnostic, even the spread of an error is part of the wide-world process by which we stumble into mere approximations to truth. It is explicable from the necessities of the case that partial illusions should arise at each successive stage of our onward movement. But if the old Faith be absolutely true, and also dependent on the catastrophe of a revelation, the whole process of the evolution of truth becomes hopelessly unintelligible. The new ideas which stir the intellectual movement of the world are regarded with suspicion, for God may again be leaving the field to the Devil as it was left of old. The corruption of our nature may be once more showing itself and getting the upper hand. Increase of knowledge shakes the old creeds, and increase of wealth shakes the old structure. The sacred authority decays, and the orthodox believer has to choose between equivocating and straining and twisting the old phrases to a new meaning, or in closer conformity with the logic of his belief, announcing that the old world is once more going to the devil, and that the evil principle, disguised as an angel of intellectual light, is seducing us to close our eyes to all that is elevating and purifying.

This, as I take it, is the scepticism which really underlies the theological belief. The belief in progress has been transferred to his opponent, for the belief in progress is the popular version of the doctrine of evolution. The doctrine of evolution is the uncompromising application to all phenomena of history and thought of a genuine belief in causation, or of an expulsion of the arbitrary. The theologian, unless he elects to become a pantheist, must struggle against a mode of thought which runs counter to his fundamental assumptions. The scientific reasoner holds by the continuity and uniformity of Nature; theology accepts a dualism which implies catastrophe and the interference of a radically unknowable factor. Therefore, the belief in progress which substitutes a development of natural forces for a Second Advent, and foresight based upon knowledge of facts for a miraculous prediction of the mysterious, is essentially incongruous to theology. The theologian abandons the only clue which can lead us to some foresight here in the attempt to find a certainty in the clouds. Faith in the beyond really implies scepticism as to the present, and those who most fervently assert their belief in an omnipotent and perfect Governor of the world are, therefore, those who can speak most bitterly and with the least hopefulness of the world which He governs. They can wrap themselves in dreams of heaven, and see the blind masses plunging, possessed of devils, into the depths of destruction.

The belief in progress has its own delusions. The Socialist may be doomed to a disappointment like that which awaited the early Christian. The Son of Man did not appear in the clouds, and I fear that it will be some time before the world will be freed from all cruelty and injustice. Yet the Socialist dream has the advantage that it points to an end not by its nature unobtainable, and is therefore capable of being pursued with some hopes of slow approximation. We must, perhaps, admit that even progress cannot be infinite. After some millions of years the earth, like its satellite, must become a wandering graveyard, and men and their dreams will in that case vanish together. Our hopes, like most things, must be finite. We must be content if they are enough to stimulate to action. We must believe in a future harvest enough to encourage us to sow, and hold that honest and unselfish work will leave the world rather better off than we found it. Perhaps this is not a very sublime prospect. Life, says the most candid of theologians[12]—and he certainly tried to prove it—is, perhaps, but a poor thing. Yet it is tolerable so long as one can believe that our fellow-men have enough of healthy and noble instinct to secure a steady, if a chequered, social growth; that their instincts do not depend upon knowledge of the unknowable, and will survive our petty systems founded upon irrational guesswork. It is something to feel a confidence, based upon experience, that we have nothing to fear from unlimited inquiry and thoroughgoing destruction of fictions, and that we may hope, not merely for an increased power of man over Nature, but for a higher, more rational, social order, and more widely extended sympathies. Extension of knowledge implies also a more accurate appreciation of the conditions of human welfare and a more intelligent cultivation of the emotions and sympathies on which it depends. We can build without fearing that any infidel Samson will suddenly crush the pillars of our temple. We cannot flatter ourselves that our personal stake in the universe is more unlimited in regard to the future than in regard to the past and the distant; but that reflection may be rather consoling than otherwise to some who fancy that they and the universe will have had about enough of each other in threescore years and ten. That may be a matter of taste; but in any case, when we see daily with more clearness that all intellectual progress involves a systematic interpretation of experience and a resolute exclusion of all imaginary *a priori* data, it is desirable that we should look in the direction in which alone experience can enlighten us, and accept realities in exchange for dreams. Scepticism about the shifting phantasmagoria of theology is less paralysing than the scepticism which, when it speaks frankly, rejects realities, and when it does not, attempts to mystify us by a jargon which hopelessly confounds the two.

NOTES

1. Ezekiel, ii, 9–10.
2. Ephesians, ii, 12.
3. In Newman's *Difficulties of Anglicans* (1850), p. 199, Lecture VIII.
4. Matthew, xxi, 31. Cf. *Difficulties of Anglicans*, p. 207. The 'writer' was Bishop Samuel Wilberforce (1805–1873).
5. Matthew, v, 28.
6. In October, 1847, Wellington pressed Lord John Russell to raise a regular army of 50,000 men against the danger of French invasion. A confidential letter of his on this subject to the Inspector-General of Fortifications reached the press.
7. Juvenal, i, 74. 'Honesty is praised and grows cold'.
8. After the Fawcett-Monro duel of 1843, the Commons debated the report of the association for the suppression of duelling. In 1844 the articles of war were amended to include the cashiering of officers who promoted or fought a duel.
9. Job, xlii, 5–6.
10. 'Have no trust in the expression'.
11. See *The Tamworth Reading Room* (1841), revised from letters in *The Times*, 5–27 February 1841, by 'Catholicus'. The extracts quoted by Newman are slightly altered from the 1841 volume-version.
12. Joseph Butler, in his *The Analogy of Religion* (1736), Part II, Ch. 8, comments that the epithet poor may be applied 'to great part or the whole of human life'.

Matthew Arnold

[Matthew Arnold (1822–1888) was the most important Victorian critic of literature and society. In his various employments as poet, inspector of schools, lecturer and essayist, Arnold worked to raise the level of cultural debate. He saw it as his task, firstly, to defend the status of the humanities against the denigration of Utilitarian, scientific and other narrowly-based writers, and secondly, to show how the wide-ranging intelligence, ironic as well as serious, which he associated with the practice of criticism, could be used to cut through the accepted cant of the day, the complacency with material progress, the anomalies, the petty feuds and the prejudices. In *Culture and Anarchy*, culture is the antidote to intellectual and social anarchy, a strongly unifying force expressing the universal aspirations of humanity. In his survey of current political and religious extremes, as in his satiric treatment of the three social classes, Arnold draws attention to our basis of common humanity, the 'general *humane* spirit' which shuns class-spirit and other divisive forces, which seeks individual perfection, and 'because men are all members of one great whole' seeks to make culture, or the 'study of perfection', the common pursuit. If he does echo Carlyle's critique of mechanism, it is without Carlyle's stridency or growing infatuation with autocracy; if his appeal to ideals of self-perfection reminds us of Newman, it is made without recourse to Newman's theological solution to the doubts and difficulties of the age; a solution, as Arnold found it, 'which, to speak frankly, is impossible.']

From *Culture and Anarchy*

[Matthew Arnold's *Culture and Anarchy* developed out of an Oxford lecture of 1867, 'Culture and its Enemies'. This was published in *The Cornhill Magazine* in the same year and was followed by five other articles under the title of 'Anarchy and Authority'. In 1869 the six articles, slightly revised, were published, with an introduction, as *Culture and Anarchy: an essay in political and social criticism*. In 1875

136

Arnold revised the work, adding chapter-headings and cutting out some topical and personal allusions. The text of the first and third chapters, given below, is taken from this second edition, to avoid the density of contemporary allusions.]

Sweetness and Light

The disparagers of culture make its motive curiosity; sometimes indeed, they make its motive mere exclusiveness and vanity. The culture which is supposed to plume itself on a smattering of Greek and Latin is a culture which is begotten by nothing so intellectual as curiosity; it is valued either out of sheer vanity and ignorance, or else as an engine of social and class distinction, separating its holder, like a badge or title, from other people who have not got it. No serious man would call this *culture*, or attach any value to it, as culture, at all. To find the real ground for the very differing estimate which serious people will set upon culture, we must find some motive for culture in the terms of which may lie a real ambiguity; and such a motive the word *curiosity* gives us.

I have before now pointed out that we English do not, like the foreigners, use this word in a good sense as well as in a bad sense. With us the word is always used in a somewhat disapproving sense. A liberal and intelligent eagerness about the things of the mind may be meant by a foreigner when he speaks of curiosity, but with us the word always conveys a certain notion of frivolous and unedifying activity. In the *Quarterly Review*, some little time ago, was an estimate of the celebrated French critic, M. Sainte-Beuve,[1] and a very inadequate estimate it in my judgement was. And its inadequacy consisted chiefly in this: that in our English way it left out of sight the double sense really involved in the word *curiosity*, thinking enough was said to stamp M. Sainte-Beuve with blame if it was said that he was impelled in his operations as a critic by curiosity, and omitting either to perceive that M. Sainte-Beuve himself, and many other people with him, would consider that this was praiseworthy and not blameworthy, or to point out why it ought really to be accounted worthy of blame and not of praise. For as there is a curiosity about intellectual matters which is futile, and merely a disease, so there is certainly a curiosity,—a desire after the things of the mind simply for their own sakes and for the pleasure of seeing them as they are,—which is, in an intelligent being, natural and laudable. Nay, and the very desire to see things as they are, implies a balance and regulation of mind which is not often attained without fruitful effort, and which is the very opposite of the blind and diseased impulse of mind which is what we mean to blame when we blame curiosity. Montesquieu says:—'The first motive which ought to impel us to study is the desire to augment the excellence of our nature, and to render an intelligent being yet more intelligent.'[2] This is the true ground to assign for the genuine scientific passion, however manifested, and for culture, viewed simply as a fruit of this passion; and it is a worthy ground, even though we let the term *curiosity* stand to describe it.

But there is of culture another view, in which not solely the scientific passion, the sheer desire to see things as they are, natural and proper in an intelligent being, appears as the ground of it. There is a view in which all the love of our neighbour, the impulses towards action, help, and beneficence, the desire for removing human error, clearing human confusion, and diminishing human misery, the noble aspiration to leave the world better and happier than we found it,— motives eminently such as are called social,—come in as part of the grounds of culture, and the main and pre-eminent part. Culture is then properly described not as having its origin in curiosity, but as having its origin in the love of perfection; it is *a study of perfection*. It moves by the force, not merely or primarily of the scientific passion for pure knowledge, but also of the moral and social passion for doing good. As, in the first view of it, we took for its worthy motto Montesquieu's words: 'To render an intelligent being yet more intelligent!' so, in the second view of it, there is no better motto which it can have than these words of Bishop Wilson: 'To make reason and the will of God prevail!'[3]

Only, whereas the passion for doing good is apt to be over-hasty in determining what reason and the will of God say, because its turn is for acting rather than thinking and it wants

to be beginning to act; and whereas it is apt to take its own
conceptions, which proceed from its own state of development
and share in all the imperfections and immaturities of this, for
a basis of action; what distinguishes culture is, that it is possessed by the scientific passion, as well as by the passion of
doing good; that it demands worthy notions of reason and the
will of God, and does not readily suffer its own crude conceptions to substitute themselves for them. And knowing that no
action or institution can be salutary and stable which are
not based on reason and the will of God, it is not so bent on
acting and instituting, even with the great aim of diminishing
human error and misery ever before its thoughts, but that it
can remember that acting and instituting are of little use,
unless we know how and what we ought to act and to institute.

This culture is more interesting and more far-reaching than
that other, which is founded solely on the scientific passion for
knowing. But it needs times of faith and ardour, times when
the intellectual horizon is opening and widening all round us,
to flourish in. And is not the close and bounded intellectual
horizon within which we have long lived and moved now
lifting up, and are not new lights finding free passage to shine
in upon us? For a long time there was no passage for them to
make their way in upon us, and then it was of no use to think
of adapting the world's action to them. Where was the hope
of making reason and the will of God prevail among people
who had a routine which they had christened reason and the
will of God, in which they were inextricably bound, and beyond
which they had no power of looking? But now the iron force
of adhesion to the old routine,—social, political, religious,—
has wonderfully yielded; the iron force of exclusion of all
which is new has wonderfully yielded. The danger now is, not
that people should obstinately refuse to allow anything but
their old routine to pass for reason and the will of God, but
either that they should allow some novelty or other to pass for
these too easily, or else that they should underrate the importance of them altogether, and think it enough to follow
action for its own sake, without troubling themselves to make
reason and the will of God prevail therein. Now, then, is the
moment for culture to be of service, culture which believes in

making reason and the will of God prevail, believes in perfection, is the study and pursuit of perfection, and is no longer debarred, by a rigid invincible exclusion of whatever is new, from getting acceptance for its ideas, simply because they are new.

The moment this view of culture is seized, the moment it is regarded not solely as the endeavour to see things as they are, to draw towards a knowledge of the universal order which seems to be intended and aimed at in the world, and which it is a man's happiness to go along with or his misery to go counter to,—to learn, in short, the will of God,—the moment, I say, culture is considered not merely as the endeavour to *see* and *learn* this, but as the endeavour, also, to make it *prevail*, the moral, social, and beneficent character of culture becomes manifest. The mere endeavour to see and learn the truth for our own personal satisfaction is indeed a commencement for making it prevail, a preparing the way for this, which always serves this, and is wrongly, therefore, stamped with blame absolutely in itself and not only in its caricature and degeneration. But perhaps it has got stamped with blame, and disparaged with the dubious title of curiosity, because in comparison with this wider endeavour of such great and plain utility it looks selfish, petty, and unprofitable.

And religion, the greatest and most important of the efforts by which the human race has manifested its impulse to perfect itself,—religion, that voice of the deepest human experience,—does not only enjoin and sanction the aim which is the great aim of culture, the aim of setting ourselves to ascertain what perfection is and to make it prevail; but also, in determining generally in what human perfection consists, religion comes to a conclusion identical with that which culture,—seeking the determination of this question through all the voices of human experience which have been heard upon it, of art, science, poetry, philosophy, history, as well as of religion, in order to give a greater fulness and certainty to its solution,—likewise reaches. Religion says: *The kingdom of God is within you*; and culture, in like manner, places human perfection in an *internal* condition, in the growth and predominance of our humanity proper, as distinguished from our animality.

It places it in the ever-increasing efficacy and in the general harmonious expansion of those gifts of thought and feeling, which make the peculiar dignity, wealth, and happiness of human nature. As I have said on a former occasion: 'It is in making endless additions to itself, in the endless expansion of its powers, in endless growth in wisdom and beauty, that the spirit of the human race finds its ideal. To reach this ideal, culture is an indispensable aid, and that is the true value of culture.' Not a having and a resting, but a growing and a becoming, is the character of perfection as culture conceives it; and here, too, it coincides with religion.

And because men are all members of one great whole, and the sympathy which is in human nature will not allow one member to be indifferent to the rest, or to have a perfect welfare independent of the rest, the expansion of our humanity, to suit the idea of perfection which culture forms, must be a *general* expansion. Perfection, as culture conceives it, is not possible while the individual remains isolated. The individual is required, under pain of being stunted and enfeebled in his own development if he disobeys, to carry others along with him in his march towards perfection, to be continually doing all he can to enlarge and increase the volume of the human stream sweeping thitherward. And here, once more, culture lays on us the same obligation as religion, which says, as Bishop Wilson has admirably put it, that 'to promote the kingdom of God is to increase and hasten one's own happiness.'

But, finally, perfection,—as culture from a thorough disinterested study of human nature and human experience learns to conceive it,—is a harmonious expansion of *all* the powers which make the beauty and worth of human nature, and is not consistent with the over-development of any one power at the expense of the rest. Here culture goes beyond religion, as religion is generally conceived by us.

If culture, then, is a study of perfection, and of harmonious perfection, general perfection, and perfection which consists in becoming something rather than in having something, in an inward condition of the mind and spirit, not in an outward set of circumstances,—it is clear that culture, instead of being the frivolous and useless thing which Mr. Bright,[4] and Mr.

Frederic Harrison, and many other Liberals are apt to call it, has a very important function to fulfil for mankind. And this function is particularly important in our modern world, of which the whole civilisation is, to a much greater degree than the civilisation of Greece and Rome, mechanical and external, and tends constantly to become more so. But above all in our own country has culture a weighty part to perform, because here that mechanical character, which civilisation tends to take everywhere, is shown in the most eminent degree. Indeed nearly all the characters of perfection, as culture teaches us to fix them, meet in this country with some powerful tendency which thwarts them and sets them at defiance. The idea of perfection as an *inward* condition of the mind and spirit is at variance with the mechanical and material civilisation in esteem with us, and nowhere, as I have said, so much in esteem as with us. The idea of perfection as a *general* expansion of the human family is at variance with our strong individualism, our hatred of all limits to the unrestrained swing of the individual's personality, our maxim of 'every man for himself.' Above all, the idea of perfection as a *harmonious* expansion of human nature is at variance with our want of flexibility, with our inaptitude for seeing more than one side of a thing, with our intense energetic absorption in the particular pursuit we happen to be following. So culture has a rough task to achieve in this country. Its preachers have, and are likely long to have, a hard time of it, and they will much oftener be regarded, for a great while to come, as elegant or spurious Jeremiahs, than as friends and benefactors. That, however, will not prevent their doing in the end good service if they persevere. And, meanwhile, the mode of action they have to pursue, and the sort of habits they must fight against, ought to be made quite clear for every one to see, who may be willing to look at the matter attentively and dispassionately.

Faith in machinery is, I said, our besetting danger, often in machinery most absurdly disproportioned to the end which this machinery, if it is to do any good at all, is to serve; but always in machinery, as if it had a value in and for itself. What is freedom but machinery? what is population but machinery? what is coal but machinery? what are railroads but machinery? what is wealth but machinery? what are, even, religious organisations but machinery? Now almost every voice in England is accustomed to speak of these things as if they were precious ends in themselves, and therefore had some of the characters of perfection indisputably joined to them. I have before now noticed Mr. Roebuck's[5] stock argument for proving the greatness and happiness of England as she is, and for quite stopping the mouths of all gainsayers. Mr. Roebuck is never weary of reiterating this argument of his, so I do not know why I should be weary of noticing it. 'May not every man in England say what he likes?'—Mr. Roebuck perpetually asks; and that, he thinks, is quite sufficient, and when every man may say what he likes, our aspirations ought to be satisfied. But the aspirations of culture, which is the study of perfection, are not satisfied, unless what men say, when they may say what they like, is worth saying,—has good in it, and more good than bad. In the same way the *Times*, replying to some foreign strictures on the dress, looks, and behaviour of the English abroad, urges that the English ideal is that every one should be free to do and to look just as he likes. But culture indefatigably tries, not to make what each raw person may like, the rule by which he fashions himself; but to draw ever nearer to a sense of what is indeed beautiful, graceful, and becoming, and to get the raw person to like that.

And in the same way with respect to railroads and coal. Every one must have observed the strange language current during the late discussions as to the possible failure of our supplies of coal. Our coal, thousands of people were saying, is the real basis of our national greatness; if our coal runs short, there is an end of the greatness of England. But what *is* greatness?—culture makes us ask. Greatness is a spiritual condition worthy to excite love, interest, and admiration; and the outward proof of possessing greatness is that we excite love, interest, and admiration. If England were swallowed up by the sea tomorrow, which of the two, a hundred years hence, would most excite the love, interest, and admiration of mankind,—would most, therefore, show the evidences of having possessed greatness,—the England of the last twenty

years, or the England of Elizabeth, of a time of splendid
spiritual effort, but when our coal, and our industrial operations depending on coal, were very little developed? Well, then,
what an unsound habit of mind it must be which makes us
talk of things like coal or iron as constituting the greatness of
England, and how salutary a friend is culture, bent on seeing
things as they are; and thus dissipating delusions of this kind
and fixing standards of perfection that are real!

Wealth, again, that end to which our prodigious works for
material advantage are directed,—the commonest of commonplaces tells us how men are always apt to regard wealth as a
precious end in itself; and certainly they have never been so
apt thus to regard it as they are in England at the present time.
Never did people believe anything more firmly than nine
Englishmen out of ten at the present day believe that our
greatness and welfare are proved by our being so very rich.
Now, the use of culture is that it helps us, by means of its
spiritual standard of perfection, to regard wealth as but
machinery, and not only to say as a matter of words that we
regard wealth as but machinery, but really to perceive and
feel that it is so. If it were not for this purging effect wrought
upon our minds by culture, the whole world, the future as
well as the present, would inevitably belong to the Philistines.
The people who believe most that our greatness and welfare
are proved by our being very rich, and who must give their
lives and thoughts to becoming rich, are just the very people
whom we call Philistines. Culture says: 'Consider these people,
then, their way of life, their habits, their manners, the very
tones of their voice; look at them attentively; observe the
literature they read, the things which give them pleasure, the
words which come forth out of their mouths, the thoughts
which make the furniture of their minds; would any amount
of wealth be worth having with the condition that one was to
become just like these people by having it?' And thus culture
begets a dissatisfaction which is of the highest possible value
in stemming the common tide of men's thoughts in a wealthy
and industrial community, and which saves the future, as one
may hope, from being vulgarised, even if it cannot save the
present.

Population, again, and bodily health and vigour, are things which are nowhere treated in such an unintelligent, misleading, exaggerated way as in England. Both are really machinery; yet how many people all around us do we see rest in them and fail to look beyond them! Why, one has heard people, fresh from reading certain articles of the *Times* on the Registrar-General's returns of marriages and births in this country, who would talk of our large English families in quite a solemn strain, as if they had something in itself beautiful, elevating, and meritorious in them; as if the British Philistine would have only to present himself before the Great Judge with his twelve children, in order to be received among the sheep as a matter of right!

But bodily health and vigour, it may be said, are not to be classed with wealth and population as mere machinery; they have a more real and essential value. True; but only as they are more intimately connected with a perfect spiritual condition than wealth or population are. The moment we disjoin them from the idea of a perfect spiritual condition, and pursue them, as we do pursue them, for their own sake and as ends in themselves, our worship of them becomes a mere worship of machinery, as our worship of wealth or population, and as unintelligent and vulgarising a worship as that is. Every one with anything like an adequate idea of human perfection has distinctly marked this subordination to higher and spiritual ends of the cultivation of bodily vigour and activity. 'Bodily exercise profiteth little; but godliness is profitable unto all things,' says the author of the Epistle to Timothy.[6] And the utilitarian Franklin says just as explicitly:—'Eat and drink such an exact quantity as suits the constitution of thy body, *in reference to the services of the mind*.'[7] But the point of view of culture, keeping the mark of human perfection simply and broadly in view, and not assigning to this perfection, as religion or utilitarianism assign to it, a special and limited character,— this point of view, I say, of culture, is best given by these words of Epictetus:—[8] 'It is a sign of ἀφυΐα' says he,—that is, of a nature not finely tempered,—'to give yourselves up to things which relate to the body; to make, for instance, a great fuss about exercise, a great fuss about eating, a great fuss about drinking, a great fuss about walking, a great fuss about riding. All these things ought to be done merely by the way: the formation of the spirit and character must be our real concern!' This is admirable; and, indeed, the Greek word ε'φϋΐα, a finely tempered nature, gives exactly the notion of perfection as culture brings us to conceive it: a harmonious perfection, a perfection in which the characters of beauty and intelligence are both present, which unites 'the two noblest of things,—as Swift, who of one of the two, at any rate, had himself all too little, most happily calls them in his *Battle of the Books*,—'the two noblest of things, *sweetness and light*.' The εὐφνής is the man who tends towards sweetness and light; the ἀφνής, on the other hand, is our Philistine. The immense spiritual significance of the Greeks is due to their having been inspired with this central and happy idea of the essential character of human perfection; and Mr. Bright's misconception of culture, as a smattering of Greek and Latin, comes itself, after all, from this wonderful significance of the Greeks having affected the very machinery of our education, and is in itself a kind of homage to it.

In thus making sweetness and light to be characters of perfection, culture is of like spirit with poetry, follows one law with poetry. Far more than on our freedom, our population, and our industrialism, many amongst us rely upon our religious organisations to save us. I have called religion a yet more important manifestation of human nature than poetry, because it has worked on a broader scale for perfection, and with greater masses of men. But the idea of beauty and of a human nature perfect on all its sides, which is the dominant idea of poetry, is a true and invaluable idea, though it has not yet had the success that the idea of conquering the obvious faults of our animality, and of a human nature perfect on the moral side,—which is the dominant idea of religion,—has been enabled to have; and it is destined, adding to itself the religious idea of a devout energy, to transform and govern the other.

The best art and poetry of the Greeks, in which religion and poetry are one, in which the idea of beauty and of a human nature perfect on all sides adds to itself a religious and devout energy, and works in the strength of that, is on this account of such surpassing interest and instructiveness for us, though it was,—as, having regard to the human race in general, and, indeed, having regard to the Greeks themselves, we must own, —a premature attempt, an attempt which for success needed the moral and religious fibre in humanity to be more braced and developed than it had yet been. But Greece did not err in having the idea of beauty, harmony, and complete human perfection, so present and paramount. It is impossible to have this idea too present and paramount; only, the moral fibre, must be braced too. And we, because we have braced the moral fibre, are not on that account in the right way, if at the same time the idea of beauty, harmony, and complete human perfection, is wanting or misapprehended amongst us; and evidently it *is* wanting or misapprehended at present. And when we rely as we do on our religious organisations, which in themselves do not and cannot give us this idea, and think we have done enough if we make them spread and prevail, then, I say, we fall into our common fault of overvaluing machinery.

Nothing is more common than for people to confound the inward peace and satisfaction which follows the subduing of the obvious faults of our animality with what I may call absolute inward peace and satisfaction,—the peace and satisfaction which are reached as we draw near to complete spiritual perfection, and not merely to moral perfection, or rather to relative moral perfection. No people in the world have done more and struggled more to attain this relative moral perfection than our English race has. For no people in the world has the command to *resist the devil*, to *overcome the wicked one*, in the nearest and most obvious sense of those words, had such a pressing force and reality. And we have had our reward, not only in the great worldly prosperity which our obedience to this command has brought us, but also, and far more, in great inward peace and satisfaction. But to me few things are more pathetic than to see people, on the strength of the inward peace and satisfaction which their rudimentary efforts towards perfection have brought them, employ, concerning their incomplete perfection and the religious

organisations within which they have found it, language
which properly applies only to complete perfection, and is a
far-off echo of the human soul's prophecy of it. Religion itself,
I need hardly say, supplies them in abundance with this
grand language. And very freely do they use it; yet it is really
the severest possible criticism of such an incomplete perfection
as alone we have yet reached through our religious organisations.

The impulse of the English race towards moral development
and self-conquest has nowhere so powerfully manifested itself
as in Puritanism. Nowhere has Puritanism found so adequate
an expression as in the religious organisation of the Independents. The modern Independents have a newspaper, the
Nonconformist, written with great sincerity and ability. The
motto, the standard, the profession of faith which this organ
of theirs carries aloft, is: 'The Dissidence of Dissent and the
Protestantism of the Protestant religion.' There is sweetness
and light, and an ideal of complete harmonious human
perfection! One need not go to culture and poetry to find
language to judge it. Religion, with its instinct for perfection,
supplies language to judge it, language, too, which is in our
mouths every day. 'Finally, be of one mind, united in feeling,'
says St. Peter.[9] There is an ideal which judges the Puritan
ideal: 'The Dissidence of Dissent and the Protestantism of the
Protestant religion!' And religious organisations like this are
what people believe in, rest in, would give their lives for!
Such, I say, is the wonderful virtue of even the beginnings of
perfection, of having conquered even the plain faults of our
animality, that the religious organisation which has helped us
to do it can seem to us something precious, salutary, and to be
propagated, even when it wears such a brand of imperfection
on its forehead as this. And men have got such a habit of
giving to the language of religion a special application, of
making it a mere jargon, that for the condemnation which
religion itself passes on the shortcomings of their religious
organisations they have no ear; they are sure to cheat themselves and to explain this condemnation away. They can only
be reached by the criticism which culture, like poetry, speaking
a language not to be sophisticated, and resolutely testing these

organisations by the ideal of a human perfection complete on all sides, applies to them.

But men of culture and poetry, it will be said, are again and again failing, and failing conspicuously, in the necessary first stage to a harmonious perfection, in the subduing of the great obvious faults of our animality, which it is the glory of these religious organisations to have helped us to subdue. True, they do often so fail. They have often been without the virtues as well as the faults of the Puritan; it has been one of their dangers that they so felt the Puritan's faults that they too much neglected the practice of his virtues. I will not, however, exculpate them at the Puritan's expense. They have often failed in morality, and morality is indispensable. And they have been punished for their failure, as the Puritan has been rewarded for his performance. They have been punished wherein they erred; but their ideal of beauty, of sweetness and light, and a human nature complete on all its sides, remains the true ideal of perfection still; just as the Puritan's ideal of perfection remains narrow and inadequate, although for what he did well he has been richly rewarded. Notwithstanding the mighty results of the Pilgrim Fathers' voyage, they and their standard of perfection are rightly judged when we figure to ourselves Shakspeare or Virgil,—souls in whom sweetness and light, and all that in human nature is most humane, were eminent,—accompanying them on their voyage, and think what intolerable company Shakspeare and Virgil would have found them! In the same way let us judge the religious organisations which we see all around us. Do not let us deny the good and the happiness which they have accomplished; but do not let us fail to see clearly that their idea of human perfection is narrow and inadequate, and that the Dissidence of Dissent and the Protestantism of the Protestant religion will never bring humanity to its true goal. As I said with regard to wealth: Let us look at the life of those who live in and for it,—so I say with regard to the religious organisations. Look at the life imaged in such a newspaper as the *Nonconformist*,—a life of jealousy of the Establishment, disputes, tea-meetings, openings of chapels, sermons; and then think of it as an ideal of a human life completing itself on all sides, and aspiring with all its organs after sweetness, light, and perfection!

Another newspaper, representing, like the *Nonconformist*, one of the religious organisations of this country, was a short time ago giving an account of the crowd at Epsom on the Derby day, and of all the vice and hideousness which was to be seen in that crowd; and then the writer turned suddenly round upon Professor Huxley, and asked him how he proposed to cure all this vice and hideousness without religion. I confess I felt disposed to ask the asker this question: And how do you propose to cure it with such a religion as yours? How is the ideal of a life so unlovely, so unattractive, so incomplete, so narrow, so far removed from a true and satisfying ideal of human perfection, as is the life of your religious organisation as you yourself image it, to conquer and transform all this vice and hideousness? Indeed, the strongest plea for the study of perfection as pursued by culture, the clearest proof of the actual inadequacy of the idea of perfection held by the religious organisations,—expressing, as I have said, the most widespread effort which the human race has yet made after perfection,—is to be found in the state of our life and society with those in possession of it, and having been in possession of it I know not how many hundred years. We are all of us included in some religious organisation or other; we all call ourselves, in the sublime and aspiring language of religion which I have before noticed, *children of God*. Children of God;— it is an immense pretension!—and how are we to justify it? By the works which we do, and the words which we speak. And the work which we collective children of God do, our grand centre of life, our *city* which we have builded for us to dwell in, is London! London, with its unutterable external hideousness, and with its internal canker of *publicè egestas, privatim opulentia*,[10]—to use the words which Sallust puts into Cato's mouth about Rome,—unequalled in the world! The word, again, which we children of God speak, the voice which most hits our collective thought, the newspaper with the largest circulation in England, nay, with the largest circulation in the whole world, is the *Daily Telegraph*! I say that when our religious organisations,—which I admit to express the most considerable effort after perfection that our race has yet made, —land us in no better result than this, it is high time to examine carefully their idea of perfection, to see whether it does not leave out of account sides and forces of human nature which we might turn to great use; whether it would not be more operative if it were more complete. And I say that the English reliance on our religious organisations and on their ideas of human perfection just as they stand, is like our reliance on freedom, on muscular Christianity, on population, on coal, on wealth,—mere belief in machinery, and unfruitful; and that is wholesomely counteracted by culture, bent on seeing things as they are, and on drawing the human race onwards to a more complete, a harmonious perfection.

Culture, however, shows its single-minded love of perfection, its desire simply to make reason and the will of God prevail, its freedom from fanaticism, by its attitude towards all this machinery, even while it insists that it *is* machinery. Fanatics, seeing the mischief men do themselves by their blind belief in some machinery or other, whether it is wealth and in-dustrialism, or whether it is the cultivation of bodily strength and activity, or whether it is a political organisation, or whether it is a religious organisation,—oppose with might and main the tendency to this or that political and religious organisation, or to games and athletic exercises, or to wealth and in-dustrialism, and try violently to stop it. But the flexibility which sweetness and light give, and which is one of the rewards of culture pursued in good faith, enables a man to see that a tendency may be necessary, and even, as a preparation for something in the future, salutary, and yet that the genera-tions of individuals who obey this tendency are sacrificed to it, that they fall short of the hope of perfection by following it; and that its mischiefs are to be criticised, lest it should take too firm a hold and last after it has served its purpose.

Mr. Gladstone well pointed out, in a speech at Paris,—and others have pointed out the same thing,—how necessary is the present great movement towards wealth and industrialism, in order to lay broad foundations of material well-being for the society of the future. The worst of these justifications is, that they are generally addressed to the very people engaged, body and soul, in the movement in question; at all events, that they are always seized with the greatest avidity by these people, and taken by them as quite justifying their life; and that thus they tend to harden them in their sins. Now, culture admits the necessity of the movement towards fortune-making and exaggerated industrialism, readily allows that the future may derive benefit from it; but insists, at the same time, that the passing generations of industrialists,—forming, for the most part, the stout main body of Philistinism,—are sacrificed to it. In the same way, the result of all the games and sports which occupy the passing generation of boys and young men may be the establishment of a better and sounder physical type for the future to work with. Culture does not set itself against the games and sports; it congratulates the future, and hopes it will make a good use of its improved physical basis; but it points out that our passing generation of boys and young men is, meantime, sacrificed. Puritanism was perhaps necessary to develop the moral fibre of the English race, Nonconformity to break the yoke of ecclesiastical domination over men's minds and to prepare the way for freedom of thought in the distant future; still, culture points out that the harmonious perfection of generations of Puritans and Non-conformists have been, in consequence, sacrificed. Freedom of speech may be necessary for the society of the future, but the young lions of the *Daily Telegraph* in the meanwhile are sacrificed. A voice for every man in his country's government may be necessary for the society of the future, but meanwhile Mr. Beales and Mr. Bradlaugh[11] are sacrificed.

Oxford, the Oxford of the past, has many faults; and she has heavily paid for them in defeat, in isolation, in want of hold upon the modern world. Yet we in Oxford, brought up amidst the beauty and sweetness of that beautiful place, have not failed to seize one truth:—the truth that beauty and sweetness are essential characters of a complete human perfection. When I insist on this, I am all in the faith and tradition of Oxford. I say boldly that this our sentiment for beauty and sweetness, our sentiment against hideousness and rawness, has been at the bottom of our attachment to so many beaten causes, of our opposition to so many triumphant movements. And the sentiment is true, and has never been wholly defeated, and has shown its power even in its defeat. We have not won our political battles, we have not carried our main points, we have not stopped our adversaries' advance, we have not marched victoriously with the modern world; but we have told silently upon the mind of the country, we have prepared currents of feeling which sap our adversaries' position when it seems gained, we have kept up our own communications with the future. Look at the course of the great movement which shook Oxford to its centre some thirty years ago! It was directed, as any one who reads Dr. Newman's *Apology* may see, against what in one word may be called 'Liberalism.' Liberalism prevailed; it was the appointed force to do the work of the hour; it was necessary, it was inevitable that it should prevail. The Oxford movement was broken, it failed; our wrecks are scattered on every shore:—

Quae regio in terris nostri non plena laboris?[12]

But what was it, this liberalism, as Dr. Newman saw it, and as it really broke the Oxford movement? It was the great middle-class liberalism, which had for the cardinal points of its belief the Reform Bill of 1832, and local self-government, in politics; in the social sphere, free-trade, unrestricted competition, and the making of large industrial fortunes; in the religious sphere, the Dissidence of Dissent and the Protestantism of the Protestant religion. I do not say that other and more intelligent forces than this were not opposed to the Oxford movement: but this was the force which really beat it; this was the force which Dr. Newman felt himself fighting with; this was the force which till only the other day seemed to be the paramount force in this country, and to be in possession of the future; this was the force whose achievements fill Mr. Lowe with such inexpressible admiration, and whose rule he was so horror-struck to see threatened. And where is this great force of Philistinism now? It is thrust into the second rank, it is become a power of yesterday, it has lost the future. A new power has suddenly appeared, a power which it is impossible yet to judge fully, but which is certainly a wholly different force from middle-class liberalism; different in its cardinal points of belief, different in its tendencies in every sphere. It loves and admires neither the legislation of middle-class Parliaments, nor the local self-government of middle-class vestries, nor the unrestricted competition of middle-class industrialists, nor the dissidence of middle-class Dissent and the Protestantism of middle-class Protestant religion. I am not now praising this new force or saying that its own ideals are better; all I say is, that they are wholly different. And who will estimate how much the currents of feeling created by Dr. Newman's movement[s], the keen desire for beauty and sweetness which it nourished, the deep aversion it manifested to the hardness and vulgarity of middle-class liberalism, the strong light it turned on the hideous and grotesque illusions of middle-class Protestantism,—who will estimate how much all these contributed to swell the tide of secret dissatisfaction which has mined the ground under the self-confident liberalism of the last thirty years, and has prepared the way for its sudden collapse and supersession? It is in this manner that the sentiment of Oxford for beauty and sweetness conquers, and in this manner long may it continue to conquer!

In this manner it works to the same end as culture, and there is plenty of work for it yet to do. I have said that the new and more democratic force which is now superseding our old middle-class liberalism cannot yet be rightly judged. It has its main tendencies still to form. We hear promises of its giving us administrative reform, law reform, reform of education, and I know not what; but those promises come rather from its advocates, wishing to make a good plea for it and to justify it for superseding middle-class liberalism, than from clear tendencies which it has itself yet developed. But meanwhile it has plenty of well-intentioned friends against whom culture may with advantage continue to uphold steadily its ideal of human perfection; that this is *an inward spiritual activity, having for its characters increased sweetness, increased light, increased life, increased sympathy.* Mr. Bright, who has a foot in both worlds, the world of middle-class liberalism and the world of democracy, but who brings most of his ideas from the world of middle-class liberalism in which he was bred, always inclines to inculcate that faith in machinery to which, as we have seen,

Englishmen are so prone, and which has been the bane of middle-class liberalism. He complains with a sorrowful indignation of people who 'appear to have no proper estimate of the value of the franchise'; he leads his disciples to believe,— what the Englishman is always too ready to believe,—that the having a vote, like the having a large family, or a large business, or large muscles, has in itself some edifying and perfecting effect upon human nature. Or else he cries out to the democracy,—'the men,' as he calls them, 'upon whose shoulders the greatness of England rests,'—he cries out to them: 'See what you have done! I look over this country and see the cities you have built, the railroads you have made, the manufactures you have produced, the cargoes which freight the ships of the greatest mercantile navy the world has ever seen! I see that you have converted by your labours what was once a wilderness, these islands, into a fruitful garden; I know that you have created this wealth, and are a nation whose name is a word of power throughout all the world.' Why, this is just the very style of laudation with which Mr. Roebuck or Mr. Lowe debauch the minds of the middle classes, and make such Philistines of them. It is the same fashion of teaching a man to value himself not on what he *is*, not on his progress in sweetness and light, but on the number of the railroads he has constructed, or the bigness of the tabernacle he has built. Only the middle classes are told they have done it all with their energy, self-reliance, and capital, and the democracy are told they have done it all with their hands and sinews. But teaching the democracy to put its trust in achievements of this kind is merely training them to be Philistines to take the place of the Philistines whom they are superseding; and they too, like the middle class, will be encouraged to sit down at the banquet of the future without having on a wedding garment, and nothing excellent can then come from them. Those who know their besetting faults, those who have watched them and listened to them, or those who will read the instructive account recently given of them by one of themselves, the *Journeyman Engineer*, will agree that the idea which culture sets before us of perfection,—an increased spiritual activity, having for its characters increased sweetness, increased light, increased life, increased sympathy,—is an idea which the new democracy needs far more than the idea of the blessedness of the franchise, or the wonderfulness of its own industrial performances.

Other well-meaning friends of this new power are for leading it, not in the old ruts of middle-class Philistinism, but in ways which are naturally alluring to the feet of democracy, though in this country they are novel and untried ways. I may call them the ways of Jacobinism. Violent indignation with the past, abstract systems of renovation applied wholesale, a new doctrine drawn up in black and white for elaborating down to the very smallest details a rational society for the future,—these are the ways of Jacobinism. Mr. Frederic Harrison and the other disciples of Comte,—one of them, Mr. Congreve,[13] is an old acquaintance of mine, and I am glad to have an opportunity of publicly expressing my respect for his talents and character,—are among the friends of democracy who are for leading it in paths of this kind. Mr. Frederic Harrison is very hostile to culture, and from a natural enough motive; for culture is the eternal opponent of the two things which are the signal marks of Jacobinism,— its fierceness, and its addiction to an abstract system. Culture is always assigning to system-makers and systems a smaller share in the bent of human destiny than their friends like. A current in people's minds sets towards new ideas; people are dissatisfied with their old narrow stock of Philistine ideas, Anglo-Saxon ideas, or any other, and some man, some Bentham or Comte, who has the real merit of having early and strongly felt and helped the new current, but who brings plenty of narrowness and mistakes of his own into his feeling and help of it, is credited with being the author of the whole current, the fit person to be entrusted with its regulation and to guide the human race.

The excellent German historian of the mythology of Rome, Preller,[14] relating the introduction at Rome under the Tarquins of the worship of Apollo, the god of light, healing, and reconciliation, will have us observe that it was not so much the Tarquins who brought to Rome the new worship of Apollo, as a current in the mind of the Roman people which set powerfully at that time towards a new worship of this kind, and away from the old run of Latin and Sabine religious ideas. In a similar way, culture directs our attention to the natural current there is in human affairs, and to its continual working, and will not let us rivet our faith upon any one man and his doings. It makes us see not only his good side, but also how much in him was of necessity limited and transient; nay, it even feels a pleasure, a sense of an increased freedom and of an ampler future, in so doing.

I remember, when I was under the influence of a mind to which I feel the greatest obligations, the mind of a man who was the very incarnation of sanity and clear sense, a man the most considerable, it seems to me, whom America has yet produced,—Benjamin Franklin,—I remember the relief with which, after long feeling the sway of Franklin's imperturbable common-sense, I came upon a project of his for a new version of the Book of Job, to replace the old version, the style of which, says Franklin, has become obsolete, and thence less agreeable. 'I give,' he continues, 'a few verses, which may serve as a sample of the kind of version I would recommend.' We all recollect the famous verse in our translation: 'Then Satan answered the Lord and said: "Doth Job fear God for nought?"' Franklin makes this: 'Does your Majesty imagine that Job's good conduct is the effect of mere personal attachment and affection?' I well remember how when first I read that, I drew a deep breath of relief, and said to myself: 'After all, there is a stretch of humanity beyond Franklin's victorious good sense!' So, after hearing Bentham cried loudly up as the renovator of modern society, and Bentham's mind and ideas proposed as the rulers of our future, I open the *Deontology*. There I read: 'While Xenophon was writing his history and Euclid teaching geometry, Socrates and Plato were talking nonsense under pretence of talking wisdom and morality. This morality of theirs consisted in words; this wisdom of theirs was the denial of matters known to every man's experience.' From the moment of reading that, I am delivered from the bondage of Bentham! the fanaticism of his adherents can touch me no longer. I feel the inadequacy of his mind and ideas for supplying the rule of human society, for perfection.

Culture tends always thus to deal with the men of a system, of disciples, of a school; with men like Comte, or the late Mr. Buckle,[15] or Mr. Mill. However much it may find to admire in these personages, or in some of them, it nevertheless remembers the text: 'Be not ye called Rabbi!'[16] and it soon passes on from any Rabbi. But Jacobinism loves a Rabbi; it does not want to pass on from its Rabbi in pursuit of a future and still unreached perfection; it wants its Rabbi and his ideas to stand for perfection, that they may with the more authority recast the world; and for Jacobinism, therefore, culture,—eternally passing onwards and seeking,—is an impertinence and an offence. But culture, just because it resists this tendency of Jacobinism to impose on us a man with limitations and errors of his own along with the true ideas of which he is the organ, really does the world and Jacobinism itself a service.

So, too, Jacobinism, in its fierce hatred of the past and of those whom it makes liable for the sins of the past, cannot away with the inexhaustible indulgence proper to culture, the consideration of circumstances, the severe judgment of actions joined to the merciful judgment of persons. 'The man of culture is in politics,' cries Mr. Frederic Harrison, 'one of the poorest mortals alive!' Mr. Frederic Harrison wants to be doing business, and he complains that the man of culture stops him with a 'turn for small fault-finding, love of selfish ease, and indecision in action.'[17] Of what use is culture, he asks, except for 'a critic of new books or a professor of *belles-lettres*?' Why, it is of use because, in presence of the fierce exasperation which breathes, or rather, I may say, hisses through the whole production in which Mr. Frederic Harrison asks that question, it reminds us that the perfection of human nature is sweetness and light. It is of use, because, like religion, —that other effort after perfection,—it testifies that, where bitter envying and strife are, there is confusion and every evil work.

The pursuit of perfection, then, is the pursuit of sweetness and light. He who works for sweetness and light, works to make reason and the will of God prevail. He who works for machinery, he who works for hatred, works only for confusion. Culture looks beyond machinery, culture hates hatred;

culture has one great passion, the passion for sweetness and
light. It has one even yet greater!—the passion for making
them *prevail*. It is not satisfied till we *all* come to a perfect man;
it knows that the sweetness and light of the few must be imperfect until the raw and unkindled masses of humanity
are touched with sweetness and light. If I have not shrunk
from saying that we must work for sweetness and light, so neither
have I shrunk from saying that we must have a broad basis,
must have sweetness and light for as many as possible. Again
and again I have insisted how those are the happy moments of
humanity, how those are the marking epochs of a people's
life, how those are the flowering times for literature and arts
and all the creative power of genius, when there is a *national*
glow of life and thought, when the whole of society is in the
fullest measure permeated by thought, sensible to beauty,
intelligent and alive. Only it must be *real* thought and *real*
beauty; *real* sweetness and *real* light. Plenty of people will try
to give the masses, as they call them, an intellectual food
prepared and adapted in the way they think proper for the
actual condition of the masses. The ordinary popular literature
is an example of this way of working on the masses. Plenty of
people will try to indoctrinate the masses with the set of ideas
and judgments constituting the creed of their own profession
or party. Our religious and political organisations give an
example of this way of working on the masses. I condemn
neither way; but culture works differently. It does not try to
teach down to the level of inferior classes; it does not try to
win them for this or that sect of its own, with ready-made
judgments and watch-words. It seeks to do away with classes;
to make the best that has been thought and known in the world
current everywhere; to make all men live in an atmosphere of
sweetness and light, where they may use ideas, as it uses them
itself, freely,—nourished, and not bound by them.

This is the *social idea*; and the men of culture are the true
apostles of equality. The great men of culture are those who
have had a passion for diffusing, for making prevail, for
carrying from one end of society to the other, the best knowledge, the best ideas of their time; who have laboured to
divest knowledge of all that was harsh, uncouth, difficult,

abstract, professional, exclusive; to humanise it, to make it
efficient outside the clique of the cultivated and learned, yet
still remaining the *best* knowledge and thought of the time,
and a true source, therefore, of sweetness and light. Such a
man was Abelard in the Middle Ages, in spite of all his imperfections; and thence the boundless emotion and enthusiasm which Abelard excited. Such were Lessing and
Herder in Germany, at the end of the last century; and their
services to Germany were in this way inestimably precious.
Generations will pass, and literary monuments will accumulate,
and works far more perfect than the works of Lessing and
Herder will be produced in Germany; and yet the names of
these two men will fill a German with a reverence and
enthusiasm such as the names of the most gifted masters will
hardly awaken. And why? Because they *humanised* knowledge;
because they broadened the basis of life and intelligence;
because they worked powerfully to diffuse sweetness and light,
to make reason and the will of God prevail. With Saint
Augustine they said: 'Let us not leave thee alone to make in
the secret of thy knowledge, as thou didst before the creation of
the firmament, the division of light from darkness; let the
children of thy spirit, placed in their firmament, make their
light shine upon the earth, mark the division of night and day,
and announce the revolution of the times; for the old order is
passed, and the new arises; the night is spent, the day is come
forth; and thou shalt crown the year with thy blessing, when
thou shalt send forth labourers into thy harvest sown by other
hands than theirs; when thou shalt send forth new labourers
to new seed-times, whereof the harvest shall be not yet.'[18]

Barbarians, Philistines, Populace

From a man without a philosophy no one can expect
philosophical completeness. Therefore I may observe without
shame, that in trying to get a distinct notion of our aristocratic,
our middle, and our working class, with a view of testing the
claims of each of these classes to become a centre of authority,
I have omitted, I find, to complete the old-fashioned analysis
which I had the fancy of applying, and have not shown in

these classes, as well as the virtuous mean and the excess, the defect also. I do not know that the omission very much matters. Still, as clearness is the one merit which a plain, unsystematic writer, without a philosophy, can hope to have, and as our notion of the three great English classes may perhaps be made clearer if we see their distinctive qualities in the defect, as well as in the excess and in the mean, let us try, before proceeding further, to remedy this omission.

It is manifest, if the perfect and virtuous mean of that fine spirit which is the distinctive quality of aristocracies, is to be found in a high, chivalrous style, and its excess in a fierce turn for resistance, that its defect must lie in a spirit not bold and high enough, and in an excessive and pusillanimous inaptness for resistance. If, again, the perfect and virtuous mean of that force by which our middle class has done its great works, and of that self-reliance with which it contemplates itself and them, is to be seen in the performances and speeches of our commercial member of Parliament, and the excess of that force and of that self-reliance in the performance and speeches of our fanatical Dissenting minister, then it is manifest that their defect must lie in a helpless inaptitude for the great works of the middle class, and in a poor and despicable lack of its self-satisfaction.

To be chosen to exemplify the happy mean of a good quality, or set of good qualities, is evidently a praise to a man; nay, to be chosen to exemplify even their excess, is a kind of praise. Therefore I could have no hesitation in taking actual personages to exemplify, respectively, the mean and the excess of aristocratic and middle-class qualities. But perhaps there might be a want of urbanity in singling out this or that personage as the representative of defect. Therefore I shall leave the defect of aristocracy unillustrated by any representative man. But with oneself one may always, without impropriety, deal quite freely; and, indeed, this sort of plain-dealing with oneself has in it, as all the moralists tell us, something very wholesome. So I will venture to humbly offer myself as an illustration of defect in those forces and qualities which make our middle class what it is. The too well-founded reproaches of my opponents declare how little I have lent a hand to the great works of the middle class; for it is evidently these works, and my slackness at them, which are meant, when I am said to 'refuse to lend a hand to the humble operation of uprooting certain definite evils' (such as church-rates and others), and that therefore 'the believers in action grow impatient' with me. The line, again, of a still unsatisfied seeker which I have followed, the idea of self-transformation, of growing towards some measure of sweetness and light not yet reached, is evidently at clean variance with the perfect self-satisfaction current in my class, the middle class, and may serve to indicate in me, therefore, the extreme defect of this feeling. But these confessions, though salutary, are bitter and unpleasant.

To pass, then, to the working class. The defect of this class would be the falling short in what Mr. Frederic Harrison calls those 'bright powers of sympathy and ready powers of action', of which we saw in Mr. Odger[19] the virtuous mean, and in Mr. Bradlaugh the excess. The working class is so fast growing and rising at the present time, that instances of this defect cannot well be now very common. Perhaps Canning's 'Needy Knife-Grinder'[20] (who is dead, and therefore cannot be pained at my taking him for an illustration) may serve to give us the notion of defect in the essential quality of a working class; or I might even cite (since, though he is alive in the flesh, he is dead to all heed of criticism) my poor old poaching friend, Zephaniah Diggs,[21] who, between his hare-snaring and his gin-drinking, has got his powers of sympathy quite dulled and his powers of action in any great movement of his class hopelessly impaired. But examples of this defect belong, as I have said, to a bygone age rather than to the present.

The same desire for clearness, which has led me thus to extend a little my first analysis of the three great classes of English society, prompts me also to improve my nomenclature for them a little, with a view to making it thereby more manageable. It is awkward and tiresome to be always saying the aristocratic class, the middle class, the working class. For the middle class, for that great body which, as we know, 'has done all the great things that have been done in all departments',[22] and which is to be conceived as moving between its two cardinal points of our commercial member of Parliament and our fanatical Protestant Dissenter,—for this class we have a designation which now has become pretty well known, and which we may as well still keep for them, the designation of Philistines. What this term means I have so often explained that I need not repeat it here. For the aristocratic class, conceived mainly as a body moving between the two cardinal points of our chivalrous lord and our defiant baronet, we have as yet got no special designation. Almost all my attention has naturally been concentrated on my own class, the middle class, with which I am in closest sympathy, and which has been, besides, the great power of our day, and has had its praises sung by all speakers and newspapers.

Still the aristocratic class is so important in itself, and the weighty functions which Mr. Carlyle proposes at the present critical time to commit to it, must add so much to its importance, that it seems neglectful, and a strong instance of that want of coherent philosophic method for which Mr. Frederic Harrison blames me, to leave the aristocratic class so much without notice and denomination. It may be thought that the characteristic which I have occasionally mentioned as proper to aristocracies,—their natural inaccessibility, as children of the established fact, to ideas,—points to our extending to this class also the designation of Philistines; the Philistine being, as is well known, the enemy of the children of light or servants of the idea. Nevertheless, there seems to be an inconvenience in thus giving one and the same designation to two very different classes; and besides, if we look into the thing closely, we shall find that the term Philistine conveys a sense which makes it more peculiarly appropriate to our middle class than to our aristocratic. For *Philistine* gives the notion of something particularly stiff-necked and perverse in the resistance to light and its children, and therein it specially suits our middle class, who not only do not pursue sweetness and light, but who even prefer to them that sort of machinery of business, chapels, tea-meetings, and addresses from Mr. Murphy,[23] which makes up the dismal and illiberal life on which I have so often touched. But the aristocratic class has actually, as we have seen, in its well-known politeness, a kind of image or shadow of sweetness; and as for light, if it does not pursue light, it is not that it perversely cherishes some dismal and illiberal existence in preference to light, but it is seduced from following light by those mighty and eternal seducers of our race which weave for this class their most irresistible charms,—by worldly splendour, security, power, and pleasure. These seducers are exterior goods, but they are goods; and he who is hindered by them from caring for light and ideas, is not so much doing what is perverse as what is too natural.

Keeping this in view. I have in my own mind often indulged myself with the fancy of employing, in order to designate our aristocratic class, the name of *the Barbarians*. The Barbarians, to whom we all owe so much, and who reinvigorated and renewed our worn-out Europe, had, as is well known, eminent merits; and in this country, where we are for the most part sprung from the Barbarians, we have never had the prejudice against them which prevails among the races of Latin origin. The Barbarians brought with them that staunch individualism, as the modern phrase is, and that passion for doing as one likes, for the assertion of personal liberty, which appears to Mr. Bright the central idea of English life, and of which we have, at any rate, a very rich supply. The stronghold and natural seat of this passion was in the nobles of whom our aristocratic class are the inheritors; and this class, accordingly, have signally manifested it, and have done much by their example to recommend it to the body of the nation, who already, indeed, had it in their blood, The Barbarians, again, had the passion for field-sports; and they have handed it on to our aristocratic class, who of this passion too, as of the passion for asserting one's personal liberty, are the great natural stronghold. The care of the Barbarians for the body, and for all manly exercises; the vigour, good looks, and fine complexion which they acquired and perpetuated in their families by these means,—all this may be observed still in our aristocratic class. The chivalry of the Barbarians, with its characteristics of high spirit, choice manners, and distinguished bearing,— what is this but the attractive commencement of the politeness of our aristocratic class? In some Barbarian noble, no doubt, one would have admired, if one could have been then alive to see it, the rudiments of our politest peer. Only, all this culture (to call it by that name) of the Barbarians was an exterior culture mainly. It consisted principally in outward gifts and graces, in looks, manners, accomplishments, prowess. The chief inward gifts which had part in it were the most exterior, so to speak, of inward gifts, those which come nearest to outward ones; they were courage, a high spirit, self-confidence. Far within, and unwakened, lay a whole range of powers of thought and feeling, to which these interesting productions of nature had, from the circumstances of their life, no access. Making allowances for the difference of the times, surely we can observe precisely the same thing now in our aristocratic class. In general its culture is exterior chiefly; all the exterior graces and accomplishments, and the more external of the inward virtues, seem to be principally its portion. It now, of course, cannot be often in contact with those studies by which, from the world of thought and feeling, true culture teaches us to fetch sweetness and light; but its hold upon these very studies appears remarkably external, and unable to exert any deep power upon its spirit. Therefore the one insufficiency which we noted in the perfect mean of this class was an insufficiency of light. And owing to the same causes, does not a subtle criticism lead us to make, even on the good looks and politeness of our aristocratic class, and of even the most fascinating half of that class, the feminine half, the one qualifying remark, that in these charming gifts there should perhaps be, for ideal perfection, a shade more *soul*?

I often, therefore, when I want to distinguish clearly the aristocratic class from the Philistines proper, or middle class, name the former, in my own mind, *the Barbarians*. And when I go through the country, and see this and that beautiful and imposing seat of theirs crowning the landscape, 'There', I say to myself, 'is a great fortified post of the Barbarians.'

It is obvious that that part of the working class which, working diligently by the light of Mrs. Gooch's Golden Rule,[24] looks forward to the happy day when it will sit on thrones with commercial members of Parliament and other middle-class potentates, to survey, as Mr. Bright beautifully says, 'the cities it has built, the railroads it has made, the manufactures it has produced, the cargoes which freight the ships of the greatest mercantile navy the world has ever seen,'—it is obvious, I say, that this part of the working class is, or is in a fair way to be, one in spirit with the industrial middle class. It is notorious that our middle-class Liberals have long looked forward to this consummation, when the working class shall join forces with them, aid them heartily to carry forward their great works, go in a body to their tea-meetings, and, in short, enable them to bring about their millennium. That part of the working class, therefore, which does really seem to lend itself to these great aims, may, with propriety, be numbered by us among the Philistines. That part of it, again, which so much occupies the attention of philanthropists at present,—the part which gives all its energies to organising itself, through trades' unions and other means, so as to constitute, first, a great working-class power independent of the middle and aristocratic classes, and then, by dint of numbers, give the law to them and itself reign absolutely,—this lively and promising part must also, according to our definition, go with the Philistines; because it is its class and its class instinct which it seeks to affirm, its ordinary self, not its best self; and it is a machinery, an industrial machinery, and power and pre-eminence and other external goods, which fill its thoughts, and not an inward perfection. It is wholly occupied, according to Plato's subtle expression, with the things of itself and not its real self, with the things of the State and not the real State. But that vast portion, lastly, of the working class which, raw and half-developed, has long lain half-hidden amidst its poverty and squalor, and is now issuing from its hiding-place to assert an Englishman's heaven-born privilege of doing as he likes, and is beginning to perplex us by marching where it likes, meeting where it likes, bawling what it likes, breaking what it likes,—to this vast residuum we may with great propriety give the name of *Populace*.

Thus we have got three distinct terms, *Barbarians, Philistines, Populace*, to denote roughly the three great classes into which our society is divided; and though this humble attempt at a scientific nomenclature falls, no doubt, very far short in precision of what might be required from a writer equipped with a complete and coherent philosophy yet, from a notoriously unsystematic and unpretending writer, it will, I trust, be accepted as sufficient.

But in using this new, and I hope, convenient division of English society, two things are to be borne in mind. The first is, that since, under all our class divisions, there is a common basis of human nature, therefore, in every one of us, whether we be properly Barbarians, Philistines, or Populace, there exists, sometimes only in germ and potentially, sometimes more or less developed, the same tendencies and passions which have made our fellow-citizens of other classes what they are. This consideration is very important, because it has great influence in begetting that spirit of indulgence which is a necessary part of sweetness, and which, indeed, when our culture is complete, is, as I have said, inexhaustible. Thus, an English Barbarian who examines himself will, in general, find himself to be not so entirely a Barbarian but that he has in him, also, something of the Philistine, and even something of the Populace as well. And the same with the Englishmen of the two other classes.

This is an experience which we may all verify every day. For instance, I myself (I again take myself as a sort of *corpus vile* to serve for illustration in a matter where serving for illustration may not by every one be thought agreeable), I myself am properly a Philistine,—Mr. Swinburne would add, the son of a Philistine. And although, through circumstances which will perhaps one day be known if ever the affecting history of my conversion comes to be written, I have, for the most part, broken with the ideas and the tea-meetings of my own class, yet I have not, on that account, been brought much the nearer to the ideas and works of the Barbarians or of the Populace. Nevertheless, I never take a gun or a fishing-rod in my hands without feeling that I have in the ground of my nature the self-same seeds which, fostered by circumstances, do so much to make the Barbarian; and that, with the Barbarian's advantages, I might have rivalled him. Place me in one of his great fortified posts, with these seeds of a love for field-sports sown in my nature, with all the means of developing them, with all pleasures at my command, with most whom I met deferring to me, everyone I met smiling on me, and with every appearance of permanence and security before me and behind me,—then I too might have grown, I feel, into a very passable child of the established fact, of commendable spirit and politeness, and, at the same time, a little inaccessible to ideas and light; not, of course, with either the eminent fine spirit of our type of aristocratic perfection, or the eminent turn for resistance of our type of aristocratic excess, but, according to the measure of the common run of mankind, something between the two. And as to the Populace, who, whether he be Barbarian or Philistine, can look at them without sympathy, when he remembers how often,—every time that we snatch up a vehement opinion in ignorance and passion, every time that we long to crush an adversary by sheer violence, every time that we are envious, every time that we are brutal, every time that we adore mere power or success, every time that we add our voice to swell a blind clamour against some unpopular personage, every time that we trample savagely on the fallen,—he has found in his own bosom the eternal spirit of the Populace, and that there needs only a little help from circumstances to make it triumph in him untameably.

The second thing to be borne in mind I have indicated several times already. It is this. All of us, so far as we are Barbarians, Philistines, or Populace, imagine happiness to consist in doing what one's ordinary self likes. What one's ordinary self likes differs according to the class to which one belongs, and has its severer and its lighter side; always, however, remaining machinery, and nothing more. The graver self of the Barbarian likes honours and consideration; his more relaxed self, field-sports and pleasure. The graver self of one kind of Philistine likes fanaticism, business, and money-making; his more relaxed self, comfort and tea-meetings. Of another kind of Philistine, the graver self likes rattening; the relaxed self, deputations, or hearing Mr. Odger speak. The sterner self of the Populace likes bawling, hustling, and smashing; the lighter self, beer. But in each class there are born a certain number of natures with a curiosity about their best self, with a bent for seeing things as they are, for disentangling themselves from machinery, for simply concerning themselves with reason and the will of God, and doing their best to make these prevail;—for the pursuit, in a word, of perfection. To certain manifestations of this love for perfection mankind have accustomed themselves to give the name of genius; implying, by this name, something original and heaven-bestowed in the passion. But the passion is to be found far beyond those manifestations of it to which the world usually gives the name of genius, and in which there is, for the most part, a *talent* of some kind or other, a special and striking faculty of execution, informed by the heaven-bestowed ardour, or genius. It is to be found in many manifestations besides these, and may best be called, as we have called it, the love and pursuit of perfection; culture being the true nurse of the pursuing love, and sweetness and light the true character of the pursued perfection. Natures with this bent emerge in all classes,—among the Barbarians, among the Philistines, among the Populace. And this bent always tends to take them out of their class, and to make their distinguishing characteristic not their Barbarianism or their Philistinism, but their *humanity*. They have, in general, a rough time of it in their lives, but they are sown more abundantly than one might think, they appear where and when one least expects it, they set up a fire which enfilades, so to speak, the class with which they are ranked; and, in general, by the extrication of their best self as the self to develop, and by the simplicity of the ends fixed by them as paramount, they hinder the unchecked predominance of that class-life which is the affirmation of our ordinary self, and seasonably disconcert mankind in their worship of machinery.

Therefore, when we speak of ourselves as divided into Barbarians, Philistines, and Populace, we must be understood always to imply that within each of these classes there are a certain number of *aliens*, if we may so call them,—persons who are mainly led, not by their class spirit, but by a general *humane* spirit, by the love of human perfection; and that this number is capable of being diminished or augmented. I mean, the number of those who will succeed in developing this happy instinct will be greater or smaller, in proportion both to the force of the original instinct within them, and to the hindrance or encouragement which it meets with from without. In almost all who have it, it is mixed with some infusion of the spirit of an ordinary self, some quantity of class-instinct, and even, as has been shown, of more than one class-instinct at the same time; so that, in general, the extrication of the best self, the pre-dominance of the *humane* instinct, will very much depend upon its meeting, or not, with what is fitted to help and elicit it. At a moment, therefore, when it is agreed that we want a source of authority, and when it seems possible that the right source is our best self, it becomes of vast importance to see whether or not the things around us are, in general, such as to help and elicit our best self, and if they are not, to see why they are not, and the most promising way of mending them.

Now, it is clear that the very absence of any powerful authority amongst us, and the prevalent doctrine of the duty and happiness of doing as one likes, and asserting our personal liberty, must tend to prevent the erection of any very strict standard of excellence, the belief in any very paramount authority of right reason, the recognition of our best self as anything very recondite and hard to come at. It may be, as I have said, a proof of our honesty that we do not attempt to give to our ordinary self, as we have it in action, predominant authority, and to impose its rule upon other people. But it is evident, also, that it is not easy, with our style of proceeding, to get beyond the notion of an ordinary self at all, or to get the paramount authority of a commanding best self, or right reason, recognised. The learned Martinus Scriblerus well says:—'The taste of the bathos is implanted by nature itself in the soul of man; till, perverted by custom or example, he is taught, or rather compelled, to relish the sublime.'[25] But with us every-thing seems directed to prevent any such perversion of us by custom or example as might compel us to relish the sublime; by all means we are encouraged to keep our natural taste for the bathos unimpaired.

I have formerly pointed out how in literature the absence of any authoritative centre, like an Academy, tends to do this. Each section of the public has its own literary organ, and the mass of the public is without any suspicion that the value of these organs is relative to their being nearer a certain ideal centre of correct information, taste and intelligence, or farther away from it. I have said that within certain limits, which any

one who is likely to read this will have no difficulty in drawing
for himself, my old adversary, the *Saturday Review*, may, on
matters of literature and taste, be fairly enough regarded,
relatively to the mass of newspapers which treat these matters,
as a kind of organ of reason. But I remember once conversing
with a company of Nonconformist admirers of some lecturer
who had let off a great firework, which the *Saturday Review*
said was all noise and false lights, and feeling my way as
tenderly as I could about the effect of this unfavourable
judgment upon those with whom I was conversing. 'Oh,'
said one who was their spokesman, with the most tranquil
air of conviction, 'it is true the *Saturday Review* abuses the lecture,
but the *British Banner*' (I am not quite sure it was the *British
Banner*, but it was some newspaper of that stamp) 'says that the
Saturday Review is quite wrong.' The speaker had evidently
no notion that there was a scale of value for judgments on
these topics, and that the judgments of the *Saturday Review*
ranked high on this scale, and those of the *British Banner* low;
the taste of the bathos implanted by nature in the literary
judgments of man had never, in my friend's case, encountered
any let or hindrance.

Just the same in religion as in literature. We have most of us
little idea of a high standard to choose our guides by, of a
great and profound spirit which is an authority while inferior
spirits are none. It is enough to give importance to things that
this or that person says them decisively, and has a large following of some strong kind when he says them. This habit of ours
is very well shown in that able and interesting work of Mr.
Hepworth Dixon's, which we were all reading lately, *The
Mormons, by One of Themselves*. Here, again, I am not quite
sure that my memory serves me as to the exact title, but I mean
the well-known book in which Mr. Hepworth Dixon described
the Mormons, and other similar religious bodies in America,
with so much detail and such warm sympathy. In this work it
seems enough for Mr. Dixon that this or that doctrine has its
Rabbi, who talks big to him, has a staunch body of disciples,
and, above all, has plenty of rifles. That there are any further
stricter tests to be applied to a doctrine, before it is pronounced
important, never seems to occur to him. 'It is easy to say,' he

writes of the Mormons, 'that these saints are dupes and
fanatics, to laugh at Joe Smith and his church, but what then?
The great facts remain. Young and his people are at Utah; a
church of 280,000 souls; an army of 20,000 rifles.' But if the
followers of a doctrine are really dupes, or worse, and its
promulgators are really fanatics, or worse, it gives the doctrine
no seriousness or authority the more that there should be
found 200,000 souls,—200,000 of the innumerable multitude
with a natural taste for the bathos,—to hold it, and 20,000
rifles to defend it. And again, of another religious organisation
in America: 'A fair and open field is not to be refused when
hosts so mighty throw down wager of battle on behalf of
what they hold to be true, however strange their faith may
seem.' A fair and open field is not to be refused to any speaker;
but this solemn way of heralding him is quite out of place,
unless he has, for the best reason and spirit of man, some
significance. 'Well, but,' says Mr. Hepworth Dixon, 'a theory
which has been accepted by men like Judge Edmonds, Dr.
Hare, Elder Frederick, and Professor Bush!' And again:
'Such are, in brief, the bases of what Newman Weeks, Sarah
Horton, Deborah Butler, and the associated brethren, proclaimed in Rolt's Hall as the new covenant!' If he was summing up an account of the doctrine of Plato, or the following
St. Paul, Mr. Hepworth Dixon could not be more earnestly
reverential. But the question is, Have personages like Judge
Edmonds, and Newman Weeks, and Elderess Polly, and
Elderess Antoinette, and the rest of Mr. Hepworth Dixon's
heroes and heroines, anything of the weight and significance
for the best reason and spirit of man that Plato and St. Paul
have? Evidently they, at present, have not; and a very small
taste of them and their doctrines ought to have convinced
Mr. Hepworth Dixon that they never could have. 'But,' says
he, 'the magnetic power which Shakerism is exercising on
American thought would of itself compel us,'—and so on. Now,
as far as real thought is concerned,—thought which affects the
best reason and spirit of man, the scientific or the imaginative
thought of the world, the only thought which deserves speaking
of in this solemn way,—America has up to the present time
been hardly more than a province of England, and even now

would not herself claim to be more than abreast of England; and of this only real human thought, English thought itself is not just now, as we must all admit, the most significant factor. Neither, then, can American thought be; and the magnetic power which Shakerism exercises on American thought is about as important, for the best reason and spirit of man, as the magnetic power which Mr. Murphy exercises on Birmingham Protestantism. And as we shall never get rid of our natural taste for the bathos in religion,—never get access to a best self and right reason which may stand as a serious authority,—by treating Mr. Murphy as his own disciples treat him, seriously, and as if he was as much an authority as any one else: so we shall never get rid of it while our able and popular writers treat their Joe Smiths and Deborah Butlers, with their so many thousand souls and so many thousand rifles, in the like exaggerated and misleading manner, and so do their best to confirm us in a bad mental habit to which we are already too prone.

If our habits make it hard for us to come at the idea of a high best self, of a paramount authority, in literature or religion, how much more do they make this hard in the sphere of politics! In other countries the governors, not depending so immediately on the favour of the governed, have everything to urge them, if they know anything of right reason (and it is at least supposed that governors should know more of this than the mass of the governed), to set it authoritatively before the community. But our whole scheme of government being representative, every one of our governors has all possible temptation, instead of setting up before the governed who elect him, and on whose favour he depends, a high standard of right reason, to accommodate himself as much as possible to their natural taste for the bathos; and even if he tries to go counter to it, to proceed in this with so much flattering and coaxing, that they shall not suspect their ignorance and prejudices to be anything very unlike right reason, or their natural taste for the bathos to differ much from a relish for the sublime. Every one is thus in every possible way encouraged to trust in his own heart; but, 'He that trusteth in his own heart,' says the Wise Man, 'is a fool'[26]; and at any rate this, which Bishop Wilson says, is undeniably true: 'The number of those who need to be awakened is far greater than that of those who need comfort.'

But in our political system everybody is comforted. Our guides and governors who have to be elected by the influence of the Barbarians, and who depend on their favour, sing the praises of the Barbarians, and say all the smooth things that can be said of them. With Mr. Tennyson, they celebrate 'the great broad-shouldered genial Englishman,' with his 'sense of duty,' his 'reverence for the laws,' and his 'patient force,' who saves us from the 'revolts, republics, revolutions, most no graver than a schoolboy's barring out,' which upset other and less broad-shouldered nations.[27] Our guides who are chosen by the Philistines and who have to look to their favour, tell the Philistines how 'all the world knows that the great middle class of this country supplies the mind, the will, and the power requisite for all the great and good things that have to be done,' and congratulate them on their 'earnest good sense, which penetrates through sophisms, ignores commonplaces, and gives to conventional illusions their true value.' Our guides who look to the favour of the Populace, tell them that 'theirs are the brightest powers of sympathy, and the readiest powers of action.'

Harsh things are said too, no doubt, against all the great classes of the community; but these things so evidently come from a hostile class, and are so manifestly dictated by the passions and prepossessions of a hostile class, and not by right reason, that they make no serious impression on those at whom they are launched, but slide easily off their minds. For instance, when the Reform League orators inveigh against our cruel and bloated aristocracy, these invectives so evidently show the passions and point of view of the Populace, that they do not sink into the minds of those at whom they are addressed, or awaken any thought or self-examination in them. Again, when our aristocratical baronet describes the Philistines and the Populace as influenced with a kind of hideous mania for emasculating the aristocracy, that reproach so clearly comes from the wrath and excited imagination of the Barbarians, that it does not much set the Philistines and the Populace thinking. Or when Mr. Lowe calls the Populace drunken and venal, he so evidently calls them this in an agony of apprehension for his Philistine or middle-class Parliament, which has done so many great and heroic works, and is now threatened with mixture and debasement, that the Populace do not lay his words seriously to heart.

So the voice which makes a permanent impression on each of our classes is the voice of its friends, and this is from the nature of things, as I have said, a comforting voice. The Barbarians remain in the belief that the great broad-shouldered genial Englishman may be well satisfied with himself; the Philistines remain in the belief that the great middle class of this country, with its earnest common-sense penetrating through sophisms and ignoring commonplaces, may be well satisfied with itself; the Populace, that the working man, with his bright powers of sympathy and ready powers of action, may be well satisfied with himself. What hope, at this rate, of extinguishing the taste of the bathos implanted by nature itself in the soul of man, or of inculcating the belief that excellence dwells among high and steep rocks, and can only be reached by those who sweat blood to reach her?

But it will be said, perhaps, that candidates for political influence and leadership, who thus caress the self-love of those whose suffrages they desire, know quite well that they are not saying the sheer truth as reason sees it, but that they are using a sort or conventional language, or what we call clap-trap, which is essential to the working of representative institutions. And therefore, I suppose, we ought rather to say with Figaro: *Qui est-ce qu'on trompe ici?*[28] Now, I admit that often, but not always, when our governors say smooth things to the self-love of the class whose political support they want, they know very well that they are overstepping, by a long stride, the bounds of truth and soberness; and while they talk, they in a manner, no doubt, put their tongue in their cheek. Not always; because, when a Barbarian appeals to his own class to make him their representative and give him political power, he, when he pleases their self-love by extolling broad-shouldered genial Englishmen with their sense of duty, reverence for the laws, and patient force, pleases his own self-love and extols himself, and is, therefore, himself ensnared by his own smooth

words. And so, too, when a Philistine wants to be sent to
Parliament by his brother Philistines, and extols the earnest
good sense which characterises Manchester and supplies the
mind, the will, and the power, as the *Daily News* eloquently
says, requisite for all the great and good things that have to be
done, he intoxicates and deludes himself as well as his brother
Philistines who hear him.

But it is true that a Barbarian often wants the political support of the Philistines; and he unquestionably, when he flatters
the self-love of Philistinism, and extols, in the approved fashion,
its energy, enterprise, and self-reliance, knows that he is talking
clap-trap, and, so to say, puts his tongue in his cheek. On all
matters where Nonconformity and its catchwords are concerned, this insincerity of Barbarians needing Nonconformist
support, and, therefore, flattering the self-love of Nonconformity
and repeating its catchwords without the least real belief in
them, is very noticeable. When the Nonconformists, in a
transport of blind zeal, threw out Sir James Graham's useful
Education Clauses in 1843, one-half of their Parliamentary
advocates, no doubt, who cried aloud against 'trampling on
the religious liberty of the Dissenters by taking the money of
Dissenters to teach the tenets of the Church of England,' put
their tongue in their cheek while they so cried out. And perhaps
there is even a sort of motion of Mr. Frederic Harrison's tongue
towards his cheek when he talks of 'the shriek of superstition,'
and tells the working class that 'theirs are the brightest
powers of sympathy and the readiest powers of action.' But
the point on which I would insist is, that this involuntary
tribute to truth and soberness on the part of certain of our
governors and guides never reaches at all the mass of us
governed, to serve as a lesson to us, to abate our self-love, and
to awaken in us a suspicion that our favourite prejudices may
be, to a higher reason, all nonsense. Whatever by-play goes on
among the more intelligent of our leaders, we do not see it;
and we are left to believe that, not only in our own eyes, but
in the eyes of our representative and ruling men, there is
nothing more admirable than our ordinary self, whatever our
ordinary self happens to be, Barbarian, Philistine, or Populace.

Thus everything in our political life tends to hide from us that there is anything wiser than our ordinary selves, and to prevent our getting the notion of a paramount right reason. Royalty itself, in its idea the expression of the collective nation, and a sort of constituted witness to its best mind, we try to turn into a kind of grand advertising van, meant to give publicity and credit to the inventions, sound or unsound, of the ordinary self of individuals.

I remember, when I was in North Germany, having this very strongly brought to my mind in the matter of schools and their institution. In Prussia, the best schools are Crown patronage schools, as they are called; schools which have been established and endowed (and new ones are to this day being established and endowed) by the Sovereign himself out of his own revenues, to be under the direct control and management of him or of those representing him, and to serve as types of what schools should be. The Sovereign, as his position raises him above many prejudices and littlenesses, and as he can always have at his disposal the best advice, has evident advantages over private founders in well planning and directing a school; while at the same time his great means and his great influence secure, to a well-planned school of his, credit and authority. This is what, in North Germany, the governors do in the matter of education for the governed; and one may say that they thus give the governed a lesson, and draw out in them the idea of a right reason higher than the suggestions of an ordinary man's ordinary self.

But in England how different is the part which in this matter our governors are accustomed to play! The Licensed Victuallers or the Commercial Travellers propose to make a school for their children; and I suppose, in the matter of schools, one may call the Licensed Victuallers or the Commercial Travellers ordinary men, with their natural taste for the bathos still strong; and a Sovereign with the advice of men like Wilhelm von Humboldt or Schleiermacher[29] may, in this matter, be a better judge, and nearer to right reason. And it will be allowed, probably, that right reason would suggest that, to have a sheer school of Licensed Victuallers' children, or a sheer school of Commercial Travellers' children, and to bring them all up, not only at home but at school too, in a kind of odour of licensed victualism or of bagmanism, is not a wise training to give to these children. And in Germany, I have said, the action of the national guides or governors is to suggest and provide a better. But, in England, the action of the national guides or governors is, for a Royal Prince or a great Minister to go down to the opening of the Licensed Victuallers' or of the Commercial Travellers' school, to take the chair, to extol the energy and self-reliance of the Licensed Victuallers or the Commercial Travellers, to be all of their way of thinking, to predict full success to their schools, and never so much as to hint to them that they are probably doing a very foolish thing, and that the right way to go to work with their children's education is quite different. And it is the same in almost every department of affairs. While, on the Continent, the idea prevails that it is the business of the heads and representatives of the nation, by virtue of their superior means, power, and information, to set an example and to provide suggestions of right reason, among us the idea is that the business of the heads and representatives of the nation is to do nothing of the kind, but to applaud the natural taste for the bathos showing itself vigorously in any part of the community, and to encourage its works.

Now I do not say that the political system of foreign countries has not inconveniences which may outweigh the inconveniences of our own political system; nor am I the least proposing to get rid of our own political system and to adopt theirs. But a sound centre of authority being what, in this disquisition, we have been led to seek, and right reason, or our best self, appearing alone to offer such a sound centre of authority, it is necessary to take note of the chief impediments which hinder, in this country, the extrication or recognition of this right reason as a paramount authority, with a view to afterwards trying in what way they can best be removed.

This being borne in mind, I proceed to remark how not only do we get no suggestions of right reason, and no rebukes of our ordinary self, from our governors, but a kind of philosophical theory is widely spread among us to the effect that there is no such thing at all as a best self and a right reason having claim to paramount authority, or, at any rate, no such thing ascertainable and capable of being made use of; and that there is nothing but an infinite number of ideas and works of our ordinary selves, and suggestions of our natural taste for the bathos, pretty nearly equal in value, which are doomed either to an irreconcilable conflict, or else to a perpetual give and take; and that wisdom consists in choosing the give and take rather than the conflict, and in sticking to our choice with patience and good humour.

And, on the other hand, we have another philosophical theory rife among us, to the effect that without the labour of perverting ourselves by custom or example to relish right reason, but by continuing all of us to follow freely our natural taste for the bathos, we shall, by the mercy of Providence, and by a kind of natural tendency of things, come in due time to relish and follow right reason.

The great promoters of these philosophical theories are our newspapers, which, no less than our Parliamentary representatives, may be said to act the part of guides and governors to us; and these favourite doctrines of theirs I call,—or should call, if the doctrines were not preached by authorities I so much respect,—the first, a peculiarly British form of Atheism, the second, a peculiarly British form of Quietism. The first-named melancholy doctrine is preached in the *Times* with great clearness and force of style; indeed, it is well known, from the example of the poet Lucretius and others, what great masters of style the atheistic doctrine has always counted among its promulgators. 'It is of no use,' says the *Times*, 'for us to attempt to force upon our neighbours our several likings and dislikings. We must take things as they are. Everybody has his own little vision of religious or civil perfection. Under the evident impossibility of satisfying everybody, we agree to take our stand on equal laws and on a system as open and liberal as is possible. The result is that everybody has more liberty of action and of speaking here than anywhere else in the Old World.' We come again here upon Mr. Roebuck's celebrated definition of happiness, on which I have so often commented: 'I look around me and ask what is the state of England? Is not every man able to say what he likes? I ask you whether the world over, or in past history, there is anything like it? Nothing. I pray that our unrivalled happiness may last.' This is the old story of our system of checks and every Englishman doing as he likes, which we have already seen to have been convenient enough so long as there were only the Barbarians and the Philistines to do what they liked, but to be getting inconvenient, and productive of anarchy, now that the Populace wants to do what it likes too.

But for all that, I will not at once dismiss this famous doctrine, but will first quote another passage from the *Times*, applying the doctrine to a matter of which we have just been speaking,—education. 'The difficulty here' (in providing a national system of education), says the *Times*, 'does not reside in any removable arrangements. It is inherent and native in the actual and inveterate state of things in this country. All these powers and personages, all these conflicting influences and varieties of character, exist, and have long existed among us; they are fighting it out, and will long continue to fight it out without coming to that happy consummation when some one element of the British character is to destroy or to absorb all the rest.' There it is! the various promptings of the natural taste for the bathos in this man and that amongst us are fighting it out; and the day will never come (and, indeed, why should we wish it to come?) when one man's particular sort of taste for the bathos shall tyrannise over another man's; nor when right reason (if that may be called an element of the British character) shall absorb and rule them all. 'The whole system of this country, like the constitution we boast to inherit, and are glad to uphold, is made up of established facts, prescriptive authorities, existing usages, powers that be, persons in possession, and communities or classes that have won dominion for themselves, and will hold it against all comers.' Every force in the world, evidently, except the one reconciling force, right reason! Barbarian here, Philistine there, Mr. Bradlaugh and Populace striking in!—pull devil, pull baker! Really, presented with the mastery of style of our leading journal, the sad picture, as one gazes upon it, assumes the iron and inexorable solemnity of tragic Destiny.

After this, the milder doctrine of our other philosophical teacher, the *Daily News*, has, at first, something very attractive and assuaging. The *Daily News* begins, indeed, in appearance,

to weave the iron web of necessity round us like the *Times*.
'The alternative is between a man's doing what he likes and
his doing what some one else, probably not one whit wiser
than himself, likes.' This points to the tacit compact, mentioned
in my last paper, between the Barbarians and the Philistines,
and into which it is hoped that the Populace will one day
enter; the compact, so creditable to English honesty, that
since each class has only the ideas and aims of its ordinary
self to give effect to, none of them shall, if it exercise power,
treat its ordinary self too seriously, or attempt to impose it on
others, but shall let these others,—the fanatical Protestant, for
instance, in his Papist-baiting, and the popular tribune in his
Hyde Park anarchy-mongering,—have their fling. But then
the *Daily News* suddenly lights up the gloom of necessitarianism
with bright beams of hope. 'No doubt,' it says, 'the common
reason of society ought to check the aberrations of individual
eccentricity.' This common reason of society looks very like
our best self or right reason, to which we want to give authority,
by making the action of the *State*, or nation in its collective
character, the expression of it. But of this project of ours, the
Daily News, with its subtle dialectics, makes havoc. 'Make the
State the organ of the common reason?'—it says. 'You make it
the organ of something or other, but how can you be certain
that reason will be the quality which will be embodied in it?'
You cannot be certain of it, undoubtedly, if you never try to
bring the thing about; but the question is, the action of the
State being the action of the collective nation, and the action
of the collective nation carrying naturally great publicity,
weight, and force of example with it, whether we should not
try to put into the action of the State as much as possible of
right reason or our best self, which may, in this manner, come
back to us with new force and authority; may have visibility,
form, and influence; and help to confirm us, in the many
moments when we are tempted to be our ordinary selves
merely, in resisting our natural taste of the bathos rather than
in giving way to it?

But no! says our teacher: 'It is better there should be an
infinite variety of experiments in human action; the common
reason of society will in the main check the aberrations of

individual eccentricity well enough, if left to its natural operation.' This is what I call the specially British form of Quietism, or a devout, but excessive, reliance on an over-ruling Providence. Providence, as the moralists are careful to tell us, generally works in human affairs by human means; so, when we want to make right reason act on individual inclination, our best self on our ordinary self, we seek to give it more power of doing so by giving it public recognition and authority, and embodying it, so far as we can, in the State. It seems too much to ask of Providence, that while we, on our part, leave our congenital taste for the bathos to its natural operation and its infinite variety of experiments, Providence should mysteriously guide it into the true track, and compel it to relish the sublime. At any rate, great men and great institutions have hitherto seemed necessary for producing any considerable effect of this kind. No doubt we have an infinite variety of experiments and an ever-multiplying multitude of explorers. Even in these few chapters I have enumerated many: the *British Banner*, Judge Edmonds, Newman Weeks, Deborah Butler, Elderess Polly, Brother Noyes, Mr. Murphy, the Licensed Victuallers, the Commercial Travellers, and I know not how many more; and the members of the noble army are swelling every day. But what a depth of Quietism, or rather, what an over-bold call on the direct interposition of Providence, to believe that these interesting explorers will discover the true track, or at any rate, 'will do so in the main well enough' (whatever that may mean) if left to their natural operation; that is, by going on as they are! Philosophers say, indeed, that we learn virtue by performing acts of virtue; but to say that we shall learn virtue by performing any acts to which our natural taste for the bathos carries us, that the fanatical Protestant comes at his best self by Papist-baiting, or Newman Weeks and Deborah Butler at right reason by following their noses, this certainly does appear over-sanguine.

It is true, what we want is to make right reason act on individual reason, the reason of individuals; all our search for authority has that for its end and aim. The *Daily News* says, I observe, that all my argument for authority 'has a non-intellectual root;' and from what I know of my mind and its poverty I think this so probable, that I should be inclined easily to admit it, if it were not that, in the first place, nothing of this kind, perhaps, should be admitted without examination; and in the second, a way of accounting for the charge being made, in this particular instance, without good grounds, appears to present itself. What seems to me to account here, perhaps, for the charge, is the want of flexibility of our race, on which I have so often remarked. I mean, it being admitted that the conformity of the individual reason of the fanatical Protestant or the popular rioter with right reason is our true object, and not the mere restraining them, by the strong arm of the State, from Papist-baiting, or railing-breaking,—admitting this, we English have so little flexibility that we cannot readily perceive that the State's restraining them from these in- dulgences may yet fix clearly in their minds that, to the collec- tive nation, these indulgences appear irrational and un- allowable, may make them pause and reflect, and may contri- bute to bringing, with time, their individual reason into harmony with right reason. But in no country, owing to the want of intellectual flexibility above mentioned, is the leaning which is our natural one, and, therefore, needs no recom- mending to us, so sedulously recommended, and the leaning which is not our natural one, and, therefore, does not need dispraising to us, so sedulously dispraised, as in ours. To rely on the individual being, with us, the natural leaning, we will hear of nothing but the good of relying on the individual; to act through the collective nation on the individual being not our natural leaning, we will hear nothing in recommendation of it. But the wise know that we often need to hear most of that to which we are least inclined, and even to learn to employ, in certain circumstances, that which is capable, if employed amiss, of being a danger to us.

Elsewhere, this is certainly better understood than here. In a recent number of the *Westminster Review*, an able writer, but with precisely our national want of flexibility of which I have been speaking, has unearthed, I see, for our present needs, an English translation, published some years ago, of Wilhelm von Humboldt's book, *The Sphere and Duties of Government*. Humboldt's object in this book is to show that the operation of government ought to be severely limited to what directly and immediately relates to the security of person and property. Wilhelm von Humboldt, one of the most beautiful souls that have ever existed, used to say that one's business in life was first to perfect one's self by all the means in one's power, and secondly to try and create in the world around one an aristocracy, the most numerous that one possibly could, of talents and characters. He saw, of course, that, in the end, everything comes to this,—that the individual must act for himself, and must be perfect in himself; and he lived in a country, Germany, where people were disposed to act too little for themselves, and to rely too much on the Government. But even thus, such was his flexibility, so little was he in bondage to a mere abstract maxim, that he saw very well that for his purpose itself, of enabling the individual to stand perfect on his own foundations and to do without the State, the action of the State would for long, long years be necessary. And soon after he wrote his book on *The Sphere and Duties of Government*, Wilhelm von Humboldt became Minister of Education in Prussia; and from his ministry all the great reforms which give the control of Prussian education to the State,—the transference of the management of public schools from their old boards of trustees to the State, the obligatory State-examination for schoolmasters, and the foundation of the great State-University of Berlin,—take their origin. This his English reviewer says not a word of. But, writing for a people whose dangers lie, as we have seen, on the side of their unchecked and unguided individual action, whose dangers none of them lie on the side of an over-reliance on the State, he quotes just so much of Wilhelm von Humboldt's example as can flatter them in their propensities, and do them no good; and just what might make them think, and be of use to them, he leaves on one side. This precisely recalls the manner, it will be observed, in which we have seen that our royal and noble personages proceed with the Licensed Victuallers.

In France the action of the State on individuals is yet more preponderant than in Germany; and the need which friends of human perfection feel for what may enable the individual to stand perfect on his own foundations is all the stronger.

But what says one of the staunchest of these friends, M. Renan, on State action; and even State action in that very sphere where in France it is most excessive, the sphere of education? Here are his words:—'A Liberal believes in liberty, and liberty signifies the non-intervention of the State. *But such an ideal is still a long way off from us, and the very means to remove it to an indefinite distance would be precisely the State's withdrawing its action too soon.*' [30] And this, he adds, is even truer of education than of any other department of public affairs.

We see, then, how indispensable to that human perfection which we seek is, in the opinion of good judges, some public recognition and establishment of our best self, or right reason. We see how our habits and practice oppose themselves to such a recognition, and the many inconveniences which we therefore suffer. But now let us try to go a little deeper, and to find, beneath our actual habits and practice, the very ground and cause out of which they spring.

NOTES

1. 'M. Sainte-Beuve', *Quarterly Review*, CXIX (January, 1866). The author was F. T. Marzials.
2. Charles de Montesquieu, 'Discours sur les motifs qui doivent nous encourager aux sciences'; Discours Académiques, in *Œuvres complètes*, VII, 78, ed. Laboulaye (Paris, 1879).
3. Thomas Wilson (1663–1755), Bishop of Sodor and Man, author of *Maxims of Piety and of Christianity* (1789) and *Sacra Privata* (1786). In the Preface to *Culture and Anarchy* Arnold praises Wilson's union of 'the most sincere ardour and unction' with 'downright honesty and plain good sense'.
4. John Bright (1811–1889), Quaker radical, famous for his support of Free Trade, who campaigned for the extension of the franchise in 1866.
5. J. A. Roebuck (1801–1879), Benthamite radical politician.
6. I Timothy, iv, 8.
7. One of the 'Rules of Health and Long Life' in B. Franklin's *Poor Richard, An Almanack* (1742).
8. Epictetus, a Stoic philosopher, author of *Encheiridion*.
9. I Peter, iii, 8.

10. *publicè egestas, privatim opulentia:* 'private wealth, public penury'; Sallust, *Catilina*, LII, 22.

11. Edmond Beales (1803–1881), President of the Reform League. Charles Bradlaugh (1833–1891), the famous freethinker and extreme radical.

12. 'What part of the world is not full of our endeavour?'. Virgil, *Aeneid*, I, 460.

13. Richard Congreve (1818–1899), a contemporary of Arnold's at Rugby who was greatly influenced by a meeting with Comte in Paris in 1848. He was tutor to Frederic Harrison at Wadham.

14. Ludwig Preller, *Römische Mythologie* (Berlin, 1858).

15. H. T. Buckle (1821–1862) applied a scientific method to historical problems in the *History of Civilisation in England* (1857, 1861).

16. Matthew, xxiii, 8.

17. Frederic Harrison, 'Our Venetian Constitution', in *The Fortnightly Review*, VII (1867).

18 Saint Augustine, *Confessions*, XIII, 18.

19. George Odger (1820–1877), shoemaker and trade-union official.

20. 'The Friend of Humanity and the Knife-Grinder' (*Anti-Jacobin*; November, 1797), a burlesque directed against Southey, in which the Friend becomes enraged at the Knife-Grinder's acceptance of his downtrodden condition, kicks him, overturns his wheel and exits 'in a transport of republican enthusiasm and universal philanthropy'.

21. Zephaniah Diggs, fictitious peasant in Arnold's *Friendship's Garland*.

22. Quotations from the *Daily News*, 7 December, 1864, used in *Friendship's Garland*.

23. William Murphy, inflammatory anti-Catholic orator.

24. Sir Daniel Gooch (1816–1889), chairman of the Great Western Railway, quoted to Swindon workmen his mother's daily injunction, 'Ever remember, my dear Dan, that you should look forward to being some day the manager of that concern'. Arnold refers to it in *Culture and Anarchy*, Ch. 2, as '"Be ye Perfect" done into English'.

25. Martinus Scriblerus, satiric persona used by Pope, Swift, Gay, Parnell and Arbuthnot; quotation from 'Peri Bathous or the Art of Sinking in Poetry', from *Miscellanies*, III (1728).

26. Proverbs, xxviii, 26.

27. Tennyson, *The Princess*, Conclusion.

28. 'Who is being fooled here?' Beaumarchais, *Le barbier de Séville* (Paris, 1775).

29. Wilhelm von Humboldt (1767–1835), F. D. E. Schleiermacher (1763–1834); Prussian educationalist and theologian, respectively.

30. Ernest Renan (1823–1892), 'L'instruction supérieur en France', in *Questions contemporaines* (Paris, 1868).

Evolution and Society

[Charles Robert Darwin (1809–1882) explained his hypothesis of evolution through natural selection in the *Origin of Species*. He brought together in fact two ideas already prevalent: Malthus's principle that population tends to increase beyond the resources available to it, thus making the struggle for existence inevitable, and the idea of Progress, so palpably present in the development of science and technology. The collection and sifting of evidence in Darwin's book also provided a most impressive example of those scientific methods which were acclaimed by the positivists as destroying the foundations of traditional religion and marking the new era.

Herbert Spencer (1820–1903), a respected philosophical writer in his day, can be seen as a spokesman for the doctrine of *laissez-faire*. He actually invented the phrase, 'the survival of the fittest'. Darwinism lent a scientific basis to his distrust of any interference with the efforts of the individual or with the natural conditions which rewarded or penalized them. On the other hand, Samuel Butler (1835–1902) included in his satire, *Erewhon*, a complex questioning both of the evolutionary thinking that denied a place to the will and of the blind scientific faith which seemed destined to turn man into an 'affectionate machine-tickling aphid'. Darwin's ideas were propounded most uncompromisingly by Thomas Henry Huxley (1825–1895), the biologist and educationalist. It was Huxley and John Tyndall whom the young Yeats was to detest for depriving him of the simple-minded religion of his childhood. Huxley saw man's scientific consciousness as part of an evolutionary process towards a planned social economy. He hoped that the natural man's undisciplined procreative habits might eventually be limited, but in the meantime asserted the need for a scientific social organisation of Britain to make her more effective in the forthcoming struggle among the nations. His is one of the few Victorian voices prophesying war.]

HERBERT SPENCER

From *Social Statics: or, the Conditions essential to Human Happiness specified, and the first of them developed*
[The extract, from Part III, Ch. 25, 'Poor Laws', is taken from the first edition, 1851.]

Pervading all nature we may see at work a stern discipline, which is a little cruel that it may be very kind. That state of universal warfare maintained throughout the lower creation, to the great perplexity of many worthy people, is at bottom the most merciful provision which the circumstances admit of. It is much better that the ruminant animal, when deprived by age of the vigour which made its existence a pleasure, should be killed by some beast of prey, than that it should linger out a life made painful by infirmities, and eventually die of starvation. By the destruction of all such, not only is existence ended before it becomes burdensome, but room is made for a younger generation capable of the fullest enjoyment; and, moroever, out of the very act of substitution happiness is derived for a tribe of predatory creatures. Note further, that their carnivorous enemies not only remove from herbivorous herds individuals past their prime, but also weed out the sickly, the malformed, and the least fleet or powerful. By the aid of which purifying process, as well as by the fighting so universal in the pairing season, all vitiation of the race through the multiplication of its inferior samples is prevented; and the maintenance of a constitution completely adapted to surrounding conditions, and therefore most productive of happiness, is ensured.

The development of the higher creation is a progress towards a form of being capable of a happiness undiminished by these drawbacks. It is in the human race that the consummation is to be accomplished. Civilization is the last stage of its accomplishment. And the ideal man is the man in whom all the conditions of that accomplishment are fulfilled. Meanwhile the well-being of existing humanity and the unfolding of it into this ultimate perfection, are both secured by that same beneficent, though severe discipline, to which the animate creation at large is subject: a discipline which is pitiless in the working out of good: a felicity-pursuing law which never swerves for the avoidance of partial and temporary suffering. The poverty of the incapable, the distresses that come upon the imprudent, the starvation of the idle, and those shoulder-ings aside of the weak by the strong, which leave so many "in shallows and in miseries," are the decree of a large, far-seeing benevolence. It seems hard that an unskilfullness which with all his efforts he cannot overcome, should entail hunger upon the artizan. It seems hard that a labourer incapacitated by sickness from competing with his stronger fellows, should have to bear the resulting privations. It seems hard that widows and orphans should be left to struggle for life or death. Neverthe-less, when regarded not separately, but in connexion with the interests of universal humanity, these harsh fatalities are seen to be full of the highest beneficence—the same beneficence which brings to early graves the children of diseased parents and singles out the low-spirited, the intemperate, and the debilitated as the victims of an epidemic.

There are many very amiable people—people over whom in so far as their feelings are concerned we may fitly rejoice—who have not the nerve to look this matter fairly in the face. Disabled as they are by their sympathies with present suffering, from duly regarding ultimate consequences, they pursue a course which is very injudicious, and in the end even cruel. We do not consider it true kindness in a mother to gratify her child with sweetmeats that are certain to make it ill. We should think it a very foolish sort of benevolence which led a surgeon to let his patient's disease progress to a fatal issue, rather than inflict pain by an operation. Similarly, we must call those spurious philanthropists, who, to prevent present misery, would entail greater misery upon future generations. All defenders of a poor-law must, however, be classed amongst such. That rigorous necessity which, when allowed to act on them, becomes so sharp a spur to the lazy, and so strong a bridle to the random, these paupers' friends would repeal, because of the wailings it here and there produces. Blind to the fact, that under the natural order of things society is constantly excreting its unhealthy, imbecile, slow, vacillating, faithless members, these unthinking, though well-meaning, men advocate an interference which not only stops the purifying process, but even increases the vitiation—absolutely encourages the multiplication of the reckless and incompetent by offering them an unfailing provision, and *dis*courages the multiplication of the competent and provident by heightening the prospective difficulty of maintaining a family. And thus, in their eagerness to prevent the really salutary sufferings that surround us, these sigh-wise and groan-foolish people bequeath to posterity a continually increasing curse.

CHARLES DARWIN

From *On the Origin of Species by means of Natural Selection*
[The extracts, from Ch. 4, 'Natural Selection', and Ch. 14, 'Conclusion', are taken from the first edition, 1859.]

We shall best understand the probable course of natural selection by taking the case of a country undergoing some physical change, for instance, of climate. The proportional numbers of its inhabitants would almost immediately undergo a change, and some species might become extinct. We may conclude, from what we have seen of the intimate and complex manner in which the inhabitants of each country are bound together, that any change in the numerical proportions of some of the inhabitants, independently of the change of climate itself, would most seriously affect many of the others. If the country were open on its borders, new forms would certainly immigrate, and this also would seriously disturb the relations of some of the former inhabitants. Let it be remembered how powerful the influence of a single introduced tree or mammal has been shown to be. But in the case of an island, or of a country partly surrounded by barriers, into which new and better adapted forms could not freely enter, we should then have places in the economy of nature which would assuredly be better filled up, if some of the original inhabitants were in some manner modified; for, had the area been open to immigration, these same places would have been seized on by intruders. In such a case, every slight modification, which in the course of ages chanced to arise, and which in any way favoured the individuals of any of the species, by better adapting them to their altered conditions, would tend to be preserved; and natural selection would thus have free scope for the work of improvement.

We have good reason to believe, as stated in the first chapter, that a change in the conditions of life, by specially acting on the reproductive system, causes or increases variability; and in the foregoing case the conditions are supposed to have undergone a change, and this would manifestly be favourable to natural selection, by giving a better chance of profitable variations occurring; and unless profitable variations do occur, natural selection can do nothing. Not that, as I believe, any extreme amount of variability is necessary; as man can certainly produce great results by adding up in any given direction mere individual differences, so could Nature, but far more easily, from having incomparably longer time at her disposal. Nor do I believe that any great physical change, as of climate, or any unusual degree of isolation to check immigration, is actually necessary to produce new and unoccupied places for natural selection to fill up by modifying and improving some of the varying inhabitants. For as all the inhabitants of each country are struggling together with nicely balanced forces, extremely slight modifications in the structure or habits of one inhabitant would often give it an advantage over others; and still further modifications of the same kind would often still further increase the advantage. No country can be named in which all the native inhabitants are now so perfectly adapted to each other and to the physical conditions under which they live, that none of them could anyhow be improved; for in all countries, the natives have been so far conquered by naturalised productions, that they have allowed foreigners to take firm possession of the land. And as foreigners have thus everywhere beaten some of the natives, we may safely conclude that the natives might have been modified with advantage, so as to have better resisted such intruders.

As man can produce, and certainly has produced, a great result by his methodical and unconscious means of selection, what may not nature effect? Man can act only on external and visible characters: Nature cares nothing for appearances, except in so far as they may be useful to any being. She can act on every internal organ, on every shade of constitutional difference, on the whole machinery of life. Man selects only for his own good: Nature only for that of the being which she tends. Every selected character is fully exercised by her; and the being is placed under well-suited conditions of life. Man keeps the natives of many climates in the same country; he seldom exercises each selected character in some peculiar and fitting manner; he feeds a long and a short beaked pigeon on the same food; he does not exercise a long-backed or long-legged quadruped in any peculiar manner; he exposes sheep with long and short wool to the same climate. He does not allow the most vigorous males to struggle for the females. He does not rigidly destroy all inferior animals, but protects during each varying season, as far as lies in his power, all his productions. He often begins his selection by some half-monstrous form; or at least by some modification prominent enough to catch his eye, or to be plainly useful to him. Under nature, the slightest difference of structure or constitution may well turn the nicely-balanced scale in the struggle for life, and so be preserved. How fleeting are the wishes and efforts of man! how short his time! and consequently how poor will his products be, compared with those accumulated by Nature during whole geological periods! Can we wonder then, that nature's productions should be far "truer" in character than man's productions; that they should be infinitely better adapted to the most complex conditions of life, and should plainly bear the stamp of far higher workmanship?

. . . The affinities of all the beings of the same class have sometimes been represented by a great tree. I believe this simile largely speaks the truth. The green and budding twigs may represent existing species; and those produced during each former year may represent the long succession of extinct species. At each period of growth all the growing twigs have tried to branch out on all sides, and to overtop and kill the surrounding twigs and branches, in the same manner as species and groups of species have tried to overmaster other species in the great battle for life. The limbs divided into great branches, and these into lesser and lesser branches, were themselves once, when the tree was small, budding twigs; and this connexion of the former and present buds by ramifying branches may well represent the classification of all extinct and living species in groups subordinate to groups. Of the many twigs which flourished when the tree was a mere bush, only two or three, now grown into great branches, yet survive and bear all the other branches; so with the species which lived during long-past geological periods, very few now have living and modified descendants. From the first growth of the tree, many a limb and branch has decayed and dropped off; and these lost branches of various sizes may represent those whole orders, families, and genera which have now no living representatives, and which are known to us only from having been found in a fossil state. As we here and there see a thin straggling branch springing from a fork low down in a tree, and which by some chance has been favoured and is still alive on its summit, so we occasionally see an animal like the Ornithorhynchus or Lepidosiren, which in some small degree connects by its affinities two large branches of life, and which has apparently been saved from fatal competition by having inhabited a protected station. As buds give rise by growth to fresh buds, and these, if vigorous, branch out and overtop on all sides many a feebler branch, so by generation I believe it has been with the great Tree of Life, which fills with its dead and broken branches the crust of the earth, and covers the surface with its ever branching and beautiful ramifications.

. . . Authors of the highest eminence seem to be fully satisfied with the view that each species has been independently created. To my mind it accords better with what we know of the laws impressed on matter by the Creator, that the production and extinction of the past and present inhabitants of the world should have been due to secondary causes, like those determining the birth and death of the individual. When I view all beings not as special creations, but as the lineal descendants of some few beings which lived long before the first bed of the Silurian system was deposited, they seem to me to become ennobled. Judging from the past, we may safely infer that not one living species will transmit its unaltered likeness to a distant futurity. And of the species now living very few will transmit progeny of any kind to a far distant futurity; for the manner in which all organic beings are grouped, shows that the greater number of species in each genus, and all the species of many genera, have left no descendants, but have become utterly extinct. We can so far take a prophetic glance into futurity as to foretell that it will be the common and widely-spread species, belonging to the larger and dominant groups, which will ultimately prevail and procreate new and dominant species. As all the living forms of life are the lineal descendants of those which lived long before the Silurian epoch, we may feel certain that the ordinary succession by generation has never once been broken, and that no cataclysm has desolated the whole world. Hence we may look with some confidence to a secure future of equally inappreciable length. And as natural selection works solely by and for the good of each being, all corporeal and mental endowments will tend to progress towards perfection.

It is interesting to contemplate an entangled bank, clothed with many plants of many kinds, with birds singing on the bushes, with various insects flitting about, and with worms crawling through the damp earth, and to reflect that these elaborately constructed forms, so different from each other, and dependent upon each other in so complex a manner, have all been produced by laws acting around us. These laws, taken in the largest sense, being Growth with Reproduction; Inheritance which is almost implied by reproduction; Variability from the indirect and direct action of the external conditions of life, and from use and disuse; a Ratio of Increase so high as to lead to a Struggle for Life, and as a consequence to Natural Selection, entailing Divergence of Character and the Extinction of less-improved forms. Thus, from the war of nature, from famine and death, the most exalted object which we are capable of conceiving, namely, the production of the higher animals, directly follows. There is grandeur in this view of life, with its several powers, having been originally breathed into a few forms or into one; and that, whilst this planet has gone cycling on according to the fixed law of gravity, from so simple a beginning endless forms most beautiful and most wonderful have been, and are being, evolved.

SAMUEL BUTLER

From *Erewhon or, Over the Range*

[The extracts, from Chs. 21, 22 and 23, 'The Book of the Machines', are taken from the first edition, 1872. The narrator quotes an Erewhonian philosopher who had procured the suppression of advanced machinery in Erewhon.]

"There is no security"—to quote his own words—"against the ultimate development of mechanical consciousness, in the fact of machines possessing little consciousness now. A mollusc has not much consciousness. Reflect upon the extraordinary advance which the machines have made during the last few hundred years, and note how slowly the animal and vegetable kingdoms are advancing in comparison. The more highly organised machines are creatures not so much of yesterday as of the last five minutes, so to speak, in comparison with past time. Assume for the sake of argument that conscious beings have existed for some twenty million years: see what strides machines have made in the last thousand! May not the world last twenty million years longer? If so, what will they not in the end become? Is it not safer to nip the mischief in the bud and to forbid them further progress?

"But who can say that the vapour engine has not a kind of consciousness? Where does consciousness begin, and where end? Who can draw the line? Who can draw any line? Is not every-thing interwoven with everything? Is not machinery linked with animal life in an infinite variety of ways? The shell of a hen's egg is a machine as much as an egg-cup is: the shell is a plan for holding the egg as much as the egg-cup for holding the shell: both are phases of the same function; the hen makes the shell in her inside, but it is pure pottery. She makes her nest outside of herself for convenience' sake, but the nest is not more of a machine than the egg-shell is. A 'machine' is only a 'device.'"

... "Even a potato in a dark cellar has a certain low cunning about him which serves him in excellent stead. He knows perfectly well what he wants and how to get it. He sees the light coming from the cellar window and sends his shoots crawling straight thereto: they will crawl along the floor and up the wall and out at the cellar window; if there be a little earth anywhere on the journey he will find it and use it for his own ends. What deliberation he may exercise in the matter of his roots when he is planted in the earth is a thing unknown to us, but we can imagine him saying, 'I will have a tuber here and a tuber there, and I will suck whatsoever advantage I can from all my surroundings. This neighbour I will over-shadow, and that I will undermine; and what I can do shall be the limits of what I will do. He that is stronger and better placed than I shall overcome me, and him that is weaker I will overcome.' The potato says these things by doing them, which is the best of language. What is consciousness if this is not consciousness? We find it difficult to sympathise with the emotions of a potato; so we do with those of an oyster. Neither of these things makes a noise on being boiled or opened, and noise appeals to us more strongly than anything else, because we make so much about our own sufferings. Since then they do not annoy us by any expression of pain we call them emotion-less; and so *qua* mankind they are; but mankind is not everybody."

... "*Either*," he proceeds, "a great deal of action that has been called purely mechanical and unconscious must be ad-mitted to contain more elements of consciousness than has been allowed hitherto (and in this case germs of consciousness will be found in many actions of the higher machines)—*Or* (assuming the theory of evolution but at the same time deny-ing the consciousness of vegetable and crystalline action) the race of man has descended from things which had no conscious-ness at all. In this case there is no *a priori* improbability in the descent of conscious (and more than conscious) machines from those which now exist, except that which is suggested by the apparent absence of anything like a reproductive system in the mechanical kingdom. This absence however is only apparent, as I shall presently show.

"Do not let me be misunderstood as living in fear of any actually existing machine; there is probably no known machine which is more than a prototype of future mechanical life. The present machines are to the future as the early Saurians to man. The largest of them will probably greatly diminish in size. Some of the lowest vertebrata attained a much greater bulk than has descended to their more highly organised living representatives, and in a like manner a diminution in the size of machines has often attended their development and progress. Take the watch, for example; examine its beautiful structure; observe the intelligent play of the minute members which compose it: yet this little creature is but a development of the cumbrous clocks that preceded it; it is no deterioration from them. The day might come when clocks, which certainly at the present time are not diminishing in bulk, would be superseded owing to the universal use of watches, in which case they would become as extinct as ichthyosauri, while the watch, whose tendency has for some years been to decrease in size rather than the contrary, would remain the only existing type of an extinct race."

. . . "It can be answered that even though machines should hear never so well and speak never so wisely, they will still always do the one or the other for our advantage and not for their own; that man will be the ruling spirit and the machine the servant; that as soon as a machine fails to discharge the service which man expects from it, it is doomed to extinction; that the machines stand to man simply in the relation of lower animals, the vapour-engine itself being only a more economical kind of horse: so that instead of being likely to be developed into a higher kind of life than man's, they owe their very existence and progress to their power of ministering to human wants, and must therefore both now and ever be man's inferiors.

"This is all very well. But the servant glides by imperceptible approaches into the master; and we have come to such a pass that even now man must suffer terribly on ceasing to benefit the machines. If all machines were to be annihilated at one moment, so that not a knife nor lever nor rag of clothing nor anything whatsoever were left to man but his bare body alone that he was born with, and if all knowledge of mechanical laws were taken from him so that he could make no more machines, and all machine-made food destroyed so that the race of man should be left as it were naked upon a desert island, we should become extinct in six weeks. A few miserable individuals might linger, but even these in a year or two would become worse than monkeys. Man's very soul is due to the machines; it is a machine-made thing: he thinks as he thinks and feels as he feels through the work that machines have wrought upon him, and their existence is quite as much a *sine quâ non* for his, as his for theirs. This fact precludes us from proposing the complete annihilation of machinery, but surely it indicates that we should destroy as many of them as we can possibly dispense with, lest they should tyrannize over us even more completely. It is true, from a low materialistic point of view, it would seem that those thrive best who use machinery wherever its use is possible with profit; but this is the art of the machines—they serve that they may rule. They bear no malice towards man for destroying a whole race of them provided he creates a better instead; on the contrary, they reward him liberally for having hastened their development. It is for neglecting them that he incurs their wrath, or for using inferior machines, or for not making sufficient exertions to invent new ones, or for destroying them without replacing them; yet this is what we must do, and do quickly; for though our rebellion against their infant power will cause infinite suffering, what will not things come to, if that rebellion is delayed?

"They have preyed upon man's grovelling preference for his material over his spiritual interests, and have betrayed him into supplying that element of struggle and warfare without which no race can advance. The lower animals progress because they struggle with one another; the weaker die, the stronger breed and transmit their strength. The machines being of themselves unable to struggle, have got man to do their struggling for them: as long as he fulfils this function duly, all goes well with him—at least he thinks so; but the moment he fails to do his best for the advancement of machinery by encouraging the good and destroying the bad, he is left behind in the race of competition; and this means that he will be made uncomfortable in a variety of ways, and perhaps that he will die. So that even now the machines will only serve on condition of being served, and that too upon their own terms; the moment their terms are not complied with, they jib, and either smash both themselves and all whom they can reach, or turn churlish and refuse to work at all. How many men at this hour are living in a state of bondage to the machines? How many spend their whole lives, from the cradle to the grave, in tending them by night and day? Is it not plain that the machines are gaining ground upon us, when we reflect on the increasing number of those who are bound down to them as slaves, and of those who devote their whole souls to the advancement of the mechanical kingdom?"

. . ."The misery is that man has been blind so long already. In his reliance upon the use of steam he has been betrayed into increasing and multiplying. To withdraw steam power suddenly will not have the effect of reducing us to the state in which we were before its introduction; there will be a general break-up and time of anarchy such as has never been known; it will be as though our population were suddenly doubled, with no additional means of feeding the increased number. The air we breathe is hardly more necessary for our animal life than the use of any machine, on the strength of which we have increased our numbers, is to our civilisation; it is the machines which act upon man and make him man, as much as man who has acted upon and made the machines; but we must choose between the alternative of undergoing much present suffering, or seeing ourselves gradually superseded by our own creatures, till we rank no higher in comparison with them, than the beasts of the field with ourselves.

"Herein lies our danger. For many seem inclined to acquiesce in so dishonourable a future. They say that although man should become to the machines what the horse and dog are to us, yet that he will continue to exist, and will probably

be better off in a state of domestication under the beneficent
rule of the machines than in his present wild condition. We
treat our domestic animals with much kindness. We give them
whatever we believe to be the best for them; and there can
be no doubt that our use of meat has increased their happiness
rather than detracted from it. In like manner there is reason to
hope that the machines will use us kindly, for their existence
will be in a great measure dependent upon ours; they will
rule us with a rod of iron, but they will not eat us; they will not
only require our services in the reproduction and education
of their young, but also in waiting upon them as servants; in
gathering food for them, and feeding them, in restoring them
to health when they are sick and in either burying their dead
or working up their deceased members into new forms of
mechanical existence. The nature of the motive power which
works the advancement of the machines precludes the
possibility of man's life being rendered miserable as well as
enslaved. Slaves are tolerably happy if they have good
masters, and the revolution will not occur in our time, nor
hardly in ten thousand years, or ten times that. Is it wise to be
uneasy about a contingency which is so remote? Man is not a
sentimental animal where his material interests are concerned,
and though here and there some ardent soul may look upon
himself and curse his fate that he was not born a vapour-
engine, yet the mass of mankind will acquiesce in any arrangement which gives them better food and clothing at a cheaper
rate, and will refrain from yielding to unreasonable jealousy
merely because there are other destinies more glorious than
their own. The power of custom is enormous, and so gradual
will be the change, that man's sense of what is due to himself
will be at no time rudely shocked; our bondage will steal upon
us noiselessly and by imperceptible approaches; nor will there
ever be such a clashing of desires between man and the
machines as will lead to an encounter between them. Among
themselves the machines will war eternally, but they will still
require man as the being through whose agency the struggle
will be principally conducted. In point of fact there is no
occasion for anxiety about the future happiness of man so long
as he continues to be in any way profitable to the machines;

he may become the inferior race, but he will be infinitely
better off than he is now. Is it not then both absurd and unreasonable to be envious of our benefactors? And should we
not be guilty of consummate folly if we were to reject advantages
which we cannot obtain otherwise, merely because they involve a greater gain to others than to ourselves?

"With those who can argue in this way I have nothing in
common. I shrink with as much horror from believing that
my race can ever be superseded or surpassed, as I should do
from believing that even at the remotest period my ancestors
were other than human beings. Could I believe that ten
hundred thousand years ago a single one of my ancestors was
another kind of being to myself, I should lose all self-respect,
and take no further pleasure or interest in life. I have the same
feeling with regard to my descendants, and believe it to be one
that will be felt so generally that the country will resolve upon
putting an immediate stop to all further mechanical progress,
and upon destroying all improvements that have been made
for the last three hundred years. I would not urge more than
this. We may trust ourselves to deal with those that remain,
and though I should prefer to have seen the destruction include
another two hundred years, I am aware of the necessity for
compromising, and would so far sacrifice my own individual
convictions as to be content with three hundred. Less than this
will be insufficient."

T. H. HUXLEY

From 'The Struggle for Existence: A Programme'
[This article appeared in *The Nineteenth Century*, XXIII, 161–80
(February, 1888). We omit a footnote, giving statistics.]

In the ancient world and in a large part of that in which we
live, the practice of infanticide was or is a regular and legal
custom; the steady recurrence of famine, pestilence, and war
were and are normal factors in the struggle for existence, and
have served, in a gross and brutal fashion, to mitigate the
intensity of its chief cause.

But, in the more advanced civilisations, the progress of private and public morality has steadily tended to remove all these checks. We declare infanticide murder, and punish it as such; we decree, not quite successfully, that no one shall die of hunger; we regard death from preventible causes of other kinds as a sort of constructive murder, and eliminate pestilence to the best of our ability; we declaim against the curse of war, and the wickedness of the military spirit, and we are never weary of dilating on the blessedness of peace and the innocent beneficence of Industry. In their moments of expansion, even statesmen and men of business go thus far. The finer spirits look to an ideal 'civitas Dei'; a state when, every man having reached the point of absolute self-negation, and having nothing but moral perfection to strive after, peace will truly reign, not merely among nations, but among men, and the struggle for existence will be at an end.

Whether human nature is competent, under any circumstances, to reach, or even seriously advance towards, this ideal condition, is a question which need not be discussed. It will be admitted that mankind has not yet reached this stage by a very long way, and my business is with the present. And that which I wish to point out is that, so long as the natural man increases and multiplies without restraint, so long will peace and industry not only permit, but they will necessitate, a struggle for existence as sharp as any that ever went on under the *regime* of war. If Istar[1] is to reign on the one hand, she will demand her human sacrifices on the other.

Let us look at home. For seventy years peace and industry have had their way among us with less interruption and under more favourable conditions than in any other country on the face of the earth. The wealth of Croesus was nothing to that which we have accumulated, and our prosperity has filled the world with envy. But Nemesis did not forget Croesus; has she forgotten us?

I think not. There are now 36,000,000 of people in our island, and every year considerably more than 300,000 are added to our numbers. That is to say, about every hundred seconds, or so, a new claimant to a share in the common stock of maintenance presents him or herself among us. At the present time, the produce of the soil does not suffice to feed half its population. The other moiety has to be supplied with food which must be bought from the people of food-producing countries. That is to say, we have to offer them the things which they want in exchange for the things we want. And the things they want and which we can produce better than they can are mainly manufactures—industrial products.

The insolent reproach of the first Napoleon had a very solid foundation. We not only are, but, under penalty of starvation, we are bound to be, a nation of shopkeepers. But other nations also lie under the same necessity of keeping shop, and some of them deal in the same goods as ourselves. Our customers naturally seek to get the most and the best in exchange for their produce. If our goods are inferior to those of our competitors, there is no ground compatible with the sanity of the buyers, which can be alleged, why they should not prefer the latter. And, if that result should ever take place on a large and general scale, five or six millions of us would soon have nothing to eat. We know what the cotton famine was; and we can therefore form some notion of what a dearth of customers would be.

Judged by an ethical standard, nothing can be less satisfactory than the position in which we find ourselves. In a real, though incomplete, degree we have attained the condition of peace which is the main object of social organization; and it may, for argument's sake, be assumed that we desire nothing but that which is in itself innocent and praiseworthy—namely, the enjoyment of the fruits of honest industry. And lo! in spite of ourselves, we are in reality engaged in an internecine struggle for existence with our presumably no less peaceful and well-meaning neighbours. We seek peace and we do not ensue it. The moral nature in us asks for no more than is compatible with the general good; the non-moral nature proclaims and acts upon that fine old Scottish family motto, 'Thou shalt starve ere I want.' Let us be under no illusions then. So long as unlimited multiplication goes on, no social organization which has ever been devised, or is likely to be devised; no fiddle-faddling with the distribution of wealth, will deliver society from the tendency to be destroyed by the reproduction within itself, in its intensest form, of that struggle for existence, the limitation of which is the object of society. And however shocking to the moral sense this eternal competition of man against man and of nation against nation may be; however revolting may be the accumulation of misery at the negative pole of society, in contrast with that of monstrous wealth at the positive pole; this state of things must abide, and grow continually worse, so long as Istar holds her way unchecked. It is the true riddle of the Sphinx; and every nation which does not solve it will sooner or later be devoured by the monster itself has generated.

The practical and pressing question for us just now seems to me to be how to gain time. 'Time brings counsel,' as the Teutonic proverb has it; and wiser folk among our posterity may see their way out of that which at present looks like an *impasse*.

It would be folly to entertain any ill-feeling towards those neighbours and rivals who, like ourselves, are slaves of Istar; but, if somebody is to be starved, the modern world has no Oracle of Delphi to which the nations can appeal for an indication of the victim. It is open to us to try our fortune; and if we avoid impending fate, there will be a certain ground for believing that we are the right people to escape. *Securus judicat orbis*.[2]

To this end, it is well to look into the necessary conditions of our salvation by works. They are two, one plain to all the world and hardly needing insistence; the other seemingly not so plain, since too often it has been theoretically and practically left out of sight. The obvious condition is that our produce shall be better than that of others. There is only one reason why our goods should be preferred to those of our rivals—our customers must find them better at the price. That means that we must use more knowledge, skill, and industry in producing them without a proportionate increase in the cost of production; and, as the price of labour constitutes a large element in that cost, the rate of wages must be restricted within certain limits. It is perfectly true that cheap production and cheap labour are by no means synonymous; but it is also true that wages cannot increase beyond a certain proportion without destroying cheapness. Cheapness, then, with, as part and parcel of cheapness, a moderate price of labour, is essential to our success as competitors in the markets of the world.

The second condition is really quite as plainly indispensable as the first, if one thinks seriously about the matter. It is social stability. Society is stable, when the wants of its members obtain as much satisfaction as, life being what it is, common sense and experience show may be reasonably expected. Mankind, in general, care very little for forms of government or ideal considerations of any sort; and nothing really stirs the great multitude to break with custom and incur the manifest perils of revolt except the belief that misery in this world or damnation in the next, or both, are threatened by the continuance of the state of things in which they have been brought up. But when they do attain that conviction, society becomes as unstable as a package of dynamite, and a very small matter will produce the explosion which sends it back to the chaos of savagery.

NOTES

1. Istar, Babylonian goddess of love and war.
2. *securus judicat orbis*, untroubled, the world passes judgment.

Art and Society

[John Ruskin (1819–1900) made his name as an art-critic, advocating the visual arts as worthy of the attention of a Protestant public and extolling resemblance to nature, especially in Turner's paintings. Ruskin's interest in the high moral quality of the ideas in art and architecture led him to examine the nature of societies which had produced great artists. From his long descriptive and speculative work on Venetian Gothic we have selected a passage which relates the beauty of objects to the conditions of the labour which created them. The assumptions behind Ruskin's idea of the degradation of the worker in the circumstances of industrial production are related to Carlyle's polemics. Ruskin carries his personal critique of society further in *Unto this Last*, which contains an attack on Mill's un-emotional analysis of capitalism and a compliment to Dickens for his caricaturing of Utilitarianism in *Hard Times*. In our extract Ruskin stresses the difference between humanistic and economic value-judgments. In *Sesame and Lilies* he makes recommendations which partly explain his influence on the development of adult education. He deals here with the basic needs of human welfare, relating art and culture to work rather than to leisure.

Walter Horatio Pater (1839–1894), Classical Fellow of Brasenose College, Oxford, argued for a leisured appreciation of art and literature in a manner antipathetic to a moralistic writer like Ruskin, or indeed George Eliot. Pater admired scholarly expertise, especially when it informs one's intense momentary experience of a work of art. He so valued this subjective impressionism that he was unwilling to sacrifice the experience of it to ideological causes like Comte's, which he was too sceptical to entertain. Pater's *The Renaissance* became the Golden Book of Oscar Wilde and the late Victorian aesthetes. Wilde, however, was favourable to socialism. By this time a formal commitment to the Socialist Movement was possible. One important British recruit was a writer who had been much influenced by Ruskin, William Morris (1834–1896), the designer, poet and Utopian fantasist. Morris read Marx in 1883. Morris's relations to the earlier sages are set out briefly in the autobiographical pamphlet with which we conclude the anthology.]

JOHN RUSKIN

From *The Stones of Venice*

[The text is from 'The Nature of Gothic', Ch. 6 of *The Stones of Venice*, II, 'The Sea-Stories', 1853, omitting Ruskin's paragraph-numbers.]

But the modern English mind has this much in common with that of the Greek, that it intensely desires, in all things, the utmost completion or perfection compatible with their nature. This is a noble character in the abstract, but becomes ignoble when it causes us to forget the relative dignities of that nature itself, and to prefer the perfectness of the lower nature to the imperfection of the higher; not considering that as, judged by such a rule, all the brute animals would be preferable to man, because more perfect in their functions and kind, and yet are always held inferior to him, so also in the works of man, those which are more perfect in their kind are always inferior to those which are, in their nature, liable to more faults and shortcomings. For the finer the nature, the more flaws it will show through the clearness of it; and it is a law of this universe, that the best things shall be seldomest seen in their best form. The wild grass grows well and strongly, one year with another; but the wheat is, according to the greater nobleness of its nature, liable to the bitterer blight. And therefore, while in all things that we see, or do, we are to desire perfection; and strive for it, we are nevertheless not to set the meaner thing, in its narrow accomplishment, above the nobler thing in its mighty progress; not to esteem smooth minuteness above shattered majesty; not to prefer mean victory to honourable defeat; not to lower the level of our aim, that we may the more surely enjoy the complacency of success. But above all, in our dealings with the souls of other men we are to take care how we check, by severe requirement or narrow caution, efforts which might otherwise lead to noble issue; and, still more, how we withhold our admiration from great excellences, because they are mingled with rough faults. Now, in the make and nature of every man, however rude or simple, whom we employ in manual labour, there are some powers for better things; some tardy imagination, torpid capacity of emotion, tottering steps of thought, there are, even at the worst; and in most cases it is all our own fault that they *are* tardy or torpid. But they cannot be strengthened, unless we are content to take them in their feebleness, and unless we prize and honour them in their imperfection above the best and most perfect manual skill. And this is what we have to do with all our labourers; to look for the *thoughtful* part of them, and get that out of them, whatever we lose for it, whatever faults and errors we are obliged to take with it. For the best that is in them cannot manifest itself, but in company with much error. Understand this clearly: You can teach a man to draw a straight line, and to cut one; to strike a curved line, and to carve it; and to copy and carve any number of given lines or forms, with admirable speed and perfect precision; and you find his work perfect of its kind: but if you ask him to think about any of those forms, to consider if he cannot find any better in his own head, he stops; his execution becomes hesitating; he thinks, and ten to one he thinks wrong; ten to one he makes a mistake in the first touch he gives to his work as a thinking being. But you have made a man of him for all that. He was only a machine before, an animated tool.

And observe, you are put to stern choice in this matter. You must either make a tool of the creature, or a man of him. You cannot make both. Men were not intended to work with the accuracy of tools, to be precise and perfect in all their actions. If you will have that precison out of them, and make their fingers measure degrees like cog-wheels, and their arms strike curves like compasses, you must unhumanize them. All the energy of their spirits must be given to make cogs and compasses of themselves. All their attention and strength must go to the accomplishment of the mean act. The eye of the soul must be bent upon the finger-point, and the soul's force must fill all the invisible nerves that guide it, ten hours a day, that it may not err from its steely precision, and so soul and sight be worn away, and the whole human being be lost at last—a heap of sawdust, so far as its intellectual work in this world is concerned; saved only by its Heart, which cannot go into the

form of cogs and compasses, but expands after the ten hours
are over, into fireside humanity. On the other hand, if you will
make a man of the working creature, you cannot make a tool.
Let him but begin to imagine, to think, to try to do anything
worth doing; and the engine-turned precision is lost at once.
Out come all his roughness, all his dulness, all his incapability;
shame upon shame, failure upon failure, pause after pause:
but out comes the whole majesty of him also; and we know the
height of it only, when we see the clouds settling upon him.
And, whether the clouds be bright or dark there will be
transfiguration behind and within them.

And now, reader, look round this English room of yours,
about which you have been proud so often, because the work
of it was so good and strong, and the ornaments of it so
finished. Examine again all those accurate mouldings, and
perfect polishings, and unerring adjustments of the seasoned
wood and tempered steel. Many a time you have exulted over
them, and thought how great England was, because her slightest work was done so thoroughly. Alas! if read rightly, these
perfectnesses are signs of a slavery in our England a thousand
times more bitter and more degrading than that of the
scourged African, or helot Greek. Men may be beaten,
chained, tormented, yoked like cattle, slaughtered like summer
flies, and yet remain in one sense, and the best sense, free. But
to smother their souls within them, to blight and hew into
rotting pollards the suckling branches of their human intelligence, to make the flesh and skin which, after the worm's
work on it, is to see God, into leathern thongs to yoke machinery
with,—this is to be slave-masters indeed; and there might be
more freedom in England, though her feudal lords' lightest
words were worth men's lives, and though the blood of the
vexed husbandman dropped into the furrows of her fields, than
there is while the animation of her multitudes is sent like fuel
to feed the factory smoke, and the strength of them is given
daily to be wasted into the fineness of a web, or racked into the
exactness of a line.

And, on the other hand, go forth again to gaze upon the
old cathedral front, where you have smiled so often at the
fantastic ignorance of the old sculptors: examine once more

those ugly goblins, and formless monsters, and stern statues, anatomiless and rigid; but do not mock at them, for they are signs of the life and liberty of every workman who struck the stone; a freedom of thought, and rank in scale of being, such as no laws, no charters, no charities can secure; but which it must be the first aim of all Europe at this day to regain for her children.

Let me not be thought to speak wildly or extravagantly. It is verily this degradation of the operative into a machine, which, more than any other evil of the times, is leading the mass of the nations everywhere into vain, incoherent, destructive struggling for a freedom of which they cannot explain the nature to themselves. Their universal outcry against wealth, and against nobility, is not forced from them either by the pressure of famine, or the sting of mortified pride. These do much, and have done much in all ages; but the foundations of society were never yet shaken as they are at this day. It is not that men are ill fed, but that they have no pleasure in the work by which they make their bread, and therefore look to wealth as the only means of pleasure. It is not that men are pained by the scorn of the upper classes, but they cannot endure their own; for they feel that the kind of labour to which they are condemned is verily a degrading one, and makes them less than men. Never had the upper classes so much sympathy with the lower, or charity for them, as they have at this day, and yet never were they so much hated by them: for, of old, the separation between the noble and the poor was merely a wall built by law; now it is a veritable difference in level of standing, a precipice between upper and lower grounds in the field of humanity, and there is pestilential air at the bottom of it. I know not if a day is ever to come when the nature of right freedom will be understood, and when men will see that to obey another man, to labour for him, yield reverence to him or to his place, is not slavery. It is often the best kind of liberty, —liberty from care. The man who says to one, Go, and he goeth, and to another, Come, and he cometh, has, in most cases, more sense of restraint and difficulty than the man who obeys him. The movements of the one are hindered by the burden on his shoulder; of the other, by the bridle on his lips:

there is no way by which the burden may be lightened; but
we need not suffer from the bridle if we do not champ at it. To
yield reverence to another, to hold ourselves and our lives at
his disposal, is not slavery; often, it is the noblest state in
which a man can live in this world. There is, indeed, a
reverence which is servile, that is to say irrational or selfish:
but there is also noble reverence, that is to say, reasonable and
loving; and a man is never so noble as when he is reverent
in this kind; nay, even if the feeling pass the bounds of mere
reason, so that it be loving, a man is raised by it. Which had,
in reality, most of the serf nature in him,—the Irish peasant
who was lying in wait yesterday for his landlord, with his
musket muzzle thrust through the ragged hedge; or that old
mountain servant, who, 200 years ago, at Inverkeithing,
gave up his own life and the lives of his seven sons for his
chief?[1]—as each fell, calling forth his brother to the death,
"Another for Hector!" And, therefore, in all ages and all
countries, reverence has been paid and sacrifice made by men
to each other, not only without complaint, but rejoicingly;
and famine, and peril, and sword, and all evil, and all shames,
have been borne willingly in the causes of masters and kings;
for all these gifts of the heart ennobled the men who gave, not
less than the men who received them, and nature prompted,
and God rewarded the sacrifice. But to feel their souls wither-
ing within them, unthanked, to find their whole being sunk
into an unrecognised abyss, to be counted off into a heap of
mechanism, numbered with its wheels, and weighted with its
hammer strokes;—this nature bade not,—this God blesses
not,—this humanity for no long time is able to endure.

We have much studied and much perfected, of late, the
great civilised invention of the division of labour; only we give
it a false name. It is not, truly speaking, the labour that is
divided; but the men:—Divided into mere segments of
men—broken into small fragments and crumbs of life; so that
all the little piece of intelligence that is left in a man is not
enough to make a pin, or a nail, but exhausts itself in making
the point of a pin, or the head of a nail. Now it is a good and
desirable thing, truly, to make many pins in a day; but if we
could only see with what crystal sand their points were

polished,—sand of human soul, much to be magnified before it can be discerned for what it is,—we should think there might be some loss in it also. And the great cry that rises from all our manufacturing cities, louder than their furnace blast, is all in very deed for this,—that we manufacture everything there except men; we blanch cotton, and strengthen steel, and refine sugar, and shape pottery; but to brighten to strengthen, to refine, or to form a single living spirit, never enters into our estimate of advantages. And all the evil to which that cry is urging our myriads can be met only in one way: not by teaching nor preaching, for to teach them is but to show them their misery, and to preach to them, if we do nothing more than preach, is to mock at it. It can be met only by a right understanding on the part of all classes, of what kinds of labour are good for men, raising them, and making them happy; by a determined sacrifice of such convenience, or beauty, or cheapness as is to be got only by the degradation of the workman; and by an equally determined demand for the products and results of healthy and ennobling labour.

From 'Unto this Last'

[The text is from Essay IV, *Ad Valorem*, of Ruskin's 'Unto this Last' in *The Cornhill Magazine*, II, 547–50 (November, 1860), omitting paragraph numbers. *Unto this Last* appeared in book-form in 1862.]

The real science of political economy, which has yet to be distinguished from the bastard science, as medicine from witch-craft, and astronomy from astrology, is that which teaches nations to desire and labour for the things that lead to life; and which teaches them to scorn and destroy the things that lead to destruction. And if, in a state of infancy, they suppose indifferent things, such as excrescences of shell-fish, and pieces or blue and red stone, to be valuable, and spend large measure of the labour which ought to be employed for the extension and ennobling of life, in diving or digging for them, and cutting them into various shapes,—or if, in the same state of infancy, they imagine precious and beneficent things, such as air, light and cleanliness, to be valueless,—or if, finally, they imagine the conditions of their own existence, by which alone they can truly possess or use anything, such, for instance, as peace, trust, and love, to be prudently exchange-able, when the market offers, for gold, iron, or excrescences of shells—the great and only science of Political Economy teaches them, in all these cases, what is vanity, and what substance; and how the service of Death, the Lord of Waste, and of eternal emptiness, differs from the service of Wisdom, the Lady of Saving and of eternal fulness; she who has said, 'I will cause those that love me to inherit SUBSTANCE; and I will FILL their treasures'.

The "Lady of Saving", in a profounder sense than that of the savings' bank, though that is a good one: Madonna della Salute,—Lady of Health—which though commonly spoken of as if separate from wealth, is indeed a part of wealth. This word, "wealth", it will be remembered, is the next we have to define.

'To be wealthy', says Mr. Mill, is 'to have a large stock of useful articles'.[2]

I accept this definition. Only let us perfectly understand it. My opponents often lament my not giving them enough logic: I fear I must at present use a little more than they will like; but this business of Political Economy is no light one, and we must allow no loose terms in it.

We have, therefore, to ascertain in the above definition, first, what is the meaning of "having", or the nature of Possession. Then what is the meaning of "useful", or the nature of Utility.

And first of possession. At the crossing of the transepts of Milan Cathedral has lain, for three hundred years, the embalmed body of St. Carlo Borromeo. It holds a golden crosier, and has a cross of emeralds on its breast. Admitting the crosier and emeralds to be useful articles, is the body to be considered as "having" them? Do they, in the politico-economical sense of property, belong to it? If not, and if we may, therefore, conclude generally that a dead body cannot possess property, what degree and period of animation in the body will render possession possible?

And thus: lately in a wreck of a Californian ship, one of the passengers fastened a belt about him with two hundred pounds of gold in it, with which he was found afterwards at the bottom. Now, as he was sinking—had he the gold? Or had the gold him?[3]

And if, instead of sinking him in the sea by its weight, the gold had struck him on the forehead, and therefore caused incurable disease—suppose palsy or insanity—would the gold in that case have been more a "possession" than in the first? Without pressing the inquiry up through instances of gradually increasing vital power over the gold (which I will, however, give, if they are asked for), I presume the reader will see that possession, or "having", is not an absolute, but a gradated power; and consists not only in the quantity or nature of the thing possessed, but also (and in a greater degree) in its suitableness to the person possessing it, and in his vital power to use it.

And our definition of Wealth, expanded, becomes: "The possession of useful articles, *which we can use*". This is a very serious change. For wealth, instead of depending merely on a "have", is thus seen to depend on a "can". Gladiator's death, on a "habet"; but a soldier's victory, and state's salvation, on a "quo plurimum posset". (Liv. VII, 6.)[4] And what we reasoned of only as accumulation of material, is seen to demand also accumulation of capacity.

So much for our verb. Next for our adjective. What is the meaning of "useful"?

The inquiry is closely connected with the last. For what is capable of use in the hands of some persons, is capable, in the hands of others, of the opposite of use, called commonly, "from-use", or "ab-use". And it depends on the person, much more than on the article, whether its usefulness or abusefulness will be the quality developed in it. Thus, wine, which the Greeks, in their Bacchus, make, rightly, the type of all passion, and which, when used, 'cheereth god and man' (that is to say, strengthens both the divine life, or reasoning powers, and the earthly, or carnal power, of man); yet, when abused, becomes "Dionusos", hurtful especially to the divine part of man, or reason. And again, the body itself, being equally liable to use and to abuse, and, when rightly disciplined, serviceable to the State, both for war and labour;—but when not disciplined, or abused, valueless to the State, and capable only of continuing the private or single existence of the individual (and that but feebly)—the Greeks called such a body an "idiotic" or "private" body, from their word signifying a person employed in no way directly useful to the State; whence, finally, our "idiot", meaning a person entirely occupied with his own concerns.

Hence, it follows, that if a thing is to be useful, it must be not only of an availing nature, but in availing hands. Or, in accurate terms, usefulness is value in the hands of the valiant; so that this science of wealth being, as we have just seen, when regarded as the Science of Accumulation, accumulative of capacity as well as of material,—when regarded as the Science of Distribution, is distribution not absolute, but discriminate; not of every thing to every man, but of the right thing to the right man. A difficult science, dependent on more than arithmetic.

Wealth, therefore, is "THE POSSESSION OF THE VALUABLE BY THE VALIANT"; and in considering it as a power existing in a nation, the two elements, the value of the thing, and the valour of its possessor, must be estimated together. Whence it appears that many of the persons commonly considered wealthy, are in reality no more wealthy than the locks of their own strong boxes are; they being inherently and eternally incapable of wealth; and operating for the nation, in an economical point of view, either as pools of dead water, and eddies in a stream (which, so long as the stream flows, are useless, or serve only to drown people, but may become of importance in a state of stagnation, should the stream dry); or else, as dams in a river, of which the ultimate service depends not on the dam, but the miller; or else, as mere accidental stays and impediments, acting, not as wealth, but (for we ought to have a correspondent term) as "illth", causing various devastation and trouble around them in all directions; or lastly, act not at all, but are merely animated conditions of delay, (no use being possible of anything they have until they are dead), in which last condition they are nevertheless often useful *as* delays, and "impedimenta", if a nation is apt to move too fast.

This being so, the difficulty of the true science of Political Economy lies not merely in the need of developing manly character to deal with material value, but in the fact, that while the manly character and material value only form wealth by their conjunction, they have nevertheless a mutually destructive operation on each other. For the manly character is apt to ignore, or even cast away, the material value:— whence that of Pope:—

> "Sure, of qualities demanding praise,
> More go to ruin fortunes, than to raise."[5]

And on the other hand, the material value is apt to undermine the manly character; so that it must be our work, in the issue, to examine what evidence there is of the effect of wealth on the minds of its possessors; also, what kind of person it is who usually sets himself to obtain wealth, and succeeds in doing so; and whether the world owes more gratitude to rich or to poor men, either for their moral influence upon it, or for chief goods, discoveries, and practical advancements. I, however, anticipate future conclusions so far as to state that in a community regulated only by laws of demand and supply, but protected from open violence, the persons who become rich are, generally speaking, industrious, resolute, proud, covetous, prompt, methodical, sensible, unimaginative, insensitive, and ignorant. The persons who remain poor are the entirely foolish, the entirely wise,[6] the idle, the reckless, the humble, the thoughtful, the dull, the imaginative, the sensitive, the well-informed, the improvident, the irregularly and impulsively wicked, the clumsy knave, the open thief, and the entirely merciful, just, and godly person.

From *Sesame and Lilies*

[*Sesame and Lilies* was first published in 1865, consisting of two lectures. A third, from which the following extracts come, was delivered in Dublin in 1868 as 'The Mystery of Life and its Arts' and added to the 1871 edition, which was issued as volume I of Ruskin's

Works. The text is from this 1871 volume, omitting paragraph numbers.]

In the midst of this vanity of empty religion—of tragic contemplation—of wrathful and wretched ambition, and dispute for dust, there is yet one great group of persons, by whom all these disputers live—the persons who have determined, or have had it by a beneficent Providence determined for them, that they will do something useful; that whatever may be prepared for them hereafter, or happen to them here, they will, at least, deserve the food that God gives them by winning it honourably: and that, however fallen from the purity, or far from the peace, of Eden, they will carry out the duty of human dominion, though they have lost its felicity; and dress and keep the wilderness, though they no more can dress or keep the garden.

These,—hewers of wood, and drawers of water,—these, bent under burdens, or torn of scourges—these, that dig and weave—that plant and build; workers in wood, and in marble, and in iron—by whom all food, clothing, habitation, furniture, and means of delight are produced, for themselves, and for all men beside; men, whose deeds are good, though their words may be few; men, whose lives are serviceable, be they never so short, and worthy of honour, be they never so humble;— from these, surely, at least, we may receive some clear message of teaching; and pierce, for an instant, into the mystery of life, and of its arts.

Yes; from these, at last, we do receive a lesson. But I grieve to say, or rather—for that is the deeper truth of the matter— I rejoice to say—this message of theirs can only be received by joining them—not by thinking about them.

You sent for me to talk to you of art; and I have obeyed you in coming. But the main thing I have to tell you is,—that art must not be talked about. The fact that there is talk about it at all, signifies that it is ill done, or cannot be done. No true painter ever speaks, or ever has spoken, much of his art. The greatest speak nothing. Even Reynolds is no exception, for he wrote of all that he could not himself do, and was utterly silent respecting all that he himself did.

The moment a man can really do his work he becomes speechless about it. All words become idle to him—all theories.

Does a bird need to theorize about building its nest, or boast of it when built? All good work is essentially done that way—without hesitation, without difficulty, without boasting; and in the doers of the best, there is an inner and involuntary power which approximates literally to the instinct of an animal—nay, I am certain that in the most perfect human artists, reason does *not* supersede instinct, but is added to an instinct as much more divine than that of the lower animals as the human body is more beautiful than theirs; that a great singer sings not with less instinct than the nightingale, but with more—only more various, applicable, and governable; that a great architect does not build with less instinct than the beaver or the bee, but with more—with an innate cunning of proportion that embraces all beauty, and a divine ingenuity of skill that improvises all construction. But be that as it may—be the instinct less or more than that of inferior animals like or unlike theirs, still the human art is dependent on that first, and then upon an amount of practice, of science,—and of imagination disciplined by thought, which the true possessor of it knows to be incommunicable, and the true critic of it, inexplicable, except through long process of laborious years. The journey of life's conquest, in which hills over hills, and Alps on Alps arose, and sank,—do you think you can make another trace it painlessly, by talking? Why, you cannot even carry us up an Alp, by talking. You can guide us up it, step by step, no otherwise—even so, best silently. You girls, who have been among the hills, know how the bad guide chatters and gesticulates, and it is "put your foot here", and "mind how you balance yourself there"; but the good guide walks on quietly, without a word, only with his eyes on you when need is, and his arm like an iron bar, if need be.

In that slow way, also, art can be taught—if you have faith in your guide, and will let his arm be to you as an iron bar when need is. But in what teacher of art have you such faith? Certainly not in me; for, as I told you at first, I know well enough it is only because you think I can talk, not because you think I know my business, that you let me speak to you at all. If I were to tell you anything that seemed to you strange you would not believe it, and yet it would only be in telling you strange things that I could be of use to you. I could be of great use to you—infinite use, with brief saying, if you would believe it; but you would not, just because the thing that would be of real use would displease you. You are all wild, for instance, with admiration of Gustave Doré. Well, suppose I were to tell you, in the strongest terms I could use, that Gustave Doré's art was bad—bad, not in weakness,—not in failure,—but bad with dreadful power—the power of the Furies and the Harpies mingled, enraging, and polluting; that so long as you looked at it, no perception of pure or beautiful art was possible for you. Suppose I were to tell you that! What would be the use? Would you look at Gustave Doré less? Rather, more, I fancy. On the other hand, I could soon put you into good humour with me, if I chose. I know well enough what you like and how to praise it to your better liking. I could talk to you about moonlight, and twilight, and spring flowers, and autumn leaves, and the Madonnas of Raphael— how motherly! and the Sibyls of Michael Angelo—how majestic! and the Saints of Angelico—how pious! and the Cherubs of Correggio—how delicious! Old as I am, I could play you a tune on the harp yet, that you would dance to. But neither you nor I should be a bit the better or wiser; or, if we were, our increased wisdom could be of no practical effect. For, indeed, the arts, as regards teachableness, differ from the sciences also in this, that their power is founded not merely on facts which can be communicated, but on dispositions which require to be created. Art is neither to be achieved by effort of thinking nor explained by accuracy of speaking. It is the instinctive and necessary result of powers which can only be developed through the mind of successive generations, and which finally burst into life under social conditions as slow of growth as the faculties they regulate. Whole aeras of mighty history are summed, and the passions of dead myriads are concentrated, in the existence of a noble art; and if that noble art were among us, we should feel it and rejoice; not caring in the least to hear lectures on it; and since it is not among us, be assured we have to go back to the root of it, or, at least, to the place where the stock of it is yet alive, and the branches began to die.

...."The work of men"—and what is that? Well, we may any of us know very quickly, on the condition of being wholly ready to do it. But many of us are for the most part thinking, not of what we are to do, but of what we are to get; and the best of us are sunk into the sin of Ananias,[7] and it is a mortal one—we want to keep back part of the price; and we continually talk of taking up our cross, as if the only harm in a cross was the *weight* of it—as if it was only a thing to be carried, instead of to be—crucified upon. "They that are His have crucified the flesh, with the affections and lusts."[8] Does that mean, think you, that in time of national distress, of religious trial, of crisis for every interest and hope of humanity—none of us will cease jesting, none cease idling, none put themselves to any wholesome work, none take so much as a tag of lace off their footmen's coats, to save the world? Or does it rather mean, that they are ready to leave houses, lands, and kindred—yes, and life, if need be? Life! some of us are ready enough to throw that away, joyless as we have made it. But "*station* in Life"—how many of us are ready to quit *that*? Is it not always the great objection, where there is question of finding something useful to do—"We cannot leave our stations in Life"?

Those of us who really cannot—that is to say, who can only maintain themselves by continuing in some business or salaried office, have already something to do; and all that they have to see to is, that they do it honestly and with all their might. But with most people who use that apology, "remaining in the station of life to which Providence has called them" means keeping all the carriages, and all the footmen and large houses they can possibly pay for; and, once for all, I say that if ever Providence *did* put them into stations of that sort—which is not at all a matter of certainty—Providence is just now very distinctly calling them out again. Levi's station in life was the receipt of custom;[9] and Peter's the shore of Galilee;[10] and Paul's, the antechambers of the High Priest,[11]—which "station in life" each had to leave, with brief notice.

And, whatever our station in life may be, at this crisis, those of us who mean to fulfil our duty ought, first, to live on as little as we can; and, secondly, to do all the wholesome work for it we can, and to spend all we can spare in doing all the sure good we can.

And sure good is first in feeding people, then in dressing people, then in lodging people, and lastly in rightly pleasing people, with arts, or sciences, or any other subject of thought.

I say first in feeding; and, once for all, do not let yourselves be deceived by any of the common talk of "indiscriminate charity". The order to us is not to feed the deserving hungry, nor the industrious hungry, nor the amiable and well-intentioned hungry, but simply to feed the hungry. It is quite true, infallibly true, that if any man will not work, neither should he eat—think of that, and every time you sit down to your dinner, ladies and gentlemen, say solemnly, before you ask a blessing, "How much work have I done to-day for my dinner?" But the proper way to enforce that order on those below you, as well as on yourselves, is not to leave vagabonds and honest people to starve together, but very distinctly to discern and seize your vagabond; and shut your vagabond up out of honest people's way, and very sternly then see that, until he has worked, he does *not* eat. But the first thing is to be sure you have the food to give; and, therefore, to enforce the organization of vast activities in agriculture and in commerce, for the production of the wholesomest food, and proper storing and distribution of it, so that no famine shall any more be possible among civilized beings. There is plenty of work in this business alone, and at once, for any number of people who like to engage in it.

Secondly, dressing people—that is to say, urging every one within reach of your influence to be always neat and clean, and giving them means of being so. In so far as they absolutely refuse, you must give up the effort with respect to them, only taking care that no children within your sphere of influence shall any more be brought up with such habits; and that every person who is willing to dress with propriety shall have encouragement to do so. And the first absolutely necessary step towards this is the gradual adoption of a consistent dress for different ranks of persons, so that their rank shall be known by their dress; and the restriction of the changes of fashion within certain limits. All which appears for the present quite impossible; but it is only so far even difficult as it is difficult to conquer our vanity, frivolity, and desire to appear what we are not. And it is not, nor ever shall be, creed of mine, that these mean and shallow vices are unconquerable by Christian women.

And then, thirdly, lodging people, which you may think should have been put first, but I put it third, because we must feed and clothe people where we find them, and lodge them afterwards. And providing lodgment for them means a great deal of vigorous legislature, and cutting down of vested interests that stand in the way, and after that, or before that, so far as we can get it, thorough sanitary and remedial action in the houses that we have; and then the building of more, strongly, beautifully, and in groups of limited extent, kept in proportion to their streams, and walled round, so that there may be no festering and wretched suburb anywhere, but clean and busy streets within, and the open country without, with a belt of beautiful garden and orchard round the walls, so that from any part of the city perfectly fresh air and grass, and sight of far horizon, might be reachable in a few minutes' walk. This the final aim; but in immediate action every minor and possible good to be instantly done, when, and as, we can; roofs mended that have holes in them—fences patched that have gaps in them—walls buttressed that totter—and floors propped that shake; cleanliness and order enforced with our own hands and eyes, till we are breathless, every day. And all the fine arts will healthily follow. I myself have washed a flight of stone stairs all down, with bucket and broom, in a Savoy inn, where they hadn't washed their stairs since they first went up them! and I never made a better sketch than that afternoon.

These, then, are the three first needs of civilized life; and the law for every Christian man and woman is, that they shall be in direct service towards one of these three needs, as far as is consistent with their own special occupation, and if they have no special business, then wholly in one of these services. And out of such exertion in plain duty all other good will come; for in this direct contention with material evil, you will find out the real nature of all evil; you will discern by the various kinds of resistance, what is really the fault and main antagonism to good; also you will find the most unexpected helps and profound lessons given, and truths will come thus down to us which the speculation of all our lives would never have raised us up to. You will find nearly every educational problem solved, as soon as you truly want to do something; everybody will become of use in their own fittest way, and will learn what is best for them to know in that use. Competitive examination will then, and not till then, be wholesome, because it will be daily, and calm, and in practice, and on these familiar arts, and minute, but certain and serviceable, knowledges, will be surely edified and sustained the greater arts and splendid theoretical sciences.

But much more than this. On such holy and simple practice will be founded, indeed, at last, an infallible religion. The greatest of all the mysteries of life, and the most terrible, is the corruption of even the sincerest religion, which is not daily founded on rational, effective, humble, and helpful action. Helpful action, observe! for there is just one law, which, obeyed, keeps all religions pure—forgotten, makes them all false. Whenever in any religious faith, dark or bright, we allow our minds to dwell upon the points in which we differ from other people, we are wrong, and in the devil's power. That is the essence of the Pharisee's thanksgiving—"Lord, I thank Thee that I am not as other men are." At every moment of our lives we should be trying to find out, not in what we differ from other people, but in what we agree with them; and the moment we find we can agree as to anything that should be done, kind or good, (and who but fools couldn't?) then do it; push at it together: you can't quarrel in a side-by-side push; but the moment that even the best men stop pushing, and begin talking, they mistake their pugnacity for piety, and it's all over. I will not speak of the crimes which in past times have been committed in the name of Christ, nor of the follies which are at this hour held to be consistent with obedience to Him; but I *will* speak of the morbid corruption and waste of vital power in religious sentiment, by which the pure strength of that which should be the guiding soul of every nation, the splendour

of its youthful manhood, and spotless light of its maidenhood,
is averted or cast away. You may see continually girls who have
never been taught to do a single useful thing thoroughly;
who cannot sew, who cannot cook, who cannot cast an account,
nor prepare a medicine, whose whole life has been passed
either in play or in pride—you will find girls like these, when
they are earnest-hearted, cast all their innate passion of
religious spirit, which was meant by God to support them
through the irksomeness of daily toil, into grievous and vain
meditation over the meaning of the great Book, of which no
syllable was ever yet to be understood but through a deed;
all the instinctive wisdom and mercy of their womanhood
made vain, and the glory of their pure consciences warped into
fruitless agony concerning questions which the laws of common
serviceable life would have either solved for them in an
instant, or kept out of their way. Give such a girl any true
work that will make her active in the dawn, and weary at
night, with the consciousness that her fellow-creatures have
indeed been the better for her day, and the powerless sorrow
of her enthusiasm will transform itself into a majesty of radiant
and beneficent peace.

So with our youths. We once taught them to make Latin
verses, and called them educated; now we teach them to leap
and to row, to hit a ball with a bat, and call them educated.
Can they plough, can they sow, can they plant at the right
time, or build with a steady hand? Is it the effort of their lives
to be chaste, knightly, faithful, holy in thought, lovely in
word and deed? Indeed it is, with some, nay, with many, and
the strength of England is in them, and the hope—but we have
to turn their courage from the toil of war to the toil of mercy;
and their intellect from dispute of words to discernment of
things; and their knighthood from the errantry of adventure to
the state and fidelity of a kingly power. And then, indeed,
shall abide, for them and for us, an incorruptible felicity, and
an infallible religion; shall abide for us Faith, no more to be
assailed by temptation, no more to be defended by wrath and
by fear;—shall abide with us Hope, no more to be quenched
by the years that overwhelm, or made ashamed by the shadows
that betray:—shall abide for us, and with us, the greatest of

these; the abiding will, the abiding name of our Father. For the greatest of these, is Charity.

W. H. PATER

From 'Poems by William Morris'

[Adapted later as the conclusion to his *Studies in the History of the Renaissance*, 1873, these paragraphs first appeared in Pater's 'Poems by William Morris' in *The Westminster Review*, N.S., LXVII, 309–12 (October, 1868), from which our text is taken.]

. . . To regard all things and principles of things as inconstant modes or fashions has more and more become the tendency of modern thought. Let us begin with that which is without—our physical life. Fix upon it in one of its more exquisite intervals—the moment, for instance, of delicious recoil from the flood of water in summer heat. What is the whole physical life in that moment but a combination of natural elements to which science gives their names? But those elements, phosphorus and lime, and delicate fibres, are present not in the human body alone; we detect them in places most remote from it. Our physical life is a perpetual motion of them—the passage of the blood, the wasting and repairing of the lenses of the eye, the modification of the tissues of the brain by every ray of light and sound—processes which science reduces to simpler and more elementary forces. Like the elements of which we are composed, the action of these forces extends beyond us; it rusts iron and ripens corn. Far out on every side of us these elements are broadcast, driven in many forces; and birth and gesture and death and the springing of violets from the grave are but a few out of ten thousand resulting combinations. That clear, perpetual outline of face and limb is but an image of ours under which we group them—a design in a web the actual threads of which pass out beyond it. This at least of flame-like our life has, that it is but the concurrence renewed from moment to moment of forces parting sooner or later on their ways.

Or if we begin with the inward world of thought and feeling, the whirlpool is still more rapid, the flame more eager and devouring. There it is no longer the gradual darkening of the eye, the gradual fading of colour from the wall, the movement of the shore side, where the water flows down indeed, though in apparent rest, but the race of the midstream, a drift of momentary acts of sight and passion and thought. At first sight experience seems to bury us under a flood of external objects, pressing upon us with a sharp, importunate reality, calling us out of ourselves in a thousand forms of action. But when reflection begins to act upon those objects they are dissipated under its influence; the cohesive force seems suspended like some trick of magic, each object is loosed into a group of impressions, colour, odour, texture, in the mind of the observer. And if we continue to dwell on this world, not of objects in the solidity with which language invests them, but of impressions unstable, flickering, inconsistent, which burn, and are extinguished with our consciousness of them, it contracts still further, the whole scope of observation is dwarfed into the narrow chamber of the individual mind. Experience, already reduced to a swarm of impressions, is ringed round for each one of us by that thick wall of personality through which no real voice has ever pierced on its way to us, or from us to that, which we can only conjecture to be without. Every one of those impressions is the impression of an individual in his isolation, each mind keeping as a solitary prisoner its own dream of a world.

Analysis goes a step further still, and tells us that those impressions of the individual to which, for each one of us, experience dwindles down, are in perpetual flight; that each of them is limited by time, and that as time is infinitely divisible, each of them is infinitely divisible also, all that is actual in it being a single moment, gone while we try to apprehend it, of which it may ever be more truly said that it has ceased to be than that it is. To such a tremulous wisp constantly reforming itself on the stream, to a single sharp impression, with a sense in it, a relic more or less fleeting, of such moments gone by, what is real in our life fines itself down. It is with this movement, the passage and dissolution of impressions, images, sensations, that analysis leaves off, that continual vanishing away, that strange perpetual weaving and unweaving of ourselves.

Such thoughts seem desolate at first; at times all the bitterness of life seems concentrated in them. They bring the image of one washed out beyond the bar in a sea at ebb, losing even his personality, as the elements of which he is composed pass into new combinations. Struggling, as he must, to save himself, it is himself that he loses at every moment.

Philosophiren, says Novalis, *ist dephlegmatisiren, vivificiren*.[12] The service of philosophy, and of religion and culture as well, to the human spirit, is to startle it into a sharp and eager observation. Every moment some form grows perfect in hand or face; some tone on the hills or the sea is choicer than the rest; some mood of passion or insight or intellectual excitement is irresistibly real and attractive for us for that moment only. Not the fruit of experience but experience itself is the end. A counted number of pulses only is given to us of a variegated, dramatic life. How may we see in them all that is to be seen in them by the finest senses? How can we pass most swiftly from point to point, and be present always at the focus where the greatest number of vital forces unite in their purest energy?

To burn always with this hard gem-like flame, to maintain this ecstasy, is success in life. Failure is to form habits; for habit is relative to a stereotyped world; meantime it is only the roughness of the eye that makes any two things, persons, situations—seem alike. While all melts under our feet, we may well catch at any exquisite passion, or contribution to knowledge that seems by a lifted horizon to set the spirit free for a moment, or any stirring of the senses, strange dyes, strange flowers and curious odours, or work of the artist's hands, or the face of one's friend. Not to discriminate every moment some passionate attitude in those about us and in the brilliance of their gifts some tragic dividing of forces on their ways, is on this short day of frost and sun to sleep before evening. With this sense of the splendour of our experience and of its awful brevity, gathering all we are into one desperate effort to see and touch, we shall hardly have time to make theories about the things we see and touch. What we have to do is to be for ever curiously testing opinion and courting new impressions, never acquiescing in a facile orthodoxy of Comte or of Hegel or of our own. Theories, religious or philosophical ideas, as points of view, instruments of criticism, may help us to gather up what might otherwise pass unregarded by us. "*La philosophie*", says Victor Hugo, "*c'est le microscope de la pensée*".[13] The theory or idea or system which requires of us the sacrifice of any part of this experience, in consideration of some interest into which we cannot enter, or some abstract morality we have not identified with ourselves, or of what is only conventional, has no real claim upon us.

One of the most beautiful passages in the writings of Rousseau is that in the sixth book of the Confessions, where he describes the awakening in him of the literary sense. An undefinable taint of death had clung always about him, and now in early manhood he believed himself smitten by mortal disease. He asked himself how he might make as much as possible of the interval that remained; and he was not biassed by anything in his previous life when he decided that it must be by intellectual excitement, which he found just then in the clear, fresh writings of Voltaire.[14] Well! we are all *condamnés*, as Victor Hugo somewhere says: we have an interval and then we cease to be.[15] Some spend this interval in listlessness, some in high passions, the wisest in art and song. For our one chance is in expanding that interval, in getting as many pulsations as possible into the given time. High passions give us this quickened sense of life, ecstasy and sorrow of love, political or religious enthusiasm, or the "enthusiasm of humanity". Only, be sure it is passion, that it does yield you this fruit of a quickened, multiplied consciousness. Of this wisdom, the poetic passion, the desire of beauty, the love of art for art's sake, has most; for art comes to you professing frankly to give nothing but the highest quality to your moments as they pass, and simply for those moments' sake.

From 'Notes on Leonardo Da Vinci'

[These notes, adapted for *The Renaissance* as 'Leonardo Da Vinci', first appeared in *The Fortnightly Review*, N.S., VI (November, 1869), from which our extract is taken.]

. . . La Gioconda is, in the truest sense, Leonardo's master-piece—the revealing instance of his mode of thought and work. In suggestiveness, only the Melancholia of Dürer is comparable to it; and no crude symbolism disturbs the effect of its subdued and graceful mystery. We all know the face and hands of the figure, set in its marble chair, in that cirque of fantastic rocks, as in some faint light under sea. Perhaps of all ancient pictures time has chilled it least.[16] As often happens with works in which invention seems to reach its limit, there is an element in it given to, not invented by, the master. In that inestimable folio of drawings, once in the possession of Vasari, were certain designs by Verrocchio—faces of such impressive beauty that Leonardo in his boyhood copied them many times. It is hard not to connect with these designs of the elder by-past master, as with its germinal principle, the unfathomable smile, always with a touch of something sinister in it, which plays over all Leonardo's work. Besides the picture is a portrait. From childhood we see this image defining itself on the fabric of his dreams; and but for express historical testimony, we might fancy that this was but his ideal lady, embodied and beheld at last. What was the relationship of a living Florentine to this creature of his thought? By what strange affinities had she and the dream grown thus apart, yet so closely together? Present from the first incorporeal in Leonardo's thought, dimly traced in the designs of Verrocchio, she is found present at last in Il Giocondo's house. That there is much of mere portraiture in the picture is attested by the legend that by artificial means, the presence of mimes and flute-players, that subtle expression was protracted on the face. Again, was it in four years and by renewed labour never really completed, or in four months, and as by stroke of magic, that the image was projected?

The presence that thus so strangely rose beside the waters is expressive of what in the ways of a thousand years men had come to desire. Here is the head upon which all "the ends of the world are come," and the eyelids are a little weary. It is a beauty wrought out from within upon the flesh —the deposit, little cell by cell, of strange thoughts and fantastic reveries and exquisite passions. Set it for a moment beside one of those white Greek goddesses or beautiful women of antiquity, and how would they be troubled by this beauty, into which the soul with all its maladies has passed! All the thoughts and experiences of the world have etched and moulded there, in that which they have of power to refine and make expressive the outward form—the animalism of Greece, the lust of Rome, the reverie of the Middle Age with its spiritual ambition and imaginative loves, the return of the Pagan world, the sins of the Borgias. She is older than the rocks among which she sits; like the vampire, she has been dead many times, and learned the secrets of the grave; and has been a diver in deep seas, and keeps their fallen day about her; and trafficked for strange webs with Eastern merchants; and, as Leda, was the mother of Helen of Troy, and as Saint Anne, the mother of Mary; and all this has been to her but as the sound of lyres and flutes, and lives only in the delicacy with which it has moulded the changing lineaments, and tinged the eyelids and the hands. The fancy of a perpetual life, sweeping together ten thousand experiences, is an old one; and modern philosophy has conceived the idea of humanity as wrought upon by, and summing up in itself, all modes of thought and life. Certainly Lady Lisa might stand as the embodiment of the old fancy, the symbol of the modern idea.

From 'The School of Giorgione'

[This extract is from 'The School of Giorgione', in *The Fortnightly Review*, N.S., XXII (October, 1877). The essay appeared in the second edition of *The Renaissance*, 1877.]

... *All art constantly aspires towards the condition of music.* For while in all other kinds of art it is possible to distinguish the

matter from the form and the understanding can always make
this distinction, yet it is the constant effort of art to obliterate
it. That the mere matter of a poem, for instance its subject, its
given incidents or situation; that the mere matter of a picture,
the actual circumstances of an event, the actual topography
of a landscape, should be nothing without the form, the spirit
of the handling; that this form, this mode of handling, should
become an end in itself, should penetrate every part of the
matter;—this is what all art constantly strives after, and
achieves in different degrees.

This abstract language becomes clear enough if we think
of actual examples. In an actual landscape we see a long white
road, lost suddenly on the hill-verge. That is the matter of one
of M. Legros' etchings; but in this etching it is informed by an
indwelling solemnity of expression, seen upon it or half-seen,
within the limits of an exceptional moment, or caught from
his own mood perhaps; but which he maintains as the very
essence of the thing throughout his work. Sometimes a momentary tint of stormy light may invest a homely or too familiar
scene with a character which might well have been drawn
from the deep places of the imagination. Then we might say,
This particular effect of light, this sudden inweaving of gold
thread through the texture of the haystack, and the poplars,
and the grass, gives the scene artistic qualities; it is like a
picture. And such tricks of circumstance are commonest in
landscape which has little salient character of its own, because
in such scenery the whole material detail is so easily absorbed,
or saturated by that informing expression of passing light, and
elevated throughout their whole extent to a new and delightful
effect by it. And hence the superiority for most conditions of
the picturesque of a river-side in France to a Swiss valley,
because on the French river-side mere topography, the
simple material, counts for so little, and, all being so pure,
untouched and tranquil in itself, nature has such easy work in
tuning and playing music upon it. The Venetian landscape,
on the other hand, has in its material conditions much which is
hard and definite; but the masters of the Venetian school
have shown themselves little burdened by them. Of its Alpine
background they retain certain abstracted elements only of

cool colour and tranquillising line; and they use its actual
details, the brown windy turrets, the straw-coloured fields,
the forest arabesques, but as the notes of a music which
duly accompanies the presence of their men and women,
presenting us with the spirit or essence only of a certain sort
of landscape, a country of the pure reason or half-imaginative
memory.

Poetry, again, works with words addressed in the first
instance to the mere intelligence; and it deals most often
with a definite subject or situation. Sometimes it may find
a noble and quite legitimate function in the expression of moral
or political aspiration, as often in the poetry of Victor Hugo. In
such instances it is easy enough for the understanding to
distinguish between the matter and form, however much the
matter, the subject, the element which is addressed to the
mere intelligence, has been penetrated by the informing,
artistic spirit. But the ideal types of poetry are those in which
this distinction is reduced to its *minimum*; so that lyrical poetry,
just because in it you are least able to detach the matter from
the form without a deduction of something from that matter
itself, is, at least artistically, the highest and most complete
form of poetry. And the very perfection of such poetry often
appears to depend in part on a certain suppression or vagueness
of mere subject, so that the definite meaning almost expires, or
reaches us through ways not distinctly traceable by the understanding, as in some of the most imaginative compositions
of William Blake, and often in Shakspere's songs, as pre-
eminently in that song of Mariana's page in *Measure for
Measure*, in which the kindling power and poetry of the whole
play seems to pass for a moment into an actual strain of music.

And this principle holds good of all things that partake in
any degree of artistic qualities, of the furniture of our houses
and of dress, for instance, of life itself, of gesture and speech,
and the details of daily intercourse; these also, for the wise,
being susceptible of a suavity and charm caught from the way
in which they are done, which gives them a value in themselves; wherein, indeed, lies what is valuable and justly
attractive in what is called the fashion of a time, which elevates
the trivialities of speech, and manner, and dress, into an end in

themselves, and gives them a mysterious grace and attractiveness in the doing of them.

Art, then, is thus always striving to be independent of the mere intelligence, to become a matter of pure perception, to get rid of its responsibilities to its subject or material; the ideal examples of poetry and painting being those in which the constituent elements of the composition are so welded together, that the material or subject no longer strikes the intellect only; nor the form, the eye or the ear only; but form and matter, in their union or identity, present one single effect to the imaginative reason, that complex faculty for which every thought and feeling is twin-born with its sensible analogue or symbol.

It is the art of music which most completely realises this artistic ideal this perfect identification of form and matter, this strange chemistry, uniting, in the integrity of pure light, contrasted elements. In its ideal, consummate moments, the end is not distinct from the means, the form from the matter, the subject from the expression; they inhere in and completely saturate each other; and to it, therefore, to the condition of its perfect moments, all the arts may be supposed constantly to tend and aspire. Music then, not poetry, as is so often supposed, is the true type or measure of consummate art. Therefore, although each art has its incommunicable element, its untranslatable order of impressions, its unique mode of reaching the imaginative reason, yet the arts may be represented as continually struggling after the law or principle of music, to a condition which music alone completely realises; and one of the chief functions of aesthetic criticism, dealing with the concrete products of art, new or old, is to estimate the degree in which each of those products approaches in this sense to musical law.

By no school of painters have the necessary limitations of the art of painting been so unerringly though instinctively apprehended, and the essence of what is pictorial in a picture so justly conceived, as by the school of Venice; and the train of thought suggested in what has been now said is, perhaps, a not unfitting introduction to a few pages about Giorgione, who, though much has been taken by recent criticism from what was reputed his, still, more entirely than any other, sums up, in what we know of himself and his work, the spirit of that school.

The beginnings of Venetian painting link themselves to the last, stiff, half-barbaric splendours of Byzantine decoration, and are but the introduction into the crust of marble and gold on the walls of Murano, or of Saint Mark's of a little more of human expression. And throughout the course of its later development, always subordinate to architectural effect, the work of the Venetian school never escaped from the influence of its beginnings. Unassisted, and therefore unperplexed, by naturalism, religious mysticism, philosophical theories, it had no Giotto, no Angelico, no Botticelli. Exempt from the stress of thought and sentiment, which taxed so severely the resources of the generations of Florentine artists, those earlier Venetian painters, down to Carpaccio and the Bellini, seem never for a moment to have been even tempted to lose sight of the scope of their art in its strictness, or to forget that painting must be before all things decorative, a thing for the eye, a space of colour on the wall, only more dexterously blent than the marking of its precious stone or the chance interchange of sun and shade upon it—this, to begin and end with—whatever higher matter of thought, or poetry, or religious reverie might play its part therein between. At last, with final mastery of all the technical secrets of his art, and with somewhat more than a spark of the divine fire to his share, comes Giorgione. He is the inventor of *genre*, of those easily moveable pictures which serve for uses neither of devotion nor of allegorical or historical teaching; little groups of real men and women amid congruous furniture or landscape; morsels of actual life, conversation or music or play, refined upon and idealised till they come to seem like glimpses of life from afar. Those spaces of more cunningly blent colour, obediently filling their places hitherto in a mere architectural scheme, Giorgione detaches from the wall; he frames them by the hands of some skilful carver, so that people may move them readily and take with them where they go, as one might a poem in manuscript, or a musical instrument, to be used at will for all subtle purposes of culture, stimulus or solace, coming like an animated presence, into one's cabinet, as we say, to enrich the air as with a personal aroma, and, like persons, live with us, for a day or a lifetime. Of all art like this, art which has played so large a part in men's culture since that time, Giorgione is the initiator. Yet in him, too, that old Venetian clearness or justice in the apprehension of the essential limitations of the pictorial art is still undisturbed; and while he interfuses his painted work with a high-strung sort of poetry, caught directly from a singularly rich and high-strung sort of life, yet in his selection of subject or phase of subject, in the subordination of mere subject to pictorial design, to the main purpose of a picture, he is typical of that aspiration of all the arts towards music which I have endeavoured to explain, towards the perfect identification of matter and form.

WILLIAM MORRIS

'How I became a Socialist'

[This essay, published in *Justice. The Organ of Social Democracy*, 16 June, 1894, was the third of a series under the same title, following accounts given by Hyndman and Bax.]

I am asked by the Editor to give some sort of a history of the above conversion, and I feel that it may be of some use to do so, if my readers will look upon me as a type of a certain group of people, but not so easy to do clearly, briefly, and truly. Let me, however, try. But first, I will say what I mean by being a Socialist, since I am told that the word no longer expresses definitely and with certainty what it did ten years ago. Well, what I mean by Socialism is a condition of society in which there should be neither rich nor poor, neither master nor master's man, neither idle nor overworked, neither brain-sick brain workers, nor heart-sick hand workers, in a word, in which all men would be living in equality of condition, and would manage their affairs unwastefully, and with the full consciousness that harm to one would mean harm to all—the realisation at last of the meaning of the word COMMON-WEALTH.

Now this view of Socialism, which I hold today, and hope to die holding, is what I began with; I had no transitional period, unless you may call such a brief period of political radicalism during which I saw my ideal clear enough, but had no hope of any realisation of it. That came to an end some months before I joined the (then) Democratic Federation, and the meaning of my joining that body was that I had conceived a hope of the realisation of my ideal. If you ask me how much of a hope, or what I thought we Socialists then living and working would accomplish towards it, or when there would be effected any change in the face of society, I must say, I do not know. I can only say that I did not measure my hope, nor the joy that it brought me at the time. For the rest when I took that step I was blankly ignorant of economics; I had never so much as opened Adam Smith or heard of Ricardo, or of Karl Marx. Oddly, enough, I *had* read some of Mill, to wit, those posthumous papers of his (published was it in the *Westminster Review* or the *Fortnightly?*) in which he attacks Socialism in its Fourierist guise. In those papers he put the arguments, as far as they go, clearly and honestly, and the result so far as I was concerned was to convince me that Socialism was a necessary change, and that it was possible to bring it about in our own days. Those papers put the finishing touch to my conversion to Socialism. Well, having joined a Socialist body (for the Federation soon became definitely Socialist), I put some conscience into trying to learn the economical side of Socialism, and even tackled Marx, though I must confess that, whereas I thoroughly enjoyed the historical part of "Capital," I suffered agonies of confusion of the brain over reading the pure economics of that great work. Anyhow, I read what I could, and will hope that some information stuck to me from my reading; but more, I must think, from continuous conversation with such friends as Bax[17] and Hyndman[18] and Scheu,[19] and the brisk course of propaganda meetings which were going on at the time, and in which I took my share. Such finish to what of education in practical Socialism as I am capable of I received afterwards from some of my Anarchist friends, from whom I learned, quite against their intention, that Anarchism was impossible, much as I learned from Mill against *his* intention that Socialism was necessary.

But in this telling how I fell into *practical* Socialism I have begun, as I perceive, in the middle, for in my position of a well-to-do man not suffering from the disabilities which oppress a working man at every step, I feel that I might never have been drawn into the practical side of the question if an ideal had not forced me to seek towards it. For politics as politics, i.e., not regarded as a necessary if cumbersome and disgustful means to an end, would never have attracted me, nor when I had become conscious of the wrongs of society as it now is, and the oppression of poor people, could I have ever believed in the possibility of a *partial* setting right of those wrongs. In other words, I could never have been such a fool as to believe in the happy and 'respectable' poor.

If therefore my ideal forced me to look for practical Socialism, what was it that forced me to conceive of an ideal? Now, here comes in what I said of my being (in this paper) a type of a certain group of mind.

Before the uprising of *modern* Socialism almost all intelligent people either were, or professed themselves to be, quite contented with the civilisation of this century. Again, almost all of these really were thus contented, and saw nothing to do but to perfect the said civilisation by getting rid of a few ridiculous survivals of the barbarous ages. To be short, this was the *Whig* frame of mind, natural to the modern prosperous middle-class men, who in fact as far as mechanical progress is concerned, have nothing to ask for, if only Socialism would leave them alone to enjoy their plentiful style.

But besides these contented ones there were others who were not really contented, but had a vague sentiment of repulsion to the triumph of civilisation, but were coerced into silence by the measureless power of Whiggery. Lastly there were a few who were in open rebellion against the said Whiggery—a few, say two, Carlyle and Ruskin. The latter, before my days of practical Socialism, was my master towards the ideal aforesaid, and, looking backward, I cannot help saying, by the way, how deadly dull the world would have been twenty years ago but for Ruskin! It was through him that I learned to give form to my discontent, which I must say was not by any means vague. Apart from the desire to produce beautiful things, the leading passion of my life has been and is hatred of modern civilisation. What shall I say of it now, when the words are put into my mouth, my hope of its destruction—what shall I say of its supplanting by Socialism?

What shall I say concerning its mastery of, and its waste of mechanical power, its commonwealth so poor, its enemies of the commonwealth so rich, its stupendous organization—for the misery of life! Its contempt of simple pleasures which everyone could enjoy but for its folly? Its eyeless vulgarity which has destroyed art, the one certain solace of labour? All this I felt then as now, but I did not know why it was so. The hope of the past times was gone, the struggles of mankind for many ages had produced nothing but this sordid, aimless, ugly confusion; the immediate future seemed to me likely to intensify all the present evils by sweeping away the last survivals of the days before the dull squalor of civilisation had settled down on the world. This was a bad look out indeed, and, if I may mention myself as a personality and not as a mere type, especially so to a man of my disposition, careless of metaphysics and religion, as well as of scientific analysis, but with a deep love of the earth and the life on it, and a passion for the history of the past of mankind. Think of it. Was it all to end in a counting-house on the top of a cinder-heap, with Podsnap's drawing-room in the office, and a Whig committee dealing out champagne to the rich and margarine to the poor in such convenient proportions as would make all men contented together, though the pleasure of the eyes was gone from the world, and the place of Homer was to be taken by Huxley. Yet, believe me, in my heart when I really forced myself to look towards the future, that is what I saw in it, and as far as I could tell scarce anyone seemed to think it worth while to struggle against such a consummation of civilization. So there I was in for a fine pessimistic end of life, if it had not somehow dawned on me, that amidst all this filth of civilisation the seeds of a great change, what we others call Social Revolution, were beginning to germinate. The whole face of things was changed to me by that discovery, and all I had to do then in order to become a Socialist, was to hook myself on to the practical movement, which as before said, I have tried to do as well as I could.

To sum up then, the study of history and the love and practice of art forced me into a hatred of the civilisation, which if things were to stop as they are would turn history into inconsequent nonsense, and make art a collection of the curiosities of the past, which would have no serious relation to the life of the present.

But the consciousness of revolution stirring amidst our hateful modern society prevented me, luckier than many others of artistic perceptions, from crystallising into a mere railer against "progress" on one hand, and on the other from wasting time and energy in any of the numerous schemes by which the quasi-artistic of the middle-classes hope to make art grow when it has no longer any root, and thus I became a practical Socialist.

A last word or two. Perhaps some of our friends will say, what have we to do with these matters of history and art? We want by means of Social-Democracy to win a decent livelihood, we want in some sort to live, and that at once. Surely anyone who professes to think that the question of art and cultivation must go before that of the knife and fork (and there are some who do propose that) does not understand what art means, or how that its roots must have a soil of a thriving and unanxious life. Yet it must be remembered that civilisation has reduced the workman to such a skinny and pitiful existence, that he scarcely knows how to frame a desire for any life much better than that which he now endures perforce. It is the province of art to set the true ideal of a full and reasonable life before him, a life to which the perception and creation of beauty, the enjoyment of real pleasure that is, shall be felt to be as necessary to man as his daily bread, and that no man, and no set of men can be deprived of this except by mere oppression, which should be resisted to the utmost.

NOTES

1. See preface to 'Fair Maid of Perth' (Ruskin's note); Scott wrote this preface in 1831.
2. *Principles of Political Economy*, I, 8.
3. Cf. George Herbert, *The Church Porch*, Stanza 28 (Ruskin's note).
   > Gold thou mayst safely touch; but if it stick
   > Unto thy hands, it woundeth to the quick.
4. habet, he is wounded.
   quo plurimum posset, wherein its main power lay.
   > Marcus Curtius leaped into a chasm in the forum to demonstrate that the main power of the Roman state lay in its sons' arms and valour. Livy, VII, 6, 1–5.
5. *Moral Essays*, III, ll. 201–2.
   > Yet sure, of qualities deserving praise,
   > More go to ruin fortunes, than to raise.
6. Ruskin in a note quotes Aristophanes' *Plutus*, 582, 'Zeus is indeed poor'. He regarded this phrase as a stronger expression of the idea of the superior moral worth of the poor than the words of Poverty in the same play, who says (ll. 558–9), 'my people are better in mind and body than Wealth's people.'
7. Acts, v, 1–2.
8. Galatians, v, 24.
9. Mark, ii, 14.
10. Matthew, iv, 18.
11. Acts, ix, 1.
12. Novalis (1772–1801), F. L. von Hardenburg, romantic poet and aphorist. The quotation means, 'To philosophise is to dephlegmatise, to vivify'; see *Philosophical Fragments* (1798), No. 41.
13. Source in Hugo's works untraced.
14. In Book VI of the *Confessions* (1781) Rousseau actually mentions books of devotion and science at this point, not Voltaire.
15. Cf. V. Hugo, *Le dernier jour d'un condamné* (1829), ch. 3.
16. Yet for Vasari there was some further magic of crimson in the lips and cheeks, lost for us (Pater's note).
17. E. B. Bax (1854–1926), founder, with Morris, of the Socialist League.
18. H. M. Hyndman (1842–1921), founder of the Democratic Federation.
19. Andreas Scheu, socialist exile from Austria-Hungary; d. 1927.